The Divine Office

FOR

DODOS*

Devout, Obedient Disciples of Our Savior

Madeline Pecora Nugent

A STEP-BY-STEP GUIDE TO PRAYING THE LITURGY OF THE HOURS!

Three Bean Books
www.threebeanbooks.com

THE DIVINE OFFICE FOR DODOS

Three Bean Books

P.O. Box 1814
Westerly, RI 02891
www.threebeanbooks.com

ISBN: 0-9744644-0-6

Printed in the United States of America. Distributed in the United States by Three Bean Books. For press review copies, author interviews or other publicity information, or for authorization to photocopy items for personal or organizational use, please contact Three Bean Books at 401-954-2029.

Thanks to Jerry Fuchs, of Norcross, GA (www.fooksie.com), for the illustrations of "Dora" and "Derwood" Dodo.

About the Author

Madeline Pecora Nugent prays all seven hours of the Divine Office daily. When she's not praying, she's busy being wife to Jim Nugent and mother to James, Amelia, Sister Veronica of Jesus, Michael, and Kay.

Active in prolife work since 1973, Madeline authored a book about prolife pregnancy options and assisted in opening both a right to life office and a pro-life crisis pregnancy center. In 1976, she and Jim began Prayers for Life which distributes over a dozen different prolife prayers.

Madeline, who has been writing for over forty years, holds a graduate degree in English and is a former teacher and a current speaker about the saints. She is the author of many articles, booklets, and columns as well as of two books about St. Anthony of Padua and one about St. Clare of Assisi. She has written and published over 800 brief stories of patron saints, distributed through the non-profit organization Saints' Stories, Inc., which she and Jim founded.

Madeline, Jim, and those of her family who are still at home live in Middletown, Rhode Island.

The author dedicates this book to the members of the Confraternity of Penitents who pray the Divine Office daily and most especially to her dear husband Jim who has faithfully prayed Morning and Evening Prayer with her for almost seven years. If you have questions that this manual doesn't answer, or wish to share a technique that works for you, contact the author at madeline@divineofficefordodos.com.

Dora says, "Don't forget to order your bookmarks and ribbons."

THE DIVINE OFFICE FOR DODOS uses a system of bookmarks and ribbons to help you navigate the breviary. One set comes free with this book, but you have to mail in the coupon at the end of the book to receive it. So go to page A-55, clip the coupon and mail it today! Allow 2-3 weeks for delivery. By the time you get 'em, you'll need 'em.

TABLE OF CONTENTS

SECTION TEN: PRAYING MORNING, EVENING, AND NIGHT PRAYER ON SOLEMNITIES AND FEASTS

SECTION ELEVEN: PRAYING MORNING, EVENING, AND NIGHT PRAYER ON MEMORIALS

SECTION TWELVE: THE MINOR OFFICES

SECTION THIRTEEN: OPTIONS

APPENDICES

ORDERING YOUR BOOKMARKS & RIBBONS: A-55

BEFORE YOU BEGIN
Some Interesting Stuff!

"In this section, you'll learn about ..."

Introduction to the Divine Office

Praying the Office as part of a rule of life

The author's acknowledgements

Other books by Madeline Pecora Nugent

BEFORE YOU BEGIN

Introduction

Hi! Let's start with a secret. You're not a dodo! Not only do you not have a hooked beak and fluffy gray feathers, you're even pretty smart! I mean, you know how to tie your shoe laces, brush your teeth, and set an alarm clock, don't you? But, seriously, you really do know a good deal about many things, but the Divine Office isn't one of them. Regarding the Divine Office, you might be a bit confused. Maybe more than a bit. Probably also frustrated. And maybe a little angry. You want to become a holier person. Someone told you that praying the Divine Office would be a nudge in that direction. Maybe they even tried to help you. Maybe they gave you some instructions to read. But you can't understand what to do! So you feel like a dodo.

Here's another secret. You aren't alone!

Most folks who try to pray the Divine Office experience just what you are experiencing. Confusion. Frustration. Anger. There's hope in these pages. You really are going to learn to pray the Divine Office. Honest! Then you'll join the ranks of other clergy, religious, and laity, some of whom are non-Catholic, who pray the Divine Office every day. Maybe you already know that the Divine Office is the official, formal prayer of the Church that was written to pray throughout the day. When you pray the Divine Office, your prayers are united with those who are praying the very same prayers around the world. Great graces come from such communal prayers. Maybe you knew that, too, but isn't that something?

One thing before we begin. If this book helps you, would you once in a while remember its author in your prayers? And even if it doesn't help you, would you pray for me anyway? I need the prayers. Thanks.

Oh, yes. You might be wondering about me. How did I learn to pray the Divine Office? Well, I cheated. I had help you probably don't have. In order to prepare to write a book about St. Clare of Assisi, I stayed for a week with a convent of Poor Clares. One of the sweet sisters was assigned to me to help me with the Divine Office. She very patiently took this dodo under her wing and showed me each office (and the sisters prayed all seven offices in the Divine Office) and how to pray it and where to find it. By the time the week was up, I had practiced fifty offices and knew what I was doing. If you can find a convent of Poor Clares to stay with for a week, then you won't need this book. But, if you can't, then **The Divine Office for** Dodos is your next best bet.

Praying the Divine Office as Part of a Rule of Life

So who prays the Divine Office? Clergy and religious do. So do lay people who belong to certain Third Orders and Associations. So do other lay people who just want to pray this prayer of the Church daily. Doesn't matter which category you fall into. This book will help you.

Acknowledgements

First of all, I have to thank those Poor Clares of Langhorne, PA who showed me how to pray the Divine Office. I also thank Father John Darcy, canon lawyer, and Father Peter Damian, FI, for reading and checking the first draft of this manuscript for accuracy. Father Peter also checked the second draft and made several helpful suggestions. Thanks to Fr. John of the Trinity, Erem. TOCarm, and Father Martin Mary, FI, both of whom made some helpful suggestions regarding instructions for praying the Office. Thanks, as well, to Connie Kotch, Rosemary Cross, Ellen LeGare, Doris Lucchesi, Jean Munson, Mary J. Sullivan, and Jeanne Tucciaroni for trying to learn to pray the Divine Office using the first manuscript draft. They were "guinea pig dodos" whose comments and frustrations with the first draft enabled me to clarify the confusing sections of this book. Special thanks goes to Louise F. Martin who gave the manuscript to Christine Eiva to critique. Christine had learned how to pray the Divine Office with the Sisters of Divine Providence, and her many valuable tips are included herein. Then I have to thank Mark Gordon who believed enough in this manuscript to have his company publish it.

Additional Books by the Author

Hey, I'm not embarrassed to mention some other books I've had published. If you like this one, you might want to check out some of the others. Here they are:

Having Your Baby When Others Say No! (Prayers for Life, c/o Dr. James Nugent, Salve Regina University, Newport RI 02840. Text on line at http://www.thombs.com/table.html). Free will offering. Prolife self-help book for women in crisis, how to give birth and make workable plans for themselves and their babies.

St. Anthony: Words of Fire, Life of Light (Pauline Books, 50 St. Paul's Avenue, Boston, MA 02130-3491, 800-876-4463, www.pauline.org) $13.95 St. Anthony as viewed by those who knew him. A highly acclaimed best seller on the life of the popular finder of lost objects. Uses the saint's own words as his story is told.

Praying with Anthony of Padua (originally published by St. Mary's Press, now distributed by The Word among Us, 9639 Doctor Perry Road, #126N, Ijamsville MD 21754, 1-800-775-WORD (9673), www.wau.org) $7.95. Fifteen meditations on St. Anthony using his own words and stories of his life.

St. Clare and Her Sisters: Lovers of the Poor Christ (Pauline Books, 50 St. Paul's Avenue, Boston, MA 02130-3491, 800-876-4463, www.pauline.org) $22.95. Life of St. Clare of Assisi as told by those who knew her.

Handbook of the Confraternity of Penitents (Confraternity of Penitents, 520 Oliphant Lane, Middletown RI 02842-4600, 401/849-5421). $26.00 The Confraternity of Penitents is a Catholic lay association whose members, among other things, pray the complete Divine Office as one of their prayer options. You can check out the Confraternity and its Rule at www.penitents.org.

"In this section, you'll learn about ..."

How to use this book

The Liturgy of the Hours

The Divine Office

Times of prayer

The breviary

Your Breviary's table of contents

Exploring the breviary

GETTING FAMILIAR WITH THE BREVIARY

TIPS FOR NAVIGATING THIS TOME!

1. Do the lessons in order no matter how much experience you have in praying the Divine Office or how much you already know.

2. Do each lesson's activities and answer the questions correctly before proceeding. Yes, you may look back in the lesson to find the answers! That's not cheating. It's being wise!

3. Repeat any lesson until you master it before moving on. That's being wise, too. If you have forgotten a technique, don't despair! Nobody's going to check to see if you remembered.

4. Refer back to already discussed material, using the Table of Contents to help you find what you need.

5. Take as long as you need to complete one lesson. Fully understand it before moving on.

Lesson 1: How to Use This Book

So you want to learn to pray the Divine Office? Great! Think you can spend some time to do so? Wonderful!

But you're a dodo at this, you say. Can't seem to learn new things quickly. **The Divine Office for DODOS** is for dodos just like you! The lessons are written for the most dodo-y person among us! If you are a fast learning dodo, speed up the lessons! If you are a slow learning dodo, slow them down. Just don't be an erratic dodo and skip around. Be an orderly dodo, taking the lessons in order, just as they are written, and learning the material in each before waddling on.

You might be a confused dodo who has noticed that different religious communities pray the Divine Office a bit differently. Who's right? Probably they all are! One community is using one option and another community is using a different one. **The Divine Office for DODOS** teaches the most basic and complete way of praying the Divine Office. Later it tells you about the options.

You might be a frustrated dodo who has tried to pray the Divine Office and stomped on your breviary in disgust. Can you learn to pray this? Of course! But go easy on yourself. You have much new material to learn.**The Divine Office for DODOS** will teach it to you, step by simple step. Bye, bye frustration. Ready to begin?

Wonderful.

Let's page through the manual and gawk at the pages.

Do you see that the book is divided into thirteen sections, plus several appendices. Each section focuses on one major portion of the Office. Hey, the sections are divided into LESSONS! How long do these take? For most dodos, no lesson will take more than thirty minutes and most will take considerably less time. Whew! Here's a secret. To get the maximum benefit from the lessons, follow the tips on the previous page.

That's it. But before we begin, let's talk about type styles. The typefaces in this book have a meaning.

Whenever a term is INTRODUCED, it's printed in CAPITAL LETTERS.

Is that clever or what?

Rules for understanding and praying the Divine Office are printed in bold type.

<u>Underlining emphasizes certain key points.</u>

Italics is used to print instructions that apply only to a four volume breviary. So if you are using a four volume breviary, you have more work. You ought to complete all the instructions in this book. But if you are using a one volume breviary, you can skip the instructions written in italics.

Lucky you! Oh, yes. Every section of **The Divine Office for DODOS** contains a Dodo Self-Check. You can skip this if you want to, but you'll probably learn how to pray the Divine Office a lot faster and a lot smoother if you answer the questions. It's up to you. Again, no one's checking on you but you! Here's the first Self-Check in its handy box. Look for one in each lesson.

Did you get the questions all right? Good for you! Ready for Lesson Two? Great! But before we move on, you're going to need a few things to complete this manual. One is a book that contains the Divine Office. This book is called a BREVIARY.

If you don't have a breviary, fast forward to Lesson 5, read all about 'em, and get yourself one. Then come back and do lessons 2, 3, and 4.

> **DODO SELF-CHECK #1**
>
> 1. **What are the five secrets for successfully using this manual?**
>
> 2. **When you see a word written in all CAPITALS, what does that mean?**
>
> 3. **What will it mean when you see something in bold type?**
>
> 4. <u>**How is underlining used in this book?**</u>
>
> 5. *When are italics used?*

The other things you'll need are a restful ribbon and bouncing bookmark set which come free with this manual. Yep, free, but you've got to request 'em. Right up at the front of this manual is an order form. Order yours today!

Now if you've got the breviary, ribbons, and bookmarks on hand or on order, you can dive right into Lesson 2. Ready! Go!

Lesson 2: The Liturgy of the Hours

It's good to begin any spiritual work with the Bible. Agreed? So let's look at Mark 15:25-34 and note the hours. You'll notice that Jesus was crucified at the third hour and that darkness fell over the land from the sixth to the ninth hour. What times are those in today's lingo? Well, Jesus was crucified at 9 a.m. and darkness covered the land from noon to 3 p.m.

In Bible times, people told time using the word "hours" instead of "o'clock." **THE LITURGY OF THE HOURS is a liturgy, meaning a formal rite for public worship that is prayed at certain hours of a twenty-four hour day.** In modern usage, a store or restaurant that is open for twenty-four hours a day is said to be open "around the clock." **The "Liturgy of the Hours" means "Praying Formal Prayers around the Clock."** Pretty obvious, if you think about it.

Traditionally, religious prayed the Liturgy of the Hours seven times daily. That might seem like a lot! You don't have to pray seven times a day. You might be praying the Liturgy of the Hours two or three times a day, like most lay people do! However, some people, both clergy and lay, still pray seven times daily. Why? Because they like to. Or because the seven hours are part of their religious Rule of Life. How about that!

How'd we get seven hours? They originated from careful reading of Scripture and from tradition. Psalm 119 (verse 164) states "Seven times a day I will praise you." The Bible enumerates six of these times.

People in Biblical times prayed together at the last hour of the day when lamps were lit and at the first hour of the dawn. Sort of like us praying when we get awake and before we go to sleep. OK, that's two times a day. But the Jews prayed more often than that.

In the Acts of the Apostles, the disciples came together for prayer at the third hour (9 a.m.) See Acts 1:14 coupled with Acts 2: 1-15. Taken together, these two passages indicate that the believers were gathered together in prayer on Pentecost.

DODO SELF-CHECK #2

1. What is the Liturgy of the Hours? What does the word "hour" mean? How did it come to mean this? What would be a modern translation of the term "Liturgy of the Hours"?

2. Traditionally, how many times daily did people pray the Liturgy of the Hours? How is it prayed differently today?

3. How did the seven traditional hours of prayer come about? Give the Biblical history in general terms.

4. What is the "opus Dei?"

Peter went to the housetop to pray about the sixth hour (Noon.) See Acts 10:9.

Peter and John were going up to the temple for prayer at the ninth hour (3 p.m.). See Acts 3:1.

Late at night, Paul and Silas were praying (About midnight.) See Acts 16:25.

Jesus prayed until between 3 and 6 a.m. when He ended prayer to walk across the Sea of Galilee and approach his disciples who were battling a stormy passage.

Add 'em up. Seven hours total.

Saint Benedict, the great monastic founder, wanted his monks to pray seven hours daily, to correspond with Scripture. He called the seven hours of prayer the "opus Dei," the work of God. Christians began to formally pray at these hours, thus developing the Liturgy of the Hours.

That wasn't too difficult, was it? Ready for Lesson 3? Let's go!

Lesson 3: The Divine Office

Just what is the Divine Office? And how does it differ from the Liturgy of the Hours? Read on and find out!

To pray the Liturgy of the Hours, certain prayers were composed to pray "around the clock." These formal prayers are called OFFICES. Here's where things get a little confusing. You see, many different Offices exist such as the Little Office of the Blessed Virgin and Offices written by various saints. But there is only one "official Office" written by the Church. **The "official Office" written by the Church is called the DIVINE OFFICE.** The other Offices are good. The Divine Office is the best, so good it's called Divine!

Each Office has certain parts to it. One part is prayed at one hour (a certain time) and another part at another hour (a different time) and so on. Are you with me? Now read the next line carefully! **Each part of an Office is also called an office**. Here's an easy way to understand this: Hint: Look at the capital and lower case letters. Do you notice that one Office begins with a capital and the other office doesn't? Here's an easy parallel: Scripture and scripture. If someone is reading Scripture (capitalized), they mean the entire Bible. If they are quoting a scripture (lower case), they mean a Bible verse. The capitalized word is the whole, the lower case a part. Same with Office (the whole) and office (a part). See, now you understand!

Have you ever heard the terms "Liturgy of the Hours" and "Divine Office" used interchangeably? Don't be a dodo and follow suit! These aren't the same. **The Liturgy of the Hours means <u>any</u> formal prayers said at specific times around the clock while the Divine Office is the <u>official</u> prayer composed by the Church to pray around the clock.**

DODO
SELF-CHECK #3

1. What is an Office? An office?

2. Why were Offices written?

3. How are the Liturgy of the Hours and the Divine Office different?

4. How many daily offices are there? What are their names?

5. What is the general name of the book that contains the Divine Office? Describe the three types of this book.

6. How was the Divine Office meant to be prayed? May one pray the Divine Office alone?

See the difference? Now don't you feel smart?

Here's another tip. Don't be a dodo and use the word "hour" to refer to an office. Folks don't pray the "hour of Evening Prayer"—they pray the office of prayer that is said around 6 p.m. Moreover, an "hour," as in Liturgy of the Hours, doesn't mean sixty minutes of prayer. No office takes sixty minutes, to pray. You might be glad to know that!

The Divine Office is nearly as old as the Church itself. It was meant to be prayed with others, but that doesn't happen much today outside of religious communities. Today most parish priests and laity pray the Divine Office alone. That's fine, too!

The Divine Office contains seven daily offices that correspond to the seven traditional hours of prayer in the Liturgy of the Hours. The modern names of these offices are

THE OFFICE OF READINGS
THE OFFICE OF MORNING PRAYER
THE OFFICE OF MIDMORNING PRAYER
THE OFFICE OF MIDDAY PRAYER
THE OFFICE OF MIDAFTERNOON
       PRAYER
THE OFFICE OF EVENING PRAYER

Name of Office	Traditional Name	Abbreviation
Office of Readings	Vigils or Matins	OOR
Morning Prayer	Lauds	MP
Midmorning Prayer	Terce	MMP
Midday Prayer	Sext	MDP
Midafternoon Prayer	None	MAP
Evening Prayer	Vespers	EP
Night Prayer	Compline	NP

THE OFFICE OF NIGHT PRAYER.

Where do you find the Divine Office? **The DIVINE OFFICE has been printed in a special book called a BREVIARY.** Now hold on because there is more than one kind of breviary. Here are the variations:

    * Breviary Biggie Size: Four Fat Volumes. Contains every single prayer and reading of the Divine Office.

    * Breviary Basic: One Fat Volume. For those who wish to pray only some of the offices.

    * Breviary Mini: One Thin Volume. An abbreviated form of the Divine Office that many folks take along while traveling

Which edition works with **Divine Office for Dodos**? All of them. How about that?

Lesson 4: Times of Prayer

Dodos are creatures of habit. They tend to do certain things at the same time of day. It's no diffeent with people. Religious in monasteries and cathedrals set up specific times for praying the Divine Office. Here's a nifty chart. The traditional seven hours of prayer and the traditional times prayed are charted here along with the modern name for the office and the current time to pray it. Also listed are the accepted abbreviation and approximate length of time to pray that office.

Notice anything odd about the chart? Hint: Count the offices. You've got it! There are eight hours, not seven! How come? That's because Lauds and Prime

DODO SELF-CHECK #4

1. How many offices were traditionally prayed?

2. What office is no longer prayed?

3. What is the current name of each office, its abbreviation, the length of time it takes to pray each office, and the time the office is currently prayed? You can peek while you answer.

4. Which office can be prayed at any time during the day?

5. What offices do most people pray?

Minutes to Pray	Time of Prayer	Traditional Time
15-20 minutes	Anytime during day	Midnight
10-14 minutes	6:00 - 11:00 a.m.	Dawn
5 minutes	9:00 a.m.	9:00 a.m.
5 minutes	Noon	Noon
5 minutes	3:00 p.m.	3:00 p.m.
10-14 minutes	4:00 - 11:00 p.m.	3:00 - 6:00 p.m
7-10 minutes	Before bedtime	Before bedtime

were generally prayed at the same time. Today the office of Prime has been suppressed (meaning we don't pray it now). Ta da! Seven modern day offices!

So what offices do folks pray?

Most people pray at least Morning and Evening Prayer. Many pray Night Prayer as well. Those in religious orders pray whatever offices are required by their communities.

What offices will you be praying? That's up to you!

Are you now, or are you planning to become, a religious or a member of a religious or lay Order? If so, what will you be required to pray?

Are you a lay Catholic who simply wishes to pray the Divine Office? How much time do you wish to spend in praying the Divine Office? What offices do you think you'd be praying?

Lesson 5: The Breviary

A breviary isn't very brief. It's actually pretty bulky. **A BREVIARY is a prayer book that contains the Divine Office so you're gonna need a breviary.** So which one of the three types do you get?

A. Breviary Biggie Size: The complete breviary is printed in four volumes, one volume for Lent and the Easter Season, one volume for Advent and the Christmas Season, and two volumes for Ordinary Time. It's the most expensive breviary because it's in four volumes. How come four volumes? Because most folks don't want to carry around an eight or ten pound book which is what the breviary would weigh if all the offices were printed in one volume.

The four volume breviary contains the complete Divine Office for all seven hours of the day, offering different Readings for the Office of Readings for every day of the year. It also has all year's MEMORIALS, FEASTS, AND SOLEMNITIES. Don't fret about learning what these terms mean now. We'll go over them later in detail.

Clergy, cloistered religious communities, and some other religious pray all seven hours as do some lay Catholics. If you wish to pray all seven hours, you need a four volume breviary. Maybe a few caring friends or relatives can each give you a volume for your birthday if you can't afford the cost yourself. Be sure they coordinate their gifts so you get one of each volume and not four of the same one.

B. Breviary Basic: The most widely used breviary is a one volume breviary. It contains complete Morning, Evening, and Night Prayer for the entire year as well as the most important prayers and Readings for the Memorials, Feasts, and Solemnities of the year. The Readings for the Office of Readings are a selection of those available in the four volume breviary. Some publishers include the complete Daytime Prayer Psalter while others include only a selection of the Daytime Prayer Psalms or none at all.

If you want to pray only Morning, Evening, and Night Prayer, save yourself some money and purchase the one volume breviary. It costs about a quarter of the price of the Biggie.

C. Breviary Mini: The travelers' breviary, also called SHORTER CHRISTIAN PRAYER, is a slender volume designed to fit into a briefcase, suitcase, or purse. Its Morning, Evening, and Night Prayers are complete, but it has only the barest minimum of prayers for the Feasts and Solemnities and none for the Memorials. It doesn't contain the Office of Readings or Midmorning, Midday, and Midafternoon prayer. Use the travelers' breviary when traveling, and either the Basic or Biggie the rest of the time.

When you go to order a breviary, what do you ask for? You're not going to ask for Breviary Biggie, Basic, or Mini! You're not even going to give a title for the breviary because **different publishers have different titles. Tell the bookstore clerk, "I would like to purchase a breviary that will enable me to observe the Liturgy of the Hours by praying the Divine Office of the Catholic Church."** Add whether you want a one or four volume breviary.

DODO SELF-CHECK #5

1. Compare the four volume, one volume, and travelers' breviaries. How many volumes does each contain? What offices does each contain? Which is most expensive? Why would someone purchase the four-volume breviary? The one volume breviary? The travelers' breviary?

2. What offices do you wish to pray?
3. How much money can you afford to spend? Can you save up the money you need? How?

4. Which breviary should you obtain? How can you obtain it?

5. What cautions should you observe in purchasing a breviary?

A note of caution: Some companies have published Books of Prayer based on the Divine Office and following the Liturgy of the Hours. These have adaptations and modifications and are NOT the official prayers of the Church. If you want the official prayers of the Church and are considering a book that appears to be a breviary but that is not published by the companies mentioned below, do a little sleuthing before using or purchasing. A priest or religious should be able to tell you if what you are considering is, in fact, the Divine Office as composed by the Church rather than something that has been adapted by an individual or group.

Some companies that currently distribute real, genuine breviaries are:

Pauline Books and Media (50 St. Paul's Avenue, Boston, MA 02130; phone 800-876-4463, pauline.org)—one volume breviary only.

The American Franciscan Liturgical Commission (c/o Franciscan Publishers, 165 E. Pulaski Street, P.O. Box 100, Pulaski, WI 54162-0100; phone 414/822-5833): four volume and one volume breviaries.

Catholic Book Company (77 West End Road, Totowa, New Jersey, 07512; phone: 973/890-2400): four volume, one volume, and travelers' breviary.

Here's an insider's tip. Some religious communities have unused breviaries on hand. If you ask them for one, you might get one.

Note: You'll need a breviary to continue with these instructions.

Lesson 6: Getting to Know Your Breviary's Table of Contents

In this lesson, you get to be a Breviary Doctor. You're going to examine your breviary. You don't have to give it a clean bill of health, though. You just want to see what it's all about.

If you've got a four volume breviary, select one of the volumes for ORDINARY TIME for these instructions.

Let's start poking around in a breviary. If you've got a new breviary, first look in your breviary or its package for any papers of special prayers. Place these special prayers inside the front or back cover of the breviary and remember that you have them. We'll talk about them later..

Now look at the title page. What can you learn from it?

Turn to the Table of Contents which will follow the title page. This is a real important part of your breviary. Sort of like the brain in a human body. Find the following sections in the Table of Contents and then see if you can find them in the breviary. Check off the terms as you find them:

  Proper of Seasons
  The Ordinary
  Psalter
  Proper of Saints

> **DODO
> SELF-CHECK #6**
>
> **1. What words best describe your first contact with the breviary? Hopeful? Anxious? Eager? Frustrated? Confused? Delighted? Any of these reactions is normal to a first contact with the breviary.**

Commons
Office for the Dead

Now go back and read the subheadings under each of these. Which sections are divided into months?

What can you learn by reading the subheadings under Commons?
Find Night Prayer.
Find the Complementary Psalmody (not in the travelers' breviary)
What appendices does your breviary have? What can you learn from these headings?
What indices does your breviary have? What can you learn from these?

Whew! That was some looking! Ready to nose around some more?

Let's start with the seasons of the Church year. No, they're not summer, fall, winter, and spring. **There are three seasons of the church year—Lent, Advent, and Ordinary Time. A breviary is arranged around these seasons.**

In the four volume breviary, there is one volume for Lent and Easter Seasons, one for Advent and Christmas Seasons, and two for Ordinary Time. All of these seasons are contained in some manner in the one volume and travelers' breviaries.

Leaf through your breviary. Can you find sections for Lent, Advent, and Ordinary Time? Are they in more than one place?

Lesson 7: Exploring the Breviary

Let's start off simple. Open your breviary to the Table of Contents (you remember that important, in the front section).

Can you find the heading marked Psalter? Look at the subheadings. Find Week I, Week II, Week III, and Week IV. **The Psalter is used every day throughout the year in a four week repeating cycle. These weeks are Week I, Week II, Week III, and Week IV.** This is not as confusing as it seems. After Week IV is

---

DODO SELF-CHECK #7

1. List all the new terms you found in the breviary.

2. What have you noticed about the repetition of these terms?

3. What is the Psalter? How many weeks does it contain? What happens when you finish praying Week IV?

completed, return to Week I, sort of like running laps around a track. Around and around and around. More about this later.

Time for a little "exploratory surgery." Let's look deeper into the breviary. Open your breviary to the first page of Week I. What day of the week is this? Page through this section. Look for the following headings and check them off in this book as you find them:

> Evening Prayer I
> Invitatory
> Office of Readings
> Morning Prayer
> Daytime Prayer
> Evening Prayer II.

Now go back to the first page of Week I. Page forward again, looking for the following headings. Check them off in this book as you find them:

> Hymn
> Psalmody
> Antiphon
> Psalm
> Psalm-Prayer.
> Keep paging through until you reach Monday.

What have you noticed about the frequency of the above headings? Have you noticed other headings not yet discussed? Are you feeling pretty dodo-y, not knowing what all these mean? Don't worry! You'll soon learn. A breviary is like the human body. Lots of different parts that all work together. It takes time to learn all the parts of the human body. "The leg bone's connected to the knee bone, the knee bone's connected to the shin bone, the shin bone's connected to the ankle bone." Well, you get the idea. If you want to learn about the human body, you first become familiar with the general characteristics of the body and then you start looking at the details. That's what we're doing here.

"In this section, you'll learn about ..."

Bookmarks and ribbons

Hymns

Praying aloud

Beginning and ending the Divine Office

Psalms and canticles

The responsory

Evening Prayers I & II

THE DIVINE OFFICE FOR DODOS

GENERAL INSTRUCTIONS

If you have a four volume breviary, use one of the volumes for Ordinary Time for this section.

Lesson 8: Bookmarks and Ribbons

This instructional manual uses a system of ribbons and bookmarks to help you find your place in the breviary. If you're an on the ball dodo, you've already requested your free set by using the coupon at the back of this manual. If you're a procrastinator dodo, stop procrastinating! Fill out the coupon and mail it in. Like now, man!

Let's get one thing straight right off the bat. You may not use every ribbon and bookmark. Hey, why not? Because what you use will depend on your breviary, its publisher, and the offices that you wish to pray. So what do you do with the ones you don't use? I don't know. Make Christmas ornaments or something.

You probably already noticed that your breviary comes with ribbons used to mark your place. Great. You've got some extra ribbons. Make some more ornaments. In this instruction, you'll use the free "Restful Ribbon Set" you've received or will receive via postal mail. Please insert the "restful ribbons" into your breviary by slipping the cardboard tag into the breviary's spine. We'll tell you later where to put the ribbons. **The "restful ribbons" mark prayers that are repeated frequently. Once you put a ribbon into its proper place, hands off! It's going to rest in that place forever.**

Unless you've got a mighty unusual breviary, you didn't get any bookmarks with it. This instructional manual uses a system of "Bouncing Bookmarks" to mark various parts of the offices. **The bouncing bookmarks bounce along as you pray the offices.** Please cut the bookmarks apart and keep them in a safe place, like your underwear or sock drawer, until you need them later. We'll tell you when to bounce them out.

> **DODO SELF-CHECK #8**
>
> 1. How will the "restful ribbons" be used?
>
> 2. How will the "bouncing bookmarks" be used?

If you're using a four volume breviary, you may wish to order a set of bookmarks and ribbons for each volume so that you don't have to move them from volume to volume. If you order three additional sets now, you'll probably have them on hand when you need them in this instruction.

Please contact the distributor with any questions.

Lesson 9: Hymns

A dodo didn't have the voice of a nightingale. If you're like me, you don't have the voice of a nightingale either. But whether or not you can carry a tune, you can "make a joyful noise to the Lord." Even dodos did that. This lesson will be about the "joyful noises" in the Divine Office. The joyful noises are called HYMNS and some people can actually sing them.

Every office uses a Hymn shortly after its beginning <u>whether or not a Hymn is printed or referred to in your breviary.</u>

The Hymn may be sung, but, if you don't know the tune, make one up or use a tune you do know. A Hymn may be chanted. You can create a simple chant by singing the same note for every syllable. If you want to get fancy, other more complicated chants exist. Usually a religious sister or brother can teach you some if you really want to learn them. If you can't sing or chant, just recite the Hymn. Recitation is OK, too.

How do ya find the Hymns? Depending on your breviary, they might be in different places.

Look in your breviary's Table of Contents. Some breviaries have a special Hymn section. Next look at the Psalter. Some breviaries have a Hymn printed at the beginning of each office. Sometimes more than one Hymn is printed, but **you'll use only one Hymn at the beginning of each office, even though several may be printed.**

Does your breviary have a Hymn number or page to which you should refer for that office? Some breviaries do. Do the Hymns in your breviary have only words or do they contain the notes as well? Do Hymns without notes have a notation at the bottom listing the melody to be sung? If so, page through the breviary and see if you recognize any of those melodies.

Now we get to do something fun. We get to use our first bookmark!

If you have a Hymn section, insert the Hymn bookmark into that section now and take a peek at it. What's printed on the Hynn bookmark?

If you don't have a Hymn section, don't fret. You'll get to use another book-

---

**DODO
SELF-CHECK #9**

1. How are Hymns arranged in your breviary?

2. Would you prefer to sing, chant, or recite the Hymns?

3. How will you find a Hymn when you need one?

4. How many Hymns do you use at the beginning of each office?

5. What's printed on the Hymn bookmark?

mark soon. Turn to the indices of your breviary. Does your breviary have an index of Hymns and pages they are on? Study the indices carefully. How are the Hymns arranged? What seasons do they refer to?

If your breviary has an index of Hymns, telling you which Hymns to use on certain days, insert the Hymn Index bookmark into the breviary at the beginning of the Index of Hymns.

Lesson 10: Praying Aloud

Here's something an awfully lot of folks don't know. **The Divine Office is intended to be prayed out loud.** Some folks read aloud, sing, or chant the Divine Office to help them pray better. If you can't or don't want to do that, you can at least move your lips when you pray. Moving your lips may be the wrong technique while silent reading in elementary school, but it's the right technique for praying the Divine Office.

Here's another thing an awfully lot of folks don't know. The HEADINGS, SUB-HEADINGS, and INTRODUCTIONS are not prayed. You can read 'em, but don't speak 'em.

That's great, but how can you distinguish the Office from the headings, sub-headings, and introductions? Here's how.

Take your breviary. Turn to the Psalter **and put the Psalter bookmark in place somewhere in the Psalter. Before you move on, take a peek at the Psalter bookmark. What's printed on it?.** Now page through the Psalter. You will notice many, many headings. Find Wednesday, Week IV. Look for the following headings.

Invitatory
Morning Prayer
Ant. 1
Psalm 108
Ant. 2
Canticle

Page through all of the offices for Wednesday, Week IV, moving the bookmark along as you go. What other headings do you notice?

Now use that bright dodo eye of yours. How did the publisher of your breviary distinguish the headings from the prayers? Often the headings are printed in a different color or type style (bolder, lighter, larger, smaller, italics) than the Office itself.

Now look at Morning Prayer for Wednesday, Week IV. Find Psalm 108. Under the heading "Psalm 108" will be a subheading and an introduction. These read

"Praise of God and a plea for help" and "Since the Son of God has been exalted above the heavens, his glory is proclaimed through all the earth (Arnobius)." Arnobius is the ancient writer who wrote this reflection. I bet you knew that already, didn't you?

How does the publisher of your breviary distinguish the subheading and introduction from Psalm 108? Most publishers use a different color or style of type (bolder, lighter, smaller, larger, italics) to distinguish subheadings and introductions from the Office.

Page through the remainder of the Psalter, looking for headings, subheadings, and introductions in the offices for all of Wednesday, Thursday, and Friday of Week IV. Move the Psalter bookmark along as you go. Were you able to find more examples of each of these? When praying the Divine Office, silently read the headings, subheadings, and introductions but don't say them out loud.

> **DODO**
> **SELF-CHECK #10**
>
> 1. Is the Divine Office meant to be prayed silently or aloud?
>
> 2. Is the Divine Office sometimes sung or chanted?
>
> 3. What written in the Office do you read silently? How can you distinguish these from the Office itself?
>
> 4. What does "R" mean when printed in the breviary? For now, how should you treat this instruction?

Look in the Psalter for Sunday Evening Prayer, Week IV. Page through until you come to the Canticle of Revelation 19:1-7. Look for a capital letter "R" written here and there throughout the Canticle. No, R does not mean "Restricted." **The "R" written before some lines in the breviary means "Response."** It is used as an instruction when groups are praying the office together. Right now, pay no attention to any "R's" in the breviary. Much later we will learn how to pray with them.

Lesson 11: Beginning and Ending the Office and the 'Glory Be'

Feeling brave today? I hope so because today you are going to begin to actually pray an office. I say "begin" because you'll have quite a few other lessons before you'll be praying a complete office. Today is just a beginning.

If you have a four volume breviary, use the two volumes for Ordinary Time until instructed to do otherwise.

Ready? Let's go !

First off, there are certain things that are always done, but the breviary doesn't tell you to do them. Why not? Because you're just supposed to know. Since you don't know, I'll tell you.

First thing you are supposed to know. **Every office begins and ends with the SIGN OF THE CROSS, prayed silently, even though it is not printed in the breviary.** To make the Sign of the Cross, bless yourself and <u>pray silently</u>, "In the name of the Father and of the Son and of the Holy Spirit. Amen."

Second thing you are supposed to know. **The GLORY BE is prayed after every single Psalm and Canticle, or section thereof, in the Divine Office with one exception which you will learn later. It is prayed even though the breviary does not tell you to pray it.**

Third thing you are supposed to know. The Glory Be in the Divine Office is prayed with a special ending, like this: **Glory to the Father, and to the Son, and to the Holy Spirit, as it was in the beginning is now and will be forever. Amen.** In order to show reverence, every time you pray the Glory Be, you may wish to bow while praying the words 'Glory to the Father, and to the Son, and to the Holy Spirit.' You may straighten for the remainder of the prayer.

Did you see the Glory Be printed on the Hymn bookmark? It's not cheating to look at it when you pray.

Lesson 12: Psalms and Canticles in the Psalmody

Let's nose around a bit more in the breviary. Page through the Psalter (Weeks I, II, III, and IV). Look for the section marked PSALMODY. **The PSALMODY is a section at the beginning of each office**. It follows the Hymn. Even a dodo could figure out what you'll find in a Psalmody!

Look at the Psalmody in several offices. Can you find PSALMS? CANTICLES? ANTIPHONS (abbreviated ANT.)? PSALM-PRAYERS? Go on. Find a lot of each of these. The more you find, the easier the rest of this lesson will be.

PSALMS and CANTICLES are poetic prayers found in the Bible. They were often sung. You can sing them if you want to, but you don't have to.

ANTIPHONS, often abbreviated Ant., are short, repeated prayers that accompany the Psalms and Canticles. **Antiphons are prayed before each Psalm and Canticle**. Here's an insider secret. **The Antiphons are generally prayed after each Psalm and Canticle, too**. But your breviary may not print them after, only before. Why? You'll have to ask your breviary publisher that question.

PSALM-PRAYERS are short reflections that follow some of the Psalms and Canticles. **You may pray or skip the Psalm Prayers.** We'll pray them in this instruction, but you may do as you wish.

Look in your breviary for Evening Prayer for Friday, Week III. Find the Psalmody. You will notice that it begins with an Antiphon called ANTIPHON 1 or ANT. 1. Antiphon 1 reads, "Great is the Lord, our God, transcending all other gods." Boy, isn't that the truth!

In the one volume breviary and the travelers' breviary, you will see two other Antiphons printed in smaller type following Antiphon 1. One smaller Antiphon is marked "December 17-23" and the other is marked "Easter." I bet you know what seasons those are for! For now, we'll ignore those seasonal Antiphons, even if we are in those seasons!

Do you notice that Psalm 135 has a subheading? It reads, "Praise for the wonderful things God does for us."

Psalm 135 also has an introduction that reads, "He has won us for himself . . . and you must proclaim what he has done for you. He has called you out of darkness into his own wonderful light (see 1 Peter 2:9)."

When you pray the Divine Office, will you pray aloud this heading, subheading, and introduction? Did you answer no? If so, you're correct!

Psalm 135 begins with the words, "Praise the name of the Lord." In just a moment, you'll be praying this Psalm all the way down to the words, "on his people his land he bestowed." Some breviaries have the word "Glory . . . " after this. Others don't. You know what the "Glory" means, don't you? You're right! It's a hint to pray the Glory Be here. Do you pray the Glory Be even if your breviary doesn't print the word "Glory"? You bet you do!

Some breviaries reprint Antiphon 1 following Psalm 135; others don't. In either case, Antiphon 1 is <u>often</u> prayed following the first Psalm. As noted earlier, we'll pray it both before and after in

---

DODO SELF-CHECK #12

1. What are Psalms? Antiphons? Psalm-Prayers? Canticles?

2. In praying the Divine Office, what prayer is said following each Psalm or Canticle or portion thereof?

3. Where do you pray the Antiphon for the Psalms and Canticles? If the Antiphon is not reprinted after the Psalm or Canticle, are you to pray it anyway?

4. Do you pray the Psalm-Prayer aloud?

<table>
<tr><td>

TECHNIQUE

The procedure for praying the Psalms and Canticles in the Psalmody is as follows:

  Pray Antiphon 1.
  Pray the first Psalm or Canticle.
  Say the full Glory Be.
  Pray or skip any Psalm-Prayer.
  Repeat Antiphon 1.

  Pause briefly for silent reflection.

  Pray Antiphon 2.
  Pray the second Psalm or Canticle.
  Say the full Glory-Be.
  Pray or skip any Psalm-Prayer.
  Repeat Antiphon 2.

  Pause briefly for silent reflection.

  Pray Antiphon 3.
  Pray the third Psalm or Canticle.
  Say the full Glory Be.
  Pray or skip any Psalm-Prayer.
  Repeat Antiphon 3

</td></tr>
</table>

this instruction. **After praying the Antiphon at the end of the Psalm, pause briefly for silent reflection on the Psalm itself.**

Now you're ready. Take a deep breath and pray Psalm 135, with its Antiphon and Glory Be. All done? You did it! You just prayed a Psalm from the Divine Office. Let's try another.

Find Antiphon 2. It reads, "House of Israel, bless the Lord! Sing Psalms to him, for he is merciful." Both the one volume breviary and travelers' breviary again record the December and Easter Antiphons. Ignore these for now.

Look at the Psalm. It's marked "II." Does that seem wierd? **A Psalm with the heading "II" is the second part of the preceding Psalm.** The section that begins "Lord, your name stands for ever," and that ends, "he who dwells in Jerusalem," is the second half of Psalm 135.

In some breviaries, the word "Glory . . . " is again printed after the last line of the Psalm. Whether it's printed or not, you know what to do, you smartie. Pray the "Glory Be" after the Psalm. Then you'll notice a Psalm-Prayer that begins, "Father, your name and your memory last for ever" and that ends "on us in our lowliness." In some breviaries,

Antiphon 2 is reprinted following the Psalm-Prayer. In this instruction, whether or not Antiphon 2 is reprinted, we'll pray Antiphon 2 again, then pause briefly for reflection before continuing.

Look for Antiphon 3. What does it read? Does it precede another Psalm or a Canticle? How would you pray this?

PRACTICE: Following this outline, pray the Psalmody for Friday Evening Prayer, Week III. Check how you did by referring to Appendix A.

EXTRA PRACTICE: Turn to Week II. Pray the Morning and Evening Prayer Psalmody for Monday, Tuesday, Wednesday, and Thursday. Use the outline on the left to help you.

Lesson 13: The Responsory

I bet you can figure out what a RESPONSORY is. Something you respond to, right? A RESPONSORY follows the Scripture Reading in every office.

The simplest Responsories are those for Midmorning, Midday, and Midafternoon prayer. They are only two lines long. A typical Responsory for these three little offices is:

> We do well to praise the Lord.
> To sing to you, our God most high.

To pray the Responsory if praying alone, pray the first line and then the second. Simply simple.

The responsories for Morning, Evening, and Night Prayer and the Office of Readings are longer. They also have some lines that end with a series of three dots (. . .).Most dodos know that three dots means that something is continuing. What is it? What it is, is the earlier Responsory line. **The Responsory line with three dots is to be read in full just the way it appears earlier in the Responsory.**

For example, one Responsory for the Office of Readings for the Twenty-Second Sunday in Ordinary Time is printed like this in a four volume breviary:

> I will give thanks to you, O Lord my God, with all my heart,
> for great is your mercy toward me.
> You are my God, I give you thanks; my God, I give praise to you.
> For great is . . .

The three dots mean that the fourth line is to be read in full as it appears earlier. When you pray this Responsory, you will say it as follows:

> I will give thanks to you, O Lord my God, with all my heart,
> for great is your mercy toward me.
>
> You are my God, I give you thanks; my God, I give praise to you.
> For great is your mercy toward me.

That was pretty easy, wasn't it?

The Responsories for Morning, Evening, and Night Prayer add a portion of the Glory Be to the Responsory. This is written as "Glory be to the Father . . . " Here's another secret most folks don't know. **In the Responsory, only the first line of the Glory Be is prayed—"Glory to the Father and to the Son and the Holy Spirit." The second line of the Glory Be is not prayed in the Responsory.** Why not? I don't know. I don't know everything, you'll soon discover!

In the breviary, the Responsory for Tuesday Morning Prayer, Week I, is written as follows:

> My God stands by me, my trust is in him.
> My God stands by me, my trust is in him.
>
> I find refuge in him, and I am truly free:
> all my trust is in him.
>
> Glory to the Father . . .
> My God stands . . .

DODO
SELF-CHECK #14

1. What is the name of the office that is prayed on Saturday evening?

2. What is the name of the office that is prayed on Sunday evening?

3. Why are these designations in the Psalter?

Following the guidelines earlier in this lesson, can you figure out how to pray this Responsory? Did you think it would be something like this:

> My God stands by me, my trust is in him.
> My God stands by me, my trust is in him.
>
> I find refuge in him, and I am truly free;
> all my trust is in him.
>
> Glory to the Father and to the Son and to the Holy Spirit.
> My God stands by me, all my trust is in him.

After praying the complete Responsory, it's good to pause for silent reflection before continuing to pray the office.

PRACTICE: In your breviary, find a Responsory for Morning, Evening, or Night Prayer. Using the above format as an outline, pray this Responsory. Find ten more Responsories in your breviary. Pray them, using the above instruction as a guide.

Lesson 14: Evening Prayers I and II

Evening Prayers I and II? Does this mean you have to pray two Evening Prayers? Only if you are talking about praying on two evenings.

Find your breviary's Psalter and page through it. Look for Saturday prayers. Keep going until you find an office marked "Saturday Evening Prayer."

Could you find it? Don't feel dodo-y if you couldn't. Why? Because you won't find any "Saturday Evening Prayer" unless you are using a bogus breviary.

Oh, so we don't pray Saturday Evening Prayer? Wrong! **The office prayed on**

Saturday evening is called SUNDAY, EVENING PRAYER I.

Now why in the world . . ..? The designations, Evening Prayer I and Evening Prayer II, didn't develop just to confuse folks. When they developed in medieval times, everyone knew exactly what they meant. When knights were riding about in shining armor rescuing fair damsels in distress, people considered Saturday evening as the beginning of Sunday worship. So the office for Saturday evening would naturally be called Sunday, Evening Prayer I. And the office for Sunday evening would naturally be called Sunday, Evening Prayer II. If you start to think like a knight or a damsel, you'll grasp the distinction which the Psalter has kept.

Let's find Sunday, Evening Prayer I in the Psalter. Can you find one of these offices?

Now page forward and look for Sunday, Evening Prayer II. Did you find it? Great! Before long, you'll be an expert in understanding these two offices.

"In this section, you'll learn about ..."

Introduction to Night Prayer

Beginning the Office of Night Prayer

Concluding the Office of Night Prayer

Praying the Office of Night Prayer

Night Prayer every night!

Praying Night Prayer

TECHNIQUE

For beginning every office other than the first office of the day:

1. The Sign of the Cross made silently The rest of the office prayed aloud.

2. The introduction, "God, come to my assistance. Lord, make haste to help me."

3. The Glory Be as learned in Lesson 11 and printed on the Hymn bookmark.

4. "Alleluia" prayed after the "Glory Be" except during Lent.

"Alleluia" is prayed after the Glory Be only at the <u>beginning</u> of the office. "Alleluia" is not prayed after the Glory Be when the Glory Be follows the Psalms and Canticles in the Psalmody.

The procedure for beginning the Divine Office is printed on one of the bookmarks already in your breviary.

Lesson 15: Introduction to Night Prayer

"Now I lay me down to sleep . . ." That's a night prayer, all right, but not the one in the Divine Office. Night Prayer is a very important office and here's something really great about it. It's one of the easiest offices to learn! Yipee! Let's get started!

Let's see how your breviary arranges Night Prayer.

Some breviaries begin Night Prayer with Night Prayer after Evening Prayer I on Sundays and Solemnities (this is prayed Saturday night; remember, oh you brave knight or fair damsel!) Other breviaries begin the Night Prayer section with Sunday Night Prayer. How does your breviary arrange Night Prayer. Go look!

Flip through the Night Prayer section. Check off the following terms as you fly by them:

> Hymn
> Psalmody (Psalm)
> Reading
> Responsory
> Gospel Canticle (also called the Canticle of Simeon or the Nunc Dimittis)
> Prayer
> Conclusion that reads, "May the all-powerful Lord grant us a restful night and a peaceful death" (hint: this will be either at the end of each Night Prayer or else right after Friday Night Prayer)
> Antiphons in honor of the Blessed Virgin (hint: these may be at the very end of the Night Prayer section)
> Night Prayer after Evening Prayer I on Sundays
> Night Prayer after Evening Prayer II on Sundays
> Night Prayer for Monday, Tuesday, and other weekdays to Friday

Were you able to find all these terms? If not, keep looking until you do.

Lesson 16: Beginning the Divine Office

Guess what? Every office has certain prayers that are always prayed with that particular office. That simplifies things, doesn't it? Well, not really. Because these prayers are repeated in every office, many breviaries don't write them out. Hey, that's not fair! Yes, it is, because if these prayers were printed in every single office, your breviary would be a lot thicker and a lot more expensive. Get the point?

Don't despair. The following lessons will teach you these repetitive prayers. These prayers are prayed whether or not they are printed in the proper place in the breviary. Check out the technique box on page 3-2. What repetitive prayers do you see?

Let's begin with a repetitive word. When you hear the word "Alleluia," do you think of Christmas? Or Easter? **"Alleluia" is a cry of joy. It is often used in the Divine Office. During Lent the Church keeps a somber attitude and does not pray the "Alleluia."** This is reflected in how the Divine Office begins.

First a word about the first office of the day. The first office of the day begins in a special way. Later you'll learn how to begin the very first office of the day. But now we're talking about the last office of the day. Night Prayer.

Lesson 17: Concluding the Divine Office

We're going to make a Night Prayer "sandwich." We just began our "sandwich" with the "top slice of bread," the beginning of the office. Now let's get the "bottom slice of bread," the end of the office.

Every office of the Divine Office ends with a Concluding Prayer. Called a Concluding Prayer because it concludes the office. Duh. Even a dodo can understand that! In some breviaries, this Concluding Prayer is written out in full. In others, it's not. If it's not written out in your breviary, how do you know what to pray?

Here's the process. **First ask, "Who is the Concluding Prayer addressing?"** God the Father? God the Son? God the Holy Spirit?

1. If a Concluding
Prayer is not written out
in full, how do you
determine its ending?

2. On which bookmark
can you find the endings
to the Concluding
Prayers?

If the Concluding Prayer begins by addressing God the Father or God the Holy Spirit, its ending is either "We ask this . . . " or "Grant this . . . " followed by "through our Lord Jesus Christ, your Son, who lives and reigns with you and the Holy Spirit, one God, forever and ever. Amen." See, the Son is mentioned in the conclusion.

If the Concluding Prayer begins by addressing God the Son, it concludes with "You live and reign with the Father and the Holy Spirit, one God, for ever and ever. Amen." See, the Father and Spirit are mentioned in the conclusion.

You don't have to remember these. They are printed on one of the bookmarks already in your breviary. How about looking and seeing which one?

Lesson 18: Praying Night Prayer (Part One)

Let's take a look backwards at what you've already learned. You've learned how to begin and end an office, how to pray the Glory Be, and what many of the terms and parts of the Divine Office are. You've also learned some background on the Divine Office including why the offices are named as they are and how the hours came to be designated. Do you feel as dodo-y as you used to feel? I hope not!

Now we're really going to pray a full office. Honest! First we get to use another bookmark. Can you guess which one?

Did you guess Night Prayer? Oh, you are smart! **Insert the Night Prayer bookmark in your breviary at Night Prayer After Evening Prayer One on Sundays. Hint: See Lesson 14.**

If you don't remember when this prayer is prayed, look at the Night Prayer bookmark. What's printed on there?

Aren't you glad that these bookmarks have crib notes? What's in the beginning of the Night Prayer office that's not in the beginning of any other office? You can compare the Psalter bookmark crib notes with the Night Prayer ones to find out. Did you discover something that begins with the letters EOC? Yes! Examination of Conscience. And then POF? Yes! Prayer of Forgiveness. Why do we pray these in Night Prayer? Because "if I die before I wake, I pray the Lord my soul to take." EOC POF. We want to go to bed with a clean conscience and a forgiving heart. Just in case we wake up at the Pearly Gates.

Night Prayer is the only office that contains an examination of conscience. The examination is made silently. Thankfully, especially if you are praying this office in the presence of others!

You probably have your own method of making an examination of conscience. If you don't, silently ask God to help you recall your behavior, speech, thoughts, omissions, and attitudes during the day. Examine these for any sin or failing. Ask God's forgiveness. Resolve to go to confession as soon as possible for any major sins. Ask God's grace to help you do better tomorrow.

Follow the examination of conscience with a short prayer of forgiveness. Make an Act of Contrition in a formal prayer or in your own words. You might get to use the first ribbon of the "restful ribbon" set right here. Check your breviary to see if it prints some prayers of forgiveness in a certain section (not all breviaries do). **If yours does, draw the black (for sorrow for sin) ribbon down through the breviary to mark the Prayers of Forgiveness section.**

Then sing a Hymn, if you like to sing, that is. Some breviaries print a Hymn at the beginning of each Night Prayer office. Others refer you to certain Hymns in the Hymn section which you've already bookmarked. **Some breviaries have a separate section for Night Prayer Hymns alone. If yours does, draw the orange (for sunset) ribbon down through the Night Prayer Hymn section of your breviary.**

You've learned how to begin Night Prayer. How do you conclude it? Do you think you might find some crib notes on the other side of the Night Prayer bookmark? Right! Night Prayer ends with the conclusion "May the all-powerful Lord grant us a restful night and a peaceful death. Amen" followed by the Sign of the Cross and an ANTIPHON IN HONOR OF THE BLESSED VIRGIN. Whether or not your breviary prints the conclusion to Night Prayer after each office, you know where on the bookmark to find it.

But what's that ANTIPHON IN HONOR OF THE BLESSED VIRGIN? And where is it?

The Antiphons in Honor of the Blessed Virgin are really prayers or Hymns to

> **DODO SELF-CHECK #18**
>
> 1. Could you find every section listed above? Be sure to locate them before proceeding,
>
> 2. What bookmark marks Night Prayer? What's written on that bookmark?
>
> 3. What color ribbon marks the Night Prayer Hymns?
>
> 4. What color ribbon marks the Antiphons in Honor of the Blessed Virgin?
>
> 5. What color ribbon marks the Prayers of Forgiveness?

Our Lady. You know some of them. "The Hail Mary." "Hail, Holy Queen."

Flip through the Night Prayer section of your breviary. Is an Antiphon to the Blessed Virgin written after each Night Prayer office? Or is there an Antiphon Section, usually at the end of the Night Prayer section? **If your breviary has an Antiphon Section for Antiphons in honor of the Blessed Mother, draw the pur-**

TECHNIQUE

A technique for praying Night Prayer:

> Look at the front of your Night Prayer bookmark.
> Make the Sign of the Cross.
> Read, "God, come to my assistance. Lord, make haste to help me."
> Pray the Glory Be as learned in Lesson 11 and printed on the Hymn bookmark.
> Say, "Alleluia." (Omit during Lent.)
> Make a silent examination of conscience.
> End with a prayer of forgiveness.
> Sing, chant, or recite an appropriate Hymn.
> Say the Antiphon. (In one volume breviaries, ignore for now the Antiphon marked "Easter" and pray the other Antiphon that begins "Day and night . . ..")
> Read Psalm 88. End the Psalm with the Glory Be as printed on the Hymn bookmark. Say the Antiphon (not the one marked Easter but the "Day and night" one) again.
> Pause briefly to think about Psalm 88.
> Read the Reading.
> Read the Responsory as described in Lesson 13 (In one volume breviaries, ignore for now the Responsory marked Easter).
> Pause briefly.
> Say the Antiphon that begins "Protect us, Lord." (In one volume breviaries, ignore for now the Alleluia written in parentheses after this Antiphon.)
> Make the Sign of the Cross at the first line of the Gospel Canticle from Luke 2, the line that reads, "Lord, now you let your servant go in peace."
> Read the Gospel Canticle.
> Pray the Glory Be.
> Say the Antiphon again (do not say the Alleluia in parentheses).
> Pause briefly.
> Say, "Let us pray."
> Read the prayer.
> Look at the back of your Night Prayer bookmark. Read "May the all powerful Lord grant us a restful night and a peaceful death. Amen."
> Make the Sign of the Cross.
> Pray ONE of the Antiphons in honor of the Blessed Virgin.

ple (for queenliness) ribbon from your ribbon set down through that section to mark it.

You've just completed the "upper slice of bread" and the "lower slice of bread" in the Night Prayer sandwich. First a Dodo Self Check and then we'll add the "filling."

Lesson 19: Praying Night Prayer (Part Two)

Let's start this lesson with a little pretending. **No matter what day of the week it is when you do this lesson or what time of day, pretend it's Friday evening. Move your Night Prayer bookmark to Friday Night Prayer.** Now remember, we're just pretending. You may still have to set your alarm, get up early, and go to work tomorrow.

Page through Friday Night Prayer, looking at its various parts. Where are the Night Prayer Hymns? The Prayers of Forgiveness? The Antiphons in Honor of the Blessed Mother? What color ribbon marks each of these?

The "filling" for the Night Prayer "sandwich" consists of Psalms, Antiphons, Responsory, and Canticle. You've already practiced praying those in Lessons 12 and 13. So you're ready to put it all together. Let's see what this "bedtime bite to eat" looks like. Study the technique box on page 3-6. Got it down pat? We're ready to pray Friday Night Prayer! Go ahead and try it.

Can you believe it? You've just prayed an entire office! Was it easier than you thought? This entire Office, as it would be prayed, is printed in full in Appendix B.

PRACTICE: Spend a few days praying only this particular office—Night Prayer for Friday—until you are familiar with its sections and how to use your bookmark and ribbons. Use your breviary, not Appendix B, to pray this Night Prayer. Check with this instruction or with Appendix B only to see if you are praying correctly. In learning to pray the Divine Office, it's a wise dodo who prays Night Prayer at least three to five times before proceeding with this instruction.

Lesson 20: Praying Night Prayer Every Night

Now you're really getting good. How would you like to pray Night Prayer every night? A quickie review here. Find the Night Prayer section of your breviary. On what night will you pray Night Prayer After Evening Prayer I on Sundays?

Check out Lesson 14 if you're not sure.

A few little details here and a bit more pretending. No matter what season of the year it is, pretend that it's plain, old ordinary time, like, let's say, the middle of July. Middle of July in Kansas. Ooooh, get out the fans and ice cold lemonade! Puuuleees!

Now find Night Prayer after Evening Prayer I (in some breviaries marked "Saturday") and after Evening Prayer II on Sundays (in some breviaries marked "Sunday"). Look at the Concluding Prayers to these two offices. Eeeks! Two prayers! Which one do you use? Remember, we're pretending it's the middle of July. So for now, in Night Prayer after Evening Prayer I and II on Sundays, use the first Concluding Prayer and ignore the second. We're also going to ignore any instructions that refer to any season other than Ordinary Time. Christmas and Easter seasons don't fall in July! When you get really smart, later on, you'll learn how to pray Night Prayer during these other seasons.

OK. Let's get started. Set up your breviary to pray Night Prayer tonight, on this day of the week in the middle of July.

First, find the Night Prayer that is appropriate for today. Place the "Night Prayer" bookmark at that spot. Next select a Hymn if one isn't given you. What color ribbon marks the Night Prayer hymns? (Hint: color of sunset).

Select the Prayer of Forgiveness that you wish to use. What color ribbon marks the Prayers of Forgiveness? (Hint: color of sorrow for sin).

If your breviary has a section of Antiphons in Honor of the Blessed Virgin, select the Antiphon that you wish to use. What color ribbon marks the Antiphons in honor of the Blessed Virgin? (Hint: queenly color).

PRACTICE: From now on, you might want to pray Night Prayer every night.

Night Prayer is prayed right before going to bed, whenever that might be.

"In this section, you'll learn about ..."

Getting familiar with the psalter

Morning and Evening Prayer canticles

Invitatory

Intercessions

Concluding Morning and Evening Prayer

Praying Morning and Evening Prayer

Two and three-part psalms

THE DIVINE OFFICE FOR DODOS

PRAYING MORNING AND EVENING PRAYER ON WEEKDAYS DURING ORDINARY TIME

If you have a four volume breviary, continue to use the volumes for Ordinary Time for these instructions.

Lesson 21: Growing Familiar with the Psalter

Oh, the Psalter. Does the Psalter seem kind of scary? Soon it will be an old friend.

You've already stuck the Psalter bookmark someplace in the Psalter. Flip through the Psalter, looking for the headings "Week I," "II"," III", and "IV." Now that you know where they are, move the Psalter bookmark to Monday, Week I. Find the INVITATORY for this day. It should be listed first, right under the title of the day and the week.

Put on your thinking cap. An Invitatory is a prayer that i_____ you to begin to pray. Did you fill in the word "invites?" Good for you! More about the Invitatory in a bit. Right now we want to get an overview of the Psalter.

Page through the Psalter for Monday, Week I, bouncing the bookmark along and answering the following questions as you go.

What office is listed right under the Invitaory? The Office of Readings? Morning Prayer? On a piece of paper, write the offices in order as you come to them. You might want to read these out loud a few times, just to set the order of them in your brain.

You should now be at the beginning of the office for Tuesday, Week I. Page through the offices for Tuesday, Wednesday, Thursday, and Friday, Week I. Compare them with each other and with what you've written on your paper. Do you see a pattern? Patterns make things easier, don't they?

Right here, we are going to skip a lot of stuff. In some breviaries, the Office of Readings will precede Morning Prayer, and Daytime Prayer offices will follow Morning Prayer. We're going to skip the Office of Readings and Daytime Prayer for now. Oh, we'll get to them later, all right, but right now we're concentrating on praying Morning and Evening Prayer.

Don't stop now. Keep paging through the Psalter, all the way to Saturday Morning Prayer for Week IV. Keep paging. Can you find Sunday prayers for

Week V? No. Good for you! Why? Because **there is no Week V in the Psalter. The Psalter covers only four weeks.** I bet you can figure out what to do when you complete Saturday prayers for Week IV. Think of the Psalter as a wheel. **When you finish praying the offices under Week IV of the Psalter, you return to Week I of the Psalter.** Around and around and around, Weeks I, II, III, IV, all year through. That was pretty easy, don't you think?

Let's take some examples. Suppose that on Saturday, June 5, you are praying the offices for Saturday, Week IV. When you complete these, do you throw away the book because you've finished it? Nope! You continue the Divine Office by returning to Week I of the Psalter. Where will you find the offices for Monday, June 7? In Monday, Week I of the Psalter.

DODO
SELF CHECK #21

1. What are the parts of the offices in order? You can peek when you answer.

2. How many weeks are in the Psalter? I hope you don't have to peek for this one.

3. What do you do when you complete the offices for Saturday, Week IV? Hint. Think of a circle.

So how do you pray, using the Psalter? You use it day after day, in order, until you reach the Saturday offices of Week IV. When you complete these, you roll around to Week I of the Psalter and begin all over again..

Lesson 22: Morning and Evening Prayer Canticles (Part One)

Isn't "Canticle" a beautiful word? Sounds like a song, doesn't it? That's just what a Canticle is. In Morning, Evening, and Night Prayer, there's always a Canticle to sing God's praises. You're already familiar with the Night Prayer Canticle, the song of Simeon. ("Protect us, Lord, as we stay awake . . .). What are the other two?

The other two main Canticles prayed in the Divine Office are taken from St. Luke's Gospel. You've heard them read at Sunday Mass. **THE CANTICLE OF ZECHARIAH, which is the Morning Prayer Canticle, is Zechariah's song of praise upon the birth of John the Baptist (Luke 1:68-79). THE CANTICLE OF MARY, which is the Evening Prayer Canticle, is Mary's Magnificat, sung upon visiting her cousin Elizabeth shortly after Mary conceived Our Lord (Luke 1:46-55).**

So if you look in the Morning and Evening Prayer Offices, you'll find the two Canticles, right? Wrong!

Well, why not?

Because the Canticles are more of those repeated prayers that, if printed every time you prayed them, would make your breviary very, very large.

All right. You can understand that. But where are the Canticles? Do you have to go to the Gospel of Luke every time to pray them?

Not at all. The breviary makes things easier than that, and you thought the breviary was all difficult, didn't you?

Do you recall the papers of printed prayers that come with some breviaries? You may have placed these inside either the front or back cover of your breviary. The Canticle of Zechariah and the Canticle of Mary may be printed on those cards, perhaps marked as Gospel Canticle under Morning Prayer and Evening Prayer. Check your cards and see.

If your pet goat ate the cards, or you don't have them for any other reason, it's no big deal. Look in your breviary's Table of Contents (that's right in the front of the book, for those of us who were never too good at English). In the Table of Contents, find the page for the Ordinary of the Divine Office. Flip through the Ordinary until you find the instructions for Morning Prayer. Then flip through Morning Prayer instructions, looking for the Canticle of Zechariah (Gospel Canticle). Did you find it? Good! Double check by seeing if the Bible reference on the right side above it reads Luke 1:68-79. If so, you have the right Canticle. If not, search for the proper Canticle until you do find it. Once you do find it, **draw the silver ribbon (for the silver notes of morning that greet the rising sun) from the ribbon set down through the breviary to mark the Canticle of Zechariah.**

That wasn't too difficult, was it?

Now that we're all geared up, let's find the Evening Prayer Canticle. If you suspect it's in the Ordinary, too, you're a pretty intuitive dodo. Flip through the Ordinary until you come to Evening Prayer. Page ahead in Evening Prayer, looking for the Canticle of Mary which may also be called the Gospel Canticle. Does the Bible reference at the top right of this Canticle read Luke 1:46-55? Yes? Then you've found it! If it reads something different, check through the breviary until you find the proper Canticle. **Draw the blue ribbon (blue is the color traditionally associated with Our Lady) down through the breviary to mark the Canticle of Mary.**

If you're a super intellectual dodo, you might want to compare the translations of the two Canticles in your breviary with the translations of the same Canticles in your Bible.

Now that you've marked the Canticles, how do you pray them?

We'll look at Morning Prayer first because, well, morning comes first in the day. Turn to Monday, Week I in your breviary. Find Morning Prayer and page through it until you find the Canticle of Zechariah (in some breviaries called the Benedictus or Old Testament Canticle) and mark it with the Psalter bookmark.

But, hey, in most breviaries, it's not the whole Canticle. It's only an Antiphon. The silver ribbon marks the whole Canticle.

So what do you do?

You flip from Antiphon to Canticle to Antiphon again. Isn't this fun?

Let's get specific. To pray the Morning Prayer Canticle, you first pray the Antiphon marked by the Psalter bookmark, then flip to the Canticle marked by the silver ribbon, then a Glory Be as prayed in the Office, and then flip back to the Antiphon again. Easy as breathing, right?

DODO
SELF CHECK #22

1. What is the Canticle of Zechariah?

2. What is the Canticle of Mary?

3. Where are these in your breviary?

4. What color ribbons mark each?

5. What's printed in the Morning and Evening Offices, where these Canticles are to be prayed?

Now let's try Evening Prayer. Oh, slow down! You're moving fast here. That's right, keep flipping through the office for Monday, Week I, until you get to Evening Prayer. Look for the Canticle of Mary (in some breviaries called the Magnificat or New Testament Canticle). Bet you knew it was only an Antiphon, didn't you?

Bet you know how to pray this, too? Antiphon marked by Psalter bookmark, Canticle marked by blue ribbon, Glory Be as prayed in the Office, Antiphon.

You really are doing great, you know!

Lesson 23: Morning and Evening Prayer Canticles (Part Two)

I bet you noticed that we talked about praying the Morning and Evening Prayer Canticles in the last lesson, but we didn't pray them. In this lesson, you'll learn the fine points of praying these beautiful songs.

Let's go back to where we were in the last chapter. Turn to the Psalter and find Week I, Monday, Morning Prayer. Flip ahead to the Canticle of Zechariah's Antiphon that reads, "Blessed be the Lord our God." **Place the Psalter bookmark at this spot for now.**

Before we pray, we're going on an Antiphon treasure hunt. Each one is like a little nugget of gold. How many can you find? Page ahead to Tuesday, Morning Prayer, Week I. **The guide words at the top of the pages will help you locate offices in the Psalter.** What is the Antiphon written under the Canticle of Zechariah for Tuesday, Morning Prayer, Week I?

Page ahead and look at the Antiphons for the Canticle of Zechariah on Wednesday, Thursday, and Friday Morning Prayer, Week I. Are they the same or different?

Go back to the Canticle of Zechariah for Monday, Week I, marked with the Psalter bookmark. Now you know that "Blessed be the Lord our God" is not the Canticle but only the Antiphon for the Canticle. You know, too, that the silver ribbon marks the actual Canticle. Memory jog here. Do you recall that the Glory Be is prayed after every Psalm and Canticle in the Psalter with one exception which you will learn later? How do you pray the Glory Be in the Divine Office? Hint: Consult the Hymn bookmark.

DODO
SELF CHECK #23

1. Are the Antiphons for the Canticles of Zechariah and Mary the same every day or do they change with the day?

2. How will you know which Antiphon to pray for the Canticles?

3. Is the Antiphon prayed between the verses of the Canticles?

4. What prayer is said at the end of each Canticle? Hint: It's printed on the Hymn bookmark.

5. During which office is the Canticle of Zechariah always prayed?

6. During which office is the Canticle of Mary always prayed?

TECHNIQUE

To pray the Canticle of Zechariah:

1. Say the Antiphon as printed in the Psalter.

2. Use the silver ribbon to turn to the Canticle of Zechariah (Luke 1:68-79).

3. Make the Sign of the Cross.

4. Read the whole Canticle through prayerfully.

5. At the end of the Canticle say the Glory Be in full as printed on the Hymn bookmark. Pray the Antiphon again as written in the Psalter.

Follow the technique and pray the Canticle of Zechariah for Monday, Week I. When you're done, give yourself a pat on the back, if you can reach around that far. If you can't, let your spouse or friend do it for you. Double check to see if you prayed this correctly by checking Appendix C.

Now you remember how to pray the Canticle of Mary, don't you? The same way!

Flip ahead in Monday, Week I, to Evening Prayer. Page through this until you find the Canticle of Mary. The Antiphon for the Canticle will read, "My soul proclaims the greatness of the Lord, for he has looked with favor on his lowly servant." **Move the Psalter bookmark to this spot.**

Now we're going on another treasure hunt, looking for Evening Prayer Antiphons. Page ahead in the Psalter. Find the Canticle of Mary for Tuesday, Wednesday, Thursday, and Friday of Week I. Read these Antiphons. Are they the same or different?

See how much you're learning?

In praying the Divine Office, the Canticle of Zechariah is said during every single Morning Prayer. The Canticle of Mary is said during every single Evening Prayer. The Antiphons change, but the Canticles are always the same.

Go back to Monday, Evening Prayer, Week I and find the Canticle of Mary. Well, the Antiphon for the Canticle. Where is the actual Canticle? Yep, the blue ribbon tells you.

Now pray the Canticle of Mary for Monday, Week I. How'd you do? Great? Congratulations! Check Appendix C to double check if you prayed this Office correctly.

Lesson 24: Invitatory

Here's an invitation to pray the Invitatory. Do you accept?

The INVITATORY is an invitation to praise God. It's the very first prayer of the day when praying the Divine Office.

Remember which two offices may be prayed first in the day? **The first office of the day may be either the Office of Readings or Morning Prayer. Whatever office you choose to pray first, you will begin it with the INVITATORY.**

Psalm 95 is usually said as the Invitatory Psalm.

Psalm 95 is in your breviary. I bet you know it's not printed at the beginning of every Office of Readings or every Morning Prayer. Bet you know why, too. I also bet you have an inkling of where to find the Invitatory. Either on those prayer cards that came with your breviary or in the Ordinary which you can find by looking up the page number in the Table of Contents. Oh, there it is, at the beginning of the Ordinary. Invitatory Psalm, Psalm 95.

TECHNIQUE:

To pray the Canticle of Mary:

1. Say the Antiphon as printed in the Psalter.

2. Use the blue ribbon to turn to the Canticle of Mary (Luke 1:46-55).

3. Make the Sign of the Cross.

4. Read the whole Canticle through prayerfully.

5. At the end of the Canticle say the Glory Be in full as written on the Hymn bookmark.

6. Pray the Antiphon again as written in the Psalter.

To pray the
Invitatory.

1. To pray the
Invitatory, follow
this procedure:
Make the Sign of the
Cross silently.

2. Say, "Lord, open
my lips."

3. Respond with,
"And my mouth will
proclaim your
praise."

4. Pray the Antiphon
as written in the bre-
viary and marked by
the Psalter book-
mark.

5. Pray the verses of
the Invitatory Psalm,
as marked by the
white ribbon, repeat-
ing the Antiphon
after each one. You
may wish to bow or
kneel while praying
verse 3.

6. End the Invitatory
Psalm with the
"Glory Be" as print-
ed on the Hymn
bookmark.

7. Repeat the
Antiphon.

Draw the white ribbon (white for the white dawn rising) down through the breviary to mark Psalm 95, the
Invitatory Psalm.

Let's examine Psalm 95. Notice how the verses are
separated. Your breviary may have the words
"Antiphon" or "Antiphon repeated" between each
verse. **For the Invitatory Psalm, an ANTIPHON is
prayed between each
verse. This is <u>not</u> the procedure for any other
Psalm or Canticle. In all
the other Psalms and
Canticles of the Divine
Office, the Antiphon is
said only before and after
the Psalms and Canticles
and NOT between the
verses.**

**DODO
SELF CHECK #24**

1. What is the Invitatory?
When is it said?

2. Which two offices may
be said first in the day?

3. How do you begin the
very first office that you
pray?

Read Psalm 95. Find the
third verse that begins
"Come, then, let us bow down and worship, bending
the knee before the Lord, our maker. **For the third
verse of the Invitatory, if you want to, you may either
bow or kneel while praying, then rise for the fourth
verse.** If you want to make one of these acts of reverence, you can write "Bow" or "Kneel" next to this
verse as a reminder. No one's going to scold you for
marking up your own breviary.

Let's find exactly where to pray the Invitatory. Turn to
Week I, Monday, of the Psalter. Your Psalter bookmark
is probably still in Monday, Week 1, so finding this
spot will be a breeze. Go to the very first page of these
Monday offices. Almost the very first thing written will
be the word "Invitatory." Under this will be a short
phrase ("Lord, open my lips") and an Antiphon. Did
you guess that this is the Invitatory Antiphon for
Monday, Week 1? You bet it is! Put the Psalter bookmark here.

Before going further, we're going to have an
Invitatory Antiphon treasure hunt. Page ahead in your
breviary to Tuesday, Week I. Read the Antiphon for
the Invitatory. Is it the same as Monday's? Look at the Invitatory Antiphons for
Wednesday, Thursday, and Friday? Are they all the same or do they differ from

each other?

Flip back to the Invitatory for Monday, Week I, and read what it says on the front of the Psalter bookmark. Use the technique on the left to pray the Invitatory. **The Invitatory <u>always</u> begins with the Sign of the Cross, prayed silently, and the words, "Lord, open my lips. And my mouth shall proclaim your praise." <u>This may not be written out in full in your breviary.</u> The Invitatory <u>always</u> ends with the full Glory Be <u>even though this may not be written out in your breviary.</u> This procedure is printed on the Psalter bookmark.**

PRACTICE: Using the technique at left, pray the Invitatory for Monday, Week I. Not too difficult, was it? Check with Appendix D to see if you have prayed this properly.

Lesson 25: Intercessions and Concluding Morning and Evening Prayer

You know what Intercessions are from attending Sunday Mass. **INTERCESSIONS are prayers of petition. In the Divine Office, they're prayed during Morning and Evening Prayer.**
Turn to Monday, Week I in the breviary. Yes, we'll pray from some other days in the Psalter, eventually. Honest! Right now, you're becoming an expert about Monday, Week I! Maybe you can go on a quiz show! Page along until you come to Morning Prayer for Monday, Week I. Now page through until you come to the Intercessions which follow the Canticle of Zechariah. Mark this spot with the Psalter bookmark and move on!

Keep paging until you come to Evening Prayer for Monday, Week I. Page through this until you come to the Intercessions. Did you think they'd follow the Canticle of Mary? Pretty clever, you.

Keep your finger here and turn back to the Morning Prayer Intercessions. What's similar about the two sets

---

TECHNIQUE

How to pray the Intercessions for Morning and Evening Prayer and how to end both offices:

1. Pray the first Intercessions straight through, reading one line after the next exactly as it's written. Pray the Refrain exactly where it's written and nowhere else.

2. If you wish, you <u>may</u> add Intercessions of your own at the end before the words "Our Father." <u>If you add Intercessions, pray the Refrain after each of your own added Intercessions.</u>

3. Following the Intercessions, pray the <u>entire</u> Lord's Prayer that begins "Our Father who art in heaven, hallowed be thy name . . .." <u>Pray this whole prayer through to the end even though only the first words are written in your breviary.</u>

Continued next page ...

Continued from previous...

using the ending printed on the Psalter bookmark.

6. At the end of that prayer, add the dismissal words "May the Lord bless us, protect us from all evil and bring us to everlasting life. Amen." <u>Pray this dismissal even though it's not written in your breviary.</u>

7. Make the Sign of the Cross silently <u>even though this isn't written in your breviary.</u> **This Sign of the Cross ends Morning and Evening Prayer.**

8. The conclusion of the Divine Office is printed on the Psalter bookmark.

of Intercessions? What's different? Do you notice the words "Our Father . . . " following the Intercessions? What do you think that means? If you think it means that you'll pray the "Our Father" here, you're right!

Do you like Christmas songs? Many Christmas songs have a refrain, a verse that is repeated at intervals through the song. A familiar refrain comes at the end of each verse of "Silent Night." "Sleep in heavenly peace. Sleep in heavenly peace." Another Christmas song with a refrain is "Deck the Halls." The refrain is "Fa la la la la, la la la la."

No fa la la la's in the Divine Office. But there are refrains. Let's find 'em.

Return to the Intercessions for Monday Morning Prayer, Week I. You'll notice that, **following the introduction to the Intercessions, there's a line printed in a different type. This may be in darker, lighter, smaller, larger, or** *italicized* **type. This is called the REFRAIN.** For Monday Morning Prayer, Week I, the Refrain reads, *Give us your Spirit, Lord.* This means it's repeated between the intercessions, under certain conditions (we'll tell you which in a bit).

Time for an Intercession and Refrain treasure hunt. Look ahead in your breviary to Morning Prayer and Evening Prayer for Tuesday, Wednesday, Thursday, and Friday of Week I. Are the Intercessions the same for each day or do they change? Is the Refrain the same or does it change?

Now all we have to do is find the Conclusion to the Morning and Evening Offices and we are ready to pray again. Look on the back of the Psalter bookmark. The Conclusion of the Divine Office is printed there.

DODO
SELF CHECK #25

1. What are the Intercessions?

2. May you add some Intercessions of your own?

3. What is the Refrain? How is it printed in your breviary? When do you pray the Refrain?

4. Following the Intercessions, what familiar prayer do you pray in full?

5. When do you say "Amen"?

6. What dismissal do you pray even though it's not written in the breviary?

7. How do you end Morning and Evening Prayer?

PRACTICE: Using these guidelines and your breviary, pray the Intercessions and Concluding Prayers for Monday Morning Prayer, Week I. Check how you did by comparing your praying with the Intercessions and Conclusion as written out in full in Appendix E.

EXTRA PRACTICE: Page through your breviary to Monday Evening Prayer, Week I. The very same format listed above is used to pray the Intercessions for Evening Prayer as for Morning Prayer. Pray the Intercessions and Concluding Prayers for Monday Evening Prayer, Week I, following the above guidelines. Check how you did by comparing your prayer with that in Appendix F.

Lesson 26: Praying Morning Prayer

Are you ready, really ready? Because you're going to begin to pray Morning Prayer for Ordinary Time. Honest.

Guess which office we'll use? If you guessed the ever friendly office, Monday Morning Prayer, Week I, you guessed right. Let's pretend that this will be the first prayer of your day. If you've not already done so, **move the Psalter bookmark to this Monday Morning Prayer, Week 1.**

Now a little comparison work and maybe a "gotcha." If you've not been praying Night Prayer regularly, then we "gotcha." Why? Because it's time to compare Morning Prayer with Night Prayer. Page through the Morning and Night Prayer offices. Quick now. What parts of Morning Prayer are not in Night Prayer?

TECHNIQUE

For praying Morning Prayer, Monday, Week I, as the first prayer of the day:

    1. Look at the front of the Psalter bookmark. Follow the procedure for beginning Morning Prayer.

    2. Make the Sign of the Cross, say, "Lord, open my lips." Respond, "And my mouth will proclaim your praise."

    3. Pray the Antiphon for the Invitatory, followed by the Invitatory as taught in Lesson 24. End the Invitatory with the "Glory Be" prayed in full.

    4. Sing, chant, or recite the Hymn you have chosen.

    5. Pray Antiphon 1 written in your breviary's Psalter, followed by the first Psalm (Psalm 5: 2-10, 12-13) to the end. Pray the "Glory Be" Say the Psalm-Prayer. Repeat Antiphon 1.

Continued on next page ...

---

x

Continued from previous page ...

6. Pause briefly for silent reflection.

7. Pray Antiphon 2, followed by the Canticle (1 Chronicles 29:10-13) to the end. Say the "Glory Be." Repeat Antiphon 2.

8. Pause briefly for silent reflection.

9. Say Antiphon 3, followed by the Psalm (Psalm 29) all the way through to the end. Pray the "Glory Be." Pray the Psalm-Prayer.   Repeat Antiphon 3.

10. Pause briefly for silent reflection.

11. Read the Reading, followed by the Responsory, following the guidelines in Lesson 13.

12. Pause briefly for silent reflection.

13. Pray the Antiphon for the Canticle of Zechariah, followed by the Canticle itself, as taught in Lesson 23 all the way through. Pray the full "Glory Be." Repeat the Antiphon for the Canticle of Zechariah.

14. Pause briefly for silent reflection.

15. Pray the Intercessions.   Recite the Our Father. Pray the Concluding Prayer.

16. Look at the back of your Psalter bookmark for the conclusion to the office. Pray, "May the Lord bless us, protect us from all evil, and bring us to everlasting life. Amen."

17. End with the Sign of the Cross.

Did you answer Psalm-Prayers, the Canticle of Zechariah, Intercessions, and the Our Father? And maybe the Invitatory? Good for you!

We've not talked about Psalm-Prayers yet. **PSALM-PRAYERS follow many of the Psalms and Canticles in Morning and Evening Prayer. They are prayerful reflections on the preceding Psalm or Canticle. You may read these or skip them. In this instruction, we'll consistently read them. The full GLORY BE is prayed <u>after</u> the Psalm or Canticle but <u>before</u> the Psalm-Prayer.**

Can you believe it? You're almost ready to pray Morning Prayer!. First, you've got to choose a Hymn. Some breviaries have a Hymn with the Morning Prayer.

Others have a section of Hymns with indices. You've already bookmarked the Hymn Index so look there for Hymns for Morning Prayer, Ordinary Time.

Only one Hymn is sung for Morning Prayer. Choose one suggested or a different one.

Use the "Hymn" bookmark to mark the Hymn that you've chosen.

Now, to be really ready to pray, you might want to review all the following lessons:

Lesson 9 (Hymns)
Lesson 10 (Praying Aloud)
Lesson 11 (How to Begin and End the Office and How to Pray the Glory Be)
Lessons 22 and 23 (Praying the Morning and Evening Prayer Canticles) What color ribbon marks the Canticle of Zechariah? What color ribbon marks the Canticle of Mary?
Lesson 24 (Praying the Invitatory) What color ribbon marks the Invitatory?
Lesson 25 (Praying the Intercessions and Concluding Morning and Evening   Prayer)

TECHNIQUE

For Praying Evening Prayer, Monday, Week I, Ordinary Time.

1. Look at the Psalter bookmark. Make the Sign of the Cross.   Say, "God, come to my assistance." Respond, "Lord, make haste to help me."

2. Pray the "Glory Be" all the way through to the end. Say "Alleluia." (Omit the "Alleluia" during Lent.)

3. Sing, chant, or recite the Hymn you have chosen.

4. Pray Antiphon I as written in your breviary's Psalter, followed by the first Psalm (Psalm 11) to the end. Pray the "Glory Be." Say the Psalm-Prayer. Repeat Antiphon 1.

5. Pause briefly for silent reflection.

6. Pray Antiphon 2, followed by the second Psalm (Psalm 15) to the end. Say the "Glory Be." Say the Psalm-Prayer. Repeat Antiphon 2.

Continued on next page ...

Continued from previous page ...

7. Pause briefly for silent reflection.

8. Pray Antiphon 3, followed by the Canticle (Ephesians 1: 3-10) all the way through to the end. Pray the "Glory Be." Repeat Antiphon 3.

9. Pause briefly for silent reflection.

10. Read the Reading, followed by the Responsory, following the guidelines in Lesson 13.

11. Pause briefly for silent reflection.

12. Pray the Antiphon for the Canticle of Mary, followed by the Canticle itself, as taught in Lesson 23 all the way through. Say the full "Glory Be." Repeat the Antiphon for the Canticle of Mary.

13. Pause briefly for silent reflection.

14. Pray the Intercessions.   Recite the Our Father. Pray the Concluding Prayer. Look at the back of the Psalter bookmark.

15. Pray, "May the Lord bless us, protect us from all evil, and bring us to everlasting life. Amen."

16. End with the Sign of the Cross.

Reminders on how to begin and end Morning and Evening Prayer are printed on the "Psalter" bookmark.

PRACTICE: Now you are ready to pray Morning Prayer for Monday, Week I, Ordinary Time. As you pray, move the bookmark along as you turn the pages.

Lesson 27: Beginning All the Offices Except the First Office of the Day and Praying Evening Prayer

You're moving right along, aren't you? This lesson will be a snap. Ready? Let's go!

DODO SELF CHECK #27

1. What's similar between the office of Evening Prayer and the office of Morning Prayer? What's different?

2. How does one begin the first office of the day? How does one begin all the other offices of the day?

3. Where is "Alleluia" said? During which season of the year is it omitted? Why is it omitted then?

You already know how to pray Morning Prayer. You just prayed it! Praying Evening Prayer is very similar to praying Morning Prayer. There are only two differences. One you already know. The Canticle of Mary, not the Canticle of Zechariah, is prayed during Evening Prayer.

The other difference has to do with how to begin the office of Evening Prayer. **Only the FIRST office of the day begins with the Invitatory. All the other offices except the first begin by first silently making the Sign of the Cross and then saying, "God, come to my assistance. Lord, make haste to help me." Then the full "Glory Be" is prayed. Pray "Alleluia" after the "Glory Be" unless it's Lent.** Ever hear this beginning before? Right you are! Night Prayer begins just like this. You'll find this introduction printed on the Psalter bookmark.

> **DODO**
> **SELF CHECK #28**
>
> 1. When the Psalter breaks up a Psalm or Canticle into sections, how are the sections prayed?

Let's get ready to pray Evening Prayer. Back to good ol' Monday Week I.

Page through this office until you come to Evening Prayer for Monday, Week I and move the Psalter bookmark to this spot. Select an Evening Prayer Hymn, as you did for Morning Prayer. Move the Hymn bookmark to this spot.

Now, if you want a good review, check back with the following lessons:

> Lesson 9 (Hymns)
> Lesson 10 (Praying Aloud)
> Lesson 11 (How to Begin and End the Office and How to Pray the Glory Be)
> Lessons 18 and 19 (Praying Night Prayer)
> Lessons 22 and 23 (Praying the Morning and Evening Prayer Canticles)
> Lesson 25 (Praying the Intercessions and Concluding Morning and Evening Prayer)
> You're all set to pray Evening Prayer! So let's pray! Follow the technique in the box above.

Congratulations! You've just prayed Evening Prayer!

Time for some comparisons. Compare Evening Prayer for Monday, Week I, with some other Evening Prayers in the Psalter. What's the same in these offices? What's different?

Lesson 28: Two and Three Part Psalms

Here's another easy lesson. Praying the Divine Office is a breeze, isn't it? Have you ever read the whole Book of Psalms in the Bible? If you have, you know that some Psalms are short, some are long, some are very long, and some are in between. The long and very long Psalms are broken up into sections in the Psalter. Let's find an example of this.

Check out the Psalmody for Evening Prayer, Wednesday, Week I. Did you find the first Psalm, Psalm 27? Do you see Roman Numeral I over this Psalm?

Now page ahead to the second Psalm. Do you notice that this Psalm has Roman Numeral II written over it? This means that Psalm 27, which is a long Psalm, has been broken into two parts (Part I and Part II) for the Office.

Page through the Psalter right now, looking for other offices in which a Psalm or Canticle is split into one (I), two (II), and sometimes even three (III) sections. If you find ten or more other examples, go reward yourself with a milk shake and then come back to finish the lesson!

So how do you pray these split Psalms or Canticles. Just as if they weren't split. **When you pray an office in which a Psalm or Canticle is split, many people treat each section as if it were a complete Psalm or Canticle. Pray the Antiphons as you have learned to do <u>before and after each section.</u> The Glory Be is prayed after <u>each section</u> of the Psalm or Canticle.** There is an alternate technique which you'll learn later.

PRACTICE: Here's an example. Go back to Wednesday Evening Prayer, Week I. Look at the first Psalm, Psalm 27. To pray Psalm 27 in this office, follow this procedure:

      Pray Antiphon 1,

      Pray Psalm 27 from the first line ("The Lord is my light and my help") all the way through to the last line of the first section ("I will sing and make music for the Lord").

      Pray the Glory Be.

      Repeat Antiphon I.

      Pause briefly.

      Pray Antiphon 2.

      Pray the second section of Psalm 27 straight through beginning with "O Lord, hear my voice when I call" and ending with "Hope in the Lord!"

      Pray the Glory Be.

      Read the Psalm-Prayer.

      Repeat Antiphon 2 and continue with the office as you have learned.

Lesson 29: Praying Morning Prayer and Evening Prayer Every Weekday

PRACTICE: From now on, try to pray Morning Prayer and Evening Prayer every weekday. For now, do not worry about using the proper season of the year or about any special Church celebrations. Do not pray Morning and Evening prayer on weekends just yet. Soon, you'll learn how to use your breviary to pray at all these times. For <u>right</u> <u>now</u>, however, pray Morning and Evening Prayer for Monday, Tuesday, Wednesday, Thursday, and Friday, <u>using only the Psalter</u>.

Page through the Psalter. Look for the headings that say Week I, Week II, Week III, and Week IV. How will you know which week you're in?

Make a phone call to a priest, religious, or religious community. Tell them that you're going to be praying the Divine Office. Ask them what week we're currently in (Week I, II, III, or IV). Turn to that week in the Psalter. Find today's day of the week. **Look for Morning Prayer for today. Put your Psalter bookmark at that spot.**

If it's still morning when you do this, pray Morning Prayer for today. **If it's evening, move your Psalter bookmark ahead to Evening Prayer** for today and pray Evening Prayer. And if it's in between, choose one or the other office to pray!

EXTRA PRACTICE FOR WISE DODOS: Before moving on in this instruction, you might want to take two full weeks of practice just to pray Morning and Evening Prayer for Monday, Tuesday, Wednesday, Thursday, and Friday, using the offices from the Psalter for Ordinary Time. Ignore the Saturday and Sunday offices for now. If you complete Week IV of the Psalter, you know what to do. Go back to Week I.

And remember to continue to pray Night Prayer every night.

When you're comfortable praying Morning, Evening, and Night Prayer, as instructed so far, then be my guest and proceed with these instructions.

"In this section, you'll learn about ..."

Saturday Morning and Evening Prayer

The Proper of Seasons

Sunday offices in Ordinary Time

Strophes and singing

The Canticle of Daniel

THE DIVINE OFFICE FOR DODOS

PRAYING MORNING AND EVENING PRAYER ON SATURDAYS AND SUNDAYS DURING ORDINARY TIME

Lesson 30: Saturday Morning Prayer and Saturday Evening Prayer (Sunday, Evening Prayer I)

If you have a four volume breviary, use all four volumes for these instructions.

OK. Get those dodo dancing feet ready. Why? Because we're gonna learn some fancy footwork here.

Open your breviary to Saturday Morning Prayer, Week I and examine it closely. Does it look like the same format for Monday, Tuesday, Wednesday, Thursday, and Friday Morning Prayer? Now look at Saturday Morning Prayer for Weeks II, III, and IV. Do these look like the same formats for the Morning Prayers of the week?

That was just a warm up jig because Saturday Morning Prayer is prayed in exactly the same manner as Morning Prayer on the weekdays.

We're getting ready for some new side steps here. Look for Saturday Evening Prayer, Week I. Can't find it? Remember why not? Good for you! You can't find Saturday Evening prayer because **Saturday Evening Prayer is marked Sunday, Evening Prayer I.**

DODO SELF CHECK #30

1. Compare praying Saturday Morning Prayer with praying Morning Prayer on the weekdays. How are they similar?

2. What parts of the office are not printed in the Psalter for Sunday Evening Prayer I, Sunday Morning Prayer, and Sunday Evening Prayer II? Where are these parts located?

Look in your breviary for Week I, Sunday, Evening Prayer I. Look carefully at the order of the office. What do you notice about the Canticle of Mary? What do you notice about the prayer following the Our Father?

You'll notice that these spots refer you to a section of the breviary called "THE PROPER OF SEASONS." Oh, no! What's that? Where's that? We'll dance over there in a bit but we ain't ready to leave this part of the ballroom yet. Keep dancing along through the Week I offices to Sunday Morning Prayer and Sunday Evening Prayer II. What do these say at the Canticles of Mary and Zechariah and the Prayer following the Our Father?

Jig ahead through your breviary to Weeks II, III, and IV, looking at Sunday Evening Prayer I, Sunday Morning Prayer, and Sunday Evening Prayer II. What's similar about all of them? What's different? You've not tripped over your two left feet yet, have you?

Lesson 31: The Proper of Seasons

DODO
SELF CHECK #31

1. What is the Proper of Seasons? Where is it in your breviary?

2. List five things you notice about the Proper of Seasons.

3. What is your first reaction upon studying this section of the breviary? Most people feel like they've been tossed into the middle of a Hollywood musical and they haven't the foggiest idea about the choreography. Not to worry. Pretty soon you'll be high steppin' with the best of 'em.

Aren't you dying to know what the Proper of Seasons is? It's got the word "seasons" in it. That's a clue.

THE PROPER OF SEASONS is the section of the Psalter that contains various parts of offices that change with the week and season of the year. Makes sense, right?

So where's the Proper of Seasons?

Turn to the ever popular Table of Contents in the front of your breviary. Look for the Proper of Seasons. Read all the subheadings below it. What do you notice? Keep track of them. Why? Hint: See Question 2 of the Dodo Self Check.

Now turn to the Proper of Seasons in the breviary and page through it. What do you notice? **Place the Proper of Seasons bookmark anywhere in the Proper of Seasons.**

If you have a four volume breviary, page through the Proper of Seasons in all four volumes of your breviary. What season does Volume I cover? Volume II? Volume III? Volume IV?

Still dancin'? Good for you!

Lesson 32: Sunday Offices in Ordinary Time

If you have a four volume breviary, use the two volumes for Ordinary Time for this instruction.

Keep dancing because you're about to learn some dippin' n dodgin' here.

Find the Proper of Seasons in your breviary's Table of Contents. Look under the Proper of Seasons to find the section(s) marked Ordinary Time. Turn to the section(s). Page through them, looking at the numbers of the weeks. **The guide words at the tops of the pages will help you find your place in the Proper of Seasons.** How many weeks are there in Ordinary Time? Thirty-four, right? Numbered in order from 1 to 34. That was pretty easy, wasn't it?

What is Ordinary Time? Well, it's ordinary. **Ordinary Time is the season of the Church Year that is not a Lent/Easter or Advent/Christmas season. Ordinary Time begins following the end of the Christmas season and is interrupted by Lent/Easter, resuming again following Pentecost.**

Use the Table of Contents to look for the First Sunday of Ordinary Time in the Proper of Seasons. Can you find it? No? Did your breviary publisher inadvertently leave it out? Do you have a defective breviary?

Nope, all is well. You won't find the First Sunday of Ordinary Time because the Baptism of the Lord takes place on the First Sunday of Ordinary Time. How about that?

So where's the Baptism of the Lord? It's the very last day of celebration for the Christmas Season.

Here's where we diverge a bit. Depending on your breviary, complete the following:

One Volume Breviary Instruction: In one volume breviaries, you'll notice a prayer under the title "First Week of Ordinary Time" that follows the Baptism of the Lord. The prayer reads,
> "Father of love,
> hear our prayers.
> Help us to know your will
> and to do it with courage and faith.
> Grant this through our Lord Jesus Christ, your Son,
> who lives and reigns with you and the Holy Spirit,
> one God, for ever and ever."

This prayer is all that you will see under the heading "First Week of Ordinary Time." The next heading will be "Second Sunday in Ordinary Time."

Why is this prayer here? This prayer is the Concluding Prayer for the Office of Readings for the First Week in Ordinary Time. We'll discuss how to pray the Office of Readings later in this manual. Since we're not praying the Office of Readings now, you can ignore this prayer for the time being.

Now look for the Second Sunday of Ordinary Time. It will be right after the Baptism of the Lord. What do you notice about this Sunday? Look at the

Third, Fourth, Fifth, and Sixth Sundays of Ordinary Time. How are these similar to the Second Sunday? How are they different?

Four Volume Breviary Instruction: *If you have a four volume breviary, take Volume III for the first seventeen weeks of Ordinary Time and page through the Proper of Seasons. Look for the First Week of Ordinary Time. You'll see a title for each day of the week and below that the words "Office of Readings." Under the "Office of Readings," you'll find a First Reading followed by a Responsory and then a Second Reading followed by another Rusponsory and then a Prayer.*

Look at the Office of Readings for Monday through Saturday of the First Week of Ordinary Time. Find the Concluding Prayer for the Office of Readings for each day of the First Week of Ordinary Time. You'll see that it's the very same prayer printed above under the instruction for one volume breviaries.

Now look ahead to the Second Sunday in Ordinary Time. Do you see the heading Evening Prayer I with the Canticle of Mary and Prayer printed beneath it? Now page through the Office of Readings for the Second Sunday in Ordinary Time until you come to the heading Morning Prayer. What do you see under this heading? Now page ahead and look for Evening Prayer II. What do you see under this heading?

Page through the Proper of Seasons looking at the Second Week of Ordinary Time. Compare the offices for the days of the week with the offices for the Third Sunday of Ordinary Time. Now look quickly through the Proper of Seasons in all four volumes of your breviary. What do you see?

You'll see that, <u>in the four volume breviary, every single day has two long Readings for the Office of Readings. The Readings for the Office of Readings are printed first in each office in the Proper of Seasons.</u> You'll learn how to pray the Office of Readings later in this manual. For right now, skip all the Offices of Readings that are printed in the Proper of Seasons.

Now we wish to focus on the Sunday offices of Evening Prayer I, Morning Prayer, and Evening Prayer II. Find these offices for the Fourth, Fifth, and Sixth Sundays of Ordinary Time.

Instruction for All Breviaries (One or Four Volume): OK. All breviary users are back together again in one disco. Before joining this dance, you might want to polka back to review Lesson 30. Here's what you'll find there:

For the Sundays of Ordinary Time (Sunday

DODO
SELF CHECK #32

1. What is the season of Ordinary Time? When does it begin? How many weeks are in Ordinary Time? What breaks up Ordinary Time? When does it resume?

2. What is the First Sunday of Ordinary Time?

3. What parts of the Sunday Offices are in the Proper of Seasons?

4. How does one pray the Alternative Prayer?

Evening Prayer I, Sunday Morning Prayer I, and Sunday Evening Prayer II), the Antiphons for the Canticle of Mary and the Canticle of Zechariah and the Concluding Prayer of the Sunday offices are printed in the Proper of Seasons.

You've got the Proper of Seasons marked with a bookmark. Gambol over to the Proper of Seasons. Look again at the Second Sunday in Ordinary Time. Some (not all) breviaries print both a prayer and an ALTERNATIVE PRAYER. **When praying the offices for Sunday, you may choose as a Concluding Prayer either the Prayer, which is the prayer usually said, or the ALTERNATIVE PRAYER. Only one of these prayers is prayed in each office.** Still dancing? Good!

Lesson 33: Strophes and Singing

A what-phe? Dodos were curious birds. So be curious about stophes and keep dancing. You're going to learn some tunes to dance to!

Find the Sunday offices for Week II in the Psalter. Turn to Evening Prayer for Sunday, Week II. There are, as always, three Psalms and/or Canticles. Turn to the third which is a Canticle from the Book of Revelation, Chapter 19, verses 1 to 7. Look over this Canticle. Do you see "Alleluia" sometimes written in parentheses, perhaps with a capital "R" before it? What do you think that means? (Hint: It does not mean roll over.)

Most breviaries contain some instruction right before the Canticle begins. If yours does, read the instruction. It probably says, "The following Canticle is said with the Alleluia when Evening Prayer is sung; when the office is recited, the Alleluia may be said at the beginning and end of each strophe."

There's that word again. What is a strophe (pronounced "stro-fee")? **A STRO-PHE is one section of the Psalm or Canticle. You would probably call it a verse. A space separates one strophe from the next.**

So why didn't they just say so? I have no idea. Remember, I told you that I don't know everything.

Look again at the Canticle from Revelation 19:1-7. The first strophe, as printed in your breviary, is

> Alleluia.
> Salvation, glory, and power to our God:
> (R. Alleluia)
> his judgments are honest and true.
> R. Alleluia (Alleluia).

A space separates this strophe from the second strophe. How many strophes are there in this Canticle? Yep, four.

All Psalms and Canticles are divided into strophes. Look at the first Psalm for Sunday Evening Prayer II, Week II. It's Psalm 110:1-5, 7. How many strophes in that Psalm? Right-o. Six.

DODO
SELF CHECK #33

1. What is a strophe? How can you tell how many strophes are in a Psalm or Canticle?

2. How would you pray the Canticle from Revelation 19:1-7?

Now look at the second Psalm, Psalm 115. How many strophes does it have? Nine-o, baby! Well, how about that? You've been praying strophes all these lessons and didn't know it! Isn't that a kicker?

Now read again the instruction that precedes the Canticle from Revelation. The instruction tells you that, if you sing the Evening Prayer, you are to sing all the Alleluia's. If you recite the office, you are to skip those Alleluia's that are in parentheses. If it's OK with you, since we have been reciting the office, we'll skip the Alleluia's that are in parentheses. And if it's not OK and you want to sing, you go right ahead. No one's going to stop you, are they?

PRACTICE: Pray this Canticle through as if you were <u>reciting</u> it. Therefore, skip all the Alleluia's in parentheses, unless you really want to sing. In which case, be my guest..

Lesson 34: Praying the Sunday Offices for the Second Week in Ordinary Time (Part One)

Still cha-cha ing? Good for you!

Turn to the Proper of Seasons. **Move the Proper of Seasons bookmark to mark the spot for the Second Sunday in Ordinary Time.** Right under the words "Second Sunday in Ordinary Time," your breviary has printed the words, "Psalter, Week II." This means that the Sunday offices for the Second Sunday in Ordinary Time are the Sunday offices for Week II of the Psalter. Pretty clever way to clue you in, right?

Look in the Psalter for Week II, Sunday Evening Prayer I. This will be the very first office for Week II. **Move the Psalter bookmark to this spot**. Let's see what you remember. Is this office prayed on Saturday or on Sunday evening?

Sunday Evening Prayer I is prayed on Saturday evening. Did you remember that?

Page through Sunday Evening Prayer I for Week II. If you have a one volume breviary, you'll notice that the Psalms have a variety of Antiphons listed for Advent, certain Sundays in Lent, and Easter.

If you're using a four volume breviary, you're using Volume III (Ordinary Time) and you won't see these Antiphons. That's because, in the four volume breviary, these Antiphons are in the appropriate Lent/Easter and Advent/Christmas volumes.

Time for some pretending if today happens to fall in the Advent/Christmas or Lent/Easter season.. Since we're going to <u>practice</u> praying Sunday offices for <u>Ordinary Time</u>, we're going to pretend it's Ordinary Time even if it's not. Therefore, we'll ignore all seasonal Antiphons for now. Later on you'll get to pretend it's Lent/Easter or Advent/Christmas even if it's not. What goes around comes around.

Keep paging through Sunday Evening Prayer I for Week II until you come to the Antiphon for the Canticle of Mary. Whoops! No Antiphon. Remember why? Yep, the Antiphon's in the Proper of Seasons.

Your Proper of Seasons bookmark should mark the Second Sunday in Ordinary Time in the Proper of Seasons. Good for you if it's still there. Turn there now. Do you see the Antiphon for the Canticle of Mary under Evening Prayer I?

Now use your Psalter bookmark to turn back to the Psalter. Look for the Concluding Prayer for Sunday Evening Prayer I, Week II. Oh, no. Not there. Where does the breviary refer you?

Flip back to the Proper of Seasons bookmark. In a one volume breviary, you won't see a prayer after Evening Prayer I (*it is written there in the four volume breviary*). In a one volume breviary, only one prayer (and possibly an alternative prayer) is written. It's placed after the Morning Prayer heading. *In a four volume breviary, there is also only one prayer printed after the Morning Prayer heading. If you have a four volume breviary, page ahead to the Morning Prayer heading for the Second Sunday in Ordinary Time.* **The prayer written after the Morning Prayer heading in the Proper of Seasons is the same prayer said for Evening Prayer I, Morning Prayer, and Evening Prayer II for that day.** The prayer isn't written again to avoid repetition and to save paper. You already knew that,

DODO S
SELF CHECK #34

1. Do you have the Psalter bookmark in the Psalter section? Yes? Good for you!

2. Do you have the Proper of Seasons bookmark in the Proper of Seasons section? Great!

3. What color ribbon marks the Canticle of Zechariah?

4. What color ribbon marks the Canticle of Mary?

5. When do you pray the prayer written in the Proper of Seasons? Do you pray it only after Morning Prayer or do you pray it after the other offices as well?

6. When do you pray Sunday Evening Prayer I?

didn't you?

The Proper of Seasons bookmark has a crib note printed on it. The conclusion of these concluding office prayers is printed on the Proper of Seasons bookmark. Isn't that neat?

Look in the Psalter for Sunday Morning Prayer Week II. Where's the Antiphon for the Canticle of Zechariah? Yep. Proper of Seasons. Can you find it under the Second Sunday of Ordinary Time?

Return to the Psalter. Where's the prayer that you will say to conclude Morning Prayer? Page ahead in the Psalter to Sunday Evening Prayer II for Week II. Where's the Antiphon for the Canticle of Mary? Where's the Concluding Prayer?

TECHNIQUE

For praying the Sunday Offices (Sunday Evening Prayer I, Sunday Morning Prayer, and Sunday Evening Prayer II):

　　1. Put the Psalter bookmark in the correct place in the Psalter. Put the Proper of Seasons bookmark in the correct place in the Proper of Seasons.

　　2. Choose a Hymn for the office that you will be saying and mark it with the Hymn bookmark.

　　3. The ribbons should be in place in the breviary (silver—Canticle of Zechariah; white—Invitatory; blue—Canticle of Mary)

　　4. Turn to the Psalter. Begin the office following the format printed on the front of the Psalter bookmark.

　　5. For Morning Prayer, follow the format that you learned in Lesson 26. For Evening Prayer, follow the format that you learned in Lesson 27.

　　6. When you get to the Antiphons for the Canticle of Mary and the Canticle of Zechariah, refer to the Proper of Seasons. Use the ribbons to locate the Canticles.

　　7. Continue with the offices as written in the Psalter.

　　8. Conclude with the Concluding Prayer written in the Proper of Seasons.

　　9. End the office as written on the Proper of Seasons bookmark.

Do you get the hang of this two-step rumba? Proper of Seasons to Psalter to Proper of Seasons to Psalter.

In order to pray Sunday Evening Prayer I, Sunday Morning Prayer, and Sunday Evening Prayer II, you must go to the Proper of Seasons for the Antiphons for the Canticles of Mary and Zechariah and for the Concluding Prayer. Use the bookmarks to help you rumba along through the breviary.

Lesson 35: Praying the Sunday Offices for the Second Week in Ordinary Time (Part Two)

DODO
SELF CHECK #36

1. When is the Glory Be prayed in the Psalter?

2. After which Canticle is the Glory Be not prayed? Where can you find this Canticle in the Psalter?

3. The Psalter contains two other Canticles from the Book of Daniel. Is the Glory Be prayed after these?

Have you, like a wise dodo, been praying the weekday offices for Monday, Tuesday, Wednesday, Thursday, and Friday as suggested in Lesson 29? I sure hope so. Because if you have, you're familiar with the order of these offices and how to pray the Invitatory, the Canticle of Zechariah, and the Canticle of Mary. The Sunday offices are prayed in exactly the same manner except that you must refer to the Proper of Seasons for the Antiphons for the Canticles of Mary and Zechariah and for the Concluding Prayer.

TECHNIQUE

To pray the Canticle of Daniel 3:57-88, 56, first pray the Antiphon for the Canticle. Then pray the Canticle all the way through, but do not pray the Glory Be. Pray the Antiphon again.

Here's a word to you wise dodo. Be very comfortable praying all three Sunday offices before proceeding with these instructions. Check back with or repeat some or all of Lessons 30 through 35 if you wish If you want to successfully learn to pray the Divine Office, it's real important that, before continuing, you can pray with relative ease all the offices learned so far.

Lesson 36: The Canticle of Daniel

Time for a memory jog. As you've learned, **all the Psalms and Canticles in the Psalter, with one exception, end with the prayer "Glory Be." The "Glory Be" is prayed at the end of the Psalms and Canticles <u>even though it isn't written in the breviary.</u>**

Did you wonder about that exception? Now it's time to learn about it.

Look in the Psalter for Sunday Morning Prayer, Week I. Find the Canticle of Daniel 3:57-88, 56. Read this through to the end. Does your breviary end this Canticle with a note saying that the "Glory Be to the Father" is not said at the Canticle's end?

Go to the Table of Contents. Find the section marked Psalter. Turn to the page marked Week III. Page forward until you reach Sunday Morning Prayer for Week III. Look under Sunday Morning Prayer, Week III, for the Canticle of Daniel. Yep. That's the same Canticle as in Sunday Morning Prayer Week I. And the breviary has the same ending note to the Canticle, too.

The CANTICLE OF DANIEL 3:57-88, 56 is the <u>only</u> Canticle in the Psalter after which the "Glory Be" is <u>not</u> prayed. Why not? Because the Canticle ends with a Hymn of high praise to God that is similar to the "Glory Be."

The Psalter contains two other Canticles from the Biblical Book of Daniel, Daniel 3:52-57 and Daniel 3: 26, 27. 29, and 34-41. The "Glory Be" <u>is</u> prayed after these other Canticles of Daniel.

PRACTICE: Turn to Sunday Morning Prayer Week I in the Psalter and pray the Canticle of Daniel with its Antiphons.

"In this section, you'll learn about ..."

The seasons of the church year

Navigating the seasons in the breviary

Invitatory antiphons for Lent/Easter

Invitatory antiphons for Advent/Christmas

Hymns for Lent/Easter

Hymns for Advent/Christmas

Using the Proper of Seasons

PRAYING MORNING, EVENING, AND NIGHT PRAYER THROUGHOUT THE SEASONS OF THE CHURCH YEAR

If you have a four volume breviary, you will need all four volumes to complete these lessons.

Lesson 37: The Four Volume Breviary (Part I)

This instruction is only for those who have a four volume breviary. If you have a one volume breviary, lucky you may skip this section and proceed to Lesson 40. If you have a four volume breviary, no need to fret. Complete this lesson and the two following before proceeding to Lesson 40. They're not difficult lessons but they're important.

The four volume breviary is actually one massive breviary that is printed in four volumes because it would be too large and cumbersome to be in one volume. You already knew that, right? In the instructions that follow, when you're told to "page through your breviary," you must take this to mean that you must "page through all four volumes of your breviary" until you find the section that is being discussed in the lesson. If the lesson says to "page through Ordinary Time until you come to Lent" or to another season of the Church year, then you'll need to find the volume that has that season in it.

In order to do this, you'll have to know which volume of your breviary covers which season of the year. Makes sense, right?

Some breviaries print the season of the year on the front outside cover of each volume, either on the front cover or on the spine of the book. If yours does, one outside cover will be marked "Lent/Easter," another "Christmas/Advent," one "Ordinary Time/Weeks 1-17" and another "Ordinary Time/Weeks 18-34." The volume number should also be printed on the cover. You're lucky and don't have to do one thing more here to distinguish your breviaries.

Some four volume breviaries are color coded for different seasons of the year. If your breviary is color coded, what colors are each of the seasons? Can you think of any way to associate the color with its corresponding season so that you will remember which season is in which color volume? If you've got a good memory, you've got this problem licked.

Some four volume breviaries, however, are not color coded nor do they have the titles printed on the volume covers. If your breviary is like this, don't fret. We can mark the breviaries so you can easily distinguish one from the other.

Take all four volumes and open each to the title page right in the front of the book. Your breviary may have two title pages, one with just "The Liturgy of the Hours" or the words "The Divine Office" written on it and a following page that has the same title but more information including the publisher at the bottom of the page. It is this more extensive title page that you must find.

Look at all four title pages. The seasons of the year are written on each title page. What season does Volume I cover? Volume II? Volume III? Volume IV?

Here are some ideas. You might have others. You might want to use a permanent marking pen to write the season and volume number on the front outside cover of the breviary. On the cover of the Lent/Easter breviary you might write, "Lent/Easter" and put the volume number. On the cover of the Christmas/Advent breviary, you might write, "Christmas/Advent" and the volume number. You might mark the covers of the Ordinary Time breviaries with the words "Ordinary Time/Weeks 1-17" and "Ordinary Time/Weeks 18-34" and the volume numbers. Or you might prefer to write the season on a piece of paper and tape it to your breviary's outside cover. Being able to distinguish the breviaries will help you to quickly find the breviary that you need for this instruction.

Lesson 38: The Four Volume Breviary (Part II)

In order to proceed with the instruction in this manual, it's best to have each volume of the four volume breviary marked with ribbons and bookmarks. To get one FREE set of ribbons and bookmarks, turn to the last page of this book. Just fill out the coupon there and send it to Three Bean Books, P.O. Box 1814, Westerly, RI 02891, and we'll get your freebies out to you ASAP. For additional sets of bookmarks and ribbons, use the second coupon to order as many as you would like at $5.00 per set.

When you have the ribbons and bookmarks, let's get going.

First we'll work with the ribbons. Take each of the volumes of your breviary. Look in the Table of Contents for the Ordinary. In the Ordinary of each volume:
      a. Find the Invitatory Psalm. Mark it with a white ribbon.
      b. Find the Canticle of Zechariah. Mark it with a silver ribbon.
      c. Find the Canticle of Mary. Mark it with a blue ribbon.

d. Find the Antiphons in honor of the Blessed Mother, following the Night Prayer offices. Mark these with a purple ribbon.

e. Find the Night Prayer hymns. Mark these with an orange ribbon.

f. The four volume breviary does not have Prayers of Forgiveness. It does, however, have a Poetry Section in the back of each volume. If you like, you can use a black ribbon to mark the Poetry Section.

Now we'll work with the bookmarks.

> *Bookmark Night Prayer in each volume:*
> *Bookmark the Hymn Index in each volume.*
> *Bookmark the Hymns.*

In Ordinary Time, the Hymns are printed in the Psalter on each day. However, in Advent/Christmas (Volume I) and Lent/Easter (Volume II), the Hymns are printed all together in the Proper of Seasons (not in the Psalter). Place the Hymn bookmarks in Volumes I and II. You will find the Hymns at the very beginning of the Proper of Seasons in these volumes. You only need one Hymn bookmark for each volume even though the Lenten and Advent Hymns are in a different spot from the Easter and Christmas Hymns. This is because you'll be singing these Hymns at the appropriate seasons and you can move your bookmark as needed.

> *Bookmark the Psalter in each volume.*
> *Bookmark the Proper of Seasons in each volume.*

From now on, whenever you are told to mark a section of the breviary with a ribbon or a bookmark, mark all four volumes of your breviary.

Whew! That's done! Give yourself a well-deserved pat on the back.

Lesson 39: The Four Volume Breviary (Part III)

You're moving right along and doing a great job! It's time to compare the Psalters of each volume. In each of the four volumes, find the Psalter. In each volume, find Tuesday Evening Prayer, Week III. Move the Psalter bookmark in each volume to Tuesday Evening Prayer, Week III. First compare the office in the two volumes for Ordinary Time. What's the same about the Tuesday Evening Prayer Office for Week III in both volumes of Ordinary Time? What's different? Everything's the same. Nothing's different. It's the same office.

Now compare Tuesday Evening Prayer, Week III, in the Ordinary Time volumes with Tuesday Evening Prayer, Week III, in the Lent/Easter and Christmas/Advent volumes. Compare the Hymn, Antiphons, Psalms, Psalm-Prayers, Canticles. Do you see that, in certain seasons, the Antiphons are different from those during Ordinary Time?

Now don't start giving up here because you feel a little confused. Confusion is normal for dodos at this stage of the game. You're just exploring what's in the Psalter. You don't have to memorize anything.

Now in each volume page through Tuesday Evening Prayer, Week III, until you reach the end of the Canticle of Revelation and its ending Antiphon. In the volumes for Ordinary Time, what parts of the office follow this Antiphon? Do these same parts of the office follow the Antiphon in the Lent/Easter and Advent/Christmas volumes?

In the Advent/Christmas volume, you're referred to the Proper of Seasons for the rest of the office. In the Lent/Easter volume, you're referred to the "Office of the day" for the remainder of the office. The "Office of the day" is in the Proper of Seasons as well.

Now compare, in all four volumes, these offices;
> *Friday, Morning Prayer, Week I*
> *Thursday, Evening Prayer, Week II*
> *Wednesday, Morning Prayer, Week IV*
> *What is the same about each office in each volume? What differs?*

By this comparison, you should realize that when you're in a particular season of the year, every part of the Divine Office that you'll need will be in the volume for that season. You will NOT EVER use TWO OR MORE volumes at once. You will only have to flip to different parts of ONE volume in order to pray the Divine Office for that season of the Church year. Isn't that a relief?

Lesson 40: Seasons of the Church Year

Remember when we talked about the Seasons of the Church year? They ain't summer, fall, winter, spring! The Church year is divided into special seasons of worship. So the Church year doesn't begin on January 1 like a secular year does.

The Church Year begins with the first Sunday of Advent. The seasons of the Church year are, in order: Advent, Christmas ending with the Baptism of the Lord, Ordinary Time, Lent, Easter ending with Pentecost, Continuation of Ordinary Time until first Sunday of Advent.

The Divine Office follows this cycle.

Lesson 41: The Divine Office during the Seasons of the Church Year

**DODO
SELF CHECK #40**

1. When does the Church year begin? How does this differ from what we usually think of as a year?

2. What are the seasons of the Church year? How do these differ from what we usually think of as seasons?

You'll be happy to know that praying the Divine Office during the various seasons of the Church year is somewhat like praying the Sunday Offices during

TECHNIQUE
How to treat the Proper of Seasons in praying the Divine Office:
1. During Ordinary Time, use the Psalter first. Refer to the Proper of Seasons only when told to go there.
2. During Lent/Easter and Advent/Christmas, use the Proper of Seasons first. For the parts not in the Proper of Seasons, refer to the Psalter unless directed by the breviary to refer elsewhere.

Ordinary Time.

Do you recall how, when praying the Sunday Offices (Sunday Evening Prayer I, Sunday Morning Prayer, and Sunday Evening Prayer II), you did the two step rumba by flipping back and forth from the Psalter to the Proper of Seasons to find the Antiphons for the Canticles of Zechariah and Mary and also to find the Concluding Prayer? When praying the Office during Lent/Easter and Advent/Christmas you'll be doing the two step rumba every day. You'll have to flip to the Proper of Seasons to find certain parts of some of the offices.

A convenient reminder regarding this technique is printed on the Proper of Seasons bookmark. Isn't that nifty?

Let's see how this works. **During Ordinary Time, use the Psalter first. Refer to the Proper of Seasons only when told to go there.** So, in the Psalter, look up Wednesday Morning Prayer, Week II. Pretend that it's Ordinary Time. Page through this office. Is there any place in this office that refers you to the Proper of Seasons for Ordinary Time? Nope. No place. To pray Wednesday Morning Prayer, Week II, for Ordinary Time, the Psalter is sufficient. **Place the Psalter bookmark at Wednesday Morning Prayer, Week II.**

Now hang on because things are going to get a little complicated. But you can learn the technique if you can remember one word. REPLACE. Let's say it again.

REPLACE. Got it?

REPLACE.

Let's go on. Wednesday Morning Prayer, Week II, is also the office prayed on Wednesday Morning during Holy Week. Holy Week, you'll recall, is the last week of Lent, immediately preceding Easter. **During Lent/Easter and Advent/Christmas, use the Proper of Seasons first. For the parts not in the Proper of Seasons, refer to the Psalter unless directed by the breviary to refer elsewhere.**

How does this work? Remember that key word? REPLACE. First find Wednesday Morning Prayer of Holy Week in the Proper of Seasons. In the four volume breviary, Holy Week is in the Lent/Easter Volume.

Use the Table of Contents to locate the Lenten and Holy Week offices in the Proper of Seasons. Page through this section until you find Wednesday Morning Prayer of Holy Week. **The guide words at the top of the pages will help you find your place in the Proper of Seasons. Move the Proper of Seasons bookmark to Wednesday Morning Prayer of Holy Week.** Look through this office in the Proper of Seasons. Now say that key word three times: REPLACE. REPLACE. REPLACE. Every single part of the office that is written here, in the Proper of Seasons, will REPLACE those same parts in the Psalter. If a part is not written here, in the Proper of Seasons, refer to the Psalter.

Compare the Psalter for Wednesday Morning Prayer, Week II, with Wednesday Morning Prayer of Holy Week. Some one volume breviaries have certain parts of the Wednesday Morning Prayer for Holy Week written in the Psalter but in a different type and so marked as being for Holy Week. Other one volume breviaries and most four volume breviaries have all the parts for Wednesday of Holy Week written in the Proper of Seasons. What is the format of your breviary?

And what's that key word again?

Lesson 42: Invitatory Antiphons during Lent/Easter and Advent/Christmas

**DODO
SELF CHECK #41**

1. How does one use the Proper of Seasons and the Psalter during Ordinary Time?

2. How does one use the Proper of Seasons and Psalter during Lent/Easter and Advent/Christmas?

3. How can you use the guidewords in the Proper of Seasons?

4. In your breviary, what parts of the office for Wednesday Morning of Holy Week are written in the Proper of Seasons and which are written in the Psalter?

5. What's the key word to remember in praying the offices during certain seasons of the Church year? Why is that word key?

You know the key word, don't you? We're going to start talking about some of the times we'll be REPLACING one part of the office with another. Let's dive in!

One REPLACEMENT is the Invitatory Antiphons. **Lent/Easter and Advent/Christmas use special Antiphons for the Invitatory Psalm.** Where are they? Let's find out.

How about starting with Wednesday Morning Prayer, Week II? Is any Invitatory Antiphon written there for Holy Week? If so, great. If not, look at Wednesday Morning Prayer for Holy Week in the Proper of Seasons? Is any Invitatory Antiphon written there? If so, great. If not, now what?

DODO
SELF CHECK #42

1. Which two seasons of
the year use special
Invitatory Antiphons?

2. In your breviary,
where are these
Antiphons found?

3. How can you remem-
ber to use them?

Many breviaries don't write out in the Psalter or in the Proper of Seasons the Antiphons for the Invitatory Psalm for Lent/Easter and Advent/Christmas. But they're in the breviary. Honest.

There's one other logical place to look. Any idea where? Yes! The Invitatory Psalm.

Use the white ribbon to find the Invitatory Psalm, Psalm 95, in your breviary. If you've been praying Morning Prayer for Ordinary Time, you've been praying this Psalm. Look at the several para- graphs immediately preceding Psalm 95 in the Ordinary. Read these. What have you found?

The Antiphons for the Invitatory Psalm for Lent/Easter and Advent/Christmas are printed immediately preceding Psalm 95 in the Ordinary.

Did your breviary very kindly indicate, either in the Psalter or in the Proper of Seasons, that there were special Invitatory Antiphons for Lent/Easter and Advent/Christmas? Probably not. This is one thing you are just supposed to "know." Well, now you know! But if you forget, on the Proper of Seasons bookmark is printed a reminder regarding the location of the Lent/Easter and Advent/Christmas Invitatory Antiphons. That's a nice touch, don't you think?

Lesson 43: Hymns during Lent/Easter and Advent/Christmas

Got your singin' voice ready? We're ready to tackle some new Hymns. What are they and where are they?

During Lent/Easter and Advent/Christmas, certain Hymns are sung with cer- tain offices. Other offices allow you to select an appropriate Hymn from sev- eral suggested ones. Lent/Easter and Advent/Christmas Hymns are often printed in certain special sections of the breviary. Certain celebrations may have Hymns printed with the office.
Ready to find these in your breviary? Let's go!

If you've got a one volume breviary, use the Table of Contents to find the first page of the Proper of Seasons which will be the beginning of Advent. *If you've got a four volume breviary, use the volumes for Advent/Christmas and Lent/Easter.* Go to the beginning of the Proper of Seasons in each volume.

Many breviaries list Advent Hymns at the beginning of the Proper of Seasons, telling you that they may be sung before December 17. Of course, you can sing them any time, even in August if it makes you happy. Other Hymns are traditionally sung after December 17 and still others are used in the Christmas season. Snoop around and see if you can find all these in your breviary.

Page through the Proper of Seasons, looking for actual Hymns printed with an office or referral to certain pages on which Hymns are found. Keep paging through, looking for Hymns, until you come to the beginning of Ordinary Time. Page through Ordinary Time until you come to Lent. Page through the Lent/Easter season, looking for Hymns, until you come again to Ordinary Time. Certain Hymns are used during Lent, others during Holy Week, and others for the Easter Season.

Can you find all these in your breviary?

**DODO
SELF CHECK #43**

1. How are the Hymns for Lent/Easter and Advent/Christmas arranged in your breviary?

2. Does your breviary have sections of Hymns for certain seasons? Does it refer you to a Hymn at the beginning of an office? Or does it use a combination of both techniques?

PRACTICE: Use the Proper of Seasons and Hymn sections to find Hymns that you could use for these days:

December 15
December 22
January 5
Tuesday of the Second Week of Lent
Good Friday
Easter Monday

Lesson 44: Practice in Using the Proper of Seasons

If you've got a four volume breviary, use the Lent/Easter volume for this lesson.

Time for some more pretending. No matter what season it is, and no matter where you live, imagine it's Wednesday of Holy Week in the USA. Imagine the fresh palms drying up a bit behind the bedroom crucifix, or wherever it is that you put them every year. You pull up your window shades and look out into a bright spring morning, the sun low in the sky. Should you buy a lily or a hyacinth for that special Easter plant? Or ought you go with daffodils this year? It's so beautiful at this early morning time. Maybe you'll attend the Easter Mass at Dawn this year instead of the Easter Vigil. But then, you love the Vigil Mass. Maybe you'll attend both. That sounds great!

PRACTICE: For practice in using the Proper of Seasons, we will pray Wednesday Morning Prayer during Holy Week.

       1. Choose an appropriate Hymn following the guidelines in Lesson 43 and mark it with the Hymn bookmark.

       2. Place the Psalter bookmark at Wednesday Morning Prayer, Week II.

       3. Place the Proper of Seasons bookmark at Wednesday Morning Prayer during Holy Week.

Your silver ribbon should be at the Canticle of Zechariah. Your white ribbon should be at the Invitatory Psalm. Where is the Antiphon for the Invitatory Psalm? Read the reminder on the Proper of Seasons bookmark if unsure.

Now reread Lesson 41. Remember that, in Lent/Easter and Advent/Christmas, you begin with the Proper of Seasons. Whatever is not in the Proper of Seasons is taken from the Psalter. Using the bookmarks and ribbons to help you, pray Morning Prayer for Wednesday of Holy Week. When you finish, check how you did against the entire office which is printed in Appendix G. How did you do?

"In this section, you'll learn about ..."

Morning and Evening Prayer in Advent

Morning Prayer in the Christmas Season

Evening Prayer in the Christmas Season

Night Prayer during the Christmas Octave

THE DIVINE OFFICE FOR DODOS

PRAYING MORNING, EVENING, AND NIGHT PRAYER DURING ADVENT & CHRISTMAS

If you have a four volume breviary, use the volume for Advent/Christmas to do these lessons.

Lesson 45: Morning and Evening Prayer during Advent/Christmas (Except the Octave)

The year is fast forwarding. Spring's faded into summer and summer drifted into fall. Here it is, Advent already. Where are you in the breviary?

In the Proper of Seasons, turn to the First Sunday of Advent. This will be right at the beginning of the Proper of Seasons since the Church year begins with Advent. The first office of Advent is Sunday, Evening Prayer I, which is really a Sunday office. Why? Because Sunday was seen traditionally as beginning on Saturday evening. I bet you remembered that!

> **DODO**
> **SELF CHECK #45**
>
> 1. Does your breviary combine offices or have each one printed separately?
>
> 2. Where is the Invitatory Antiphon for Advent & Christmas? Hint: Check the crib note on the Proper of Seasons bookmark.

In the Proper of Seasons, carefully study the offices for the First Sunday of Advent (Sunday Evening Prayer I, Sunday Morning Prayer, and Sunday Evening Prayer II). Does your breviary have each office printed separately or does it combine offices? It's important to know this distinction.

If your breviary combines offices, you'll know because, for example, under Sunday Evening Prayer I, you'll have listed <u>four</u> Antiphons for the Canticle of Mary (Sunday 1, 2, 3, and 4), <u>two</u> sets of Intercessions (Sundays 1 and 3 are the same and Sundays 2 and 4 are the same) and <u>four</u> Concluding Prayers (Sundays 1, 2, 3, and 4). You'll pray the Antiphon, Intercessions, and Concluding Prayer that correspond to the correct Sunday of Advent (1st, 2nd, 3rd, and 4th). Of course!

Lesson 46: Praying Morning Prayer for the Second Sunday of Advent

Advent is moving along, way too fast. You hop out of bed, the sun very low in the just lightening sky. Here it is, the Second Sunday of Advent already, and you're not even half way done with Christmas shopping. If only you could slow down time! Mass today will help you gain some perspective. It always does.

But before Mass, you want to pray Morning Prayer.

PRACTICE: Pray Morning Prayer for the Second Sunday of Advent. First, set up the breviary.

  1. Select a proper Advent Hymn and move the Hymn bookmark to that spot.

  2. Turn to Week II in the Psalter. Find Sunday Morning Prayer for Week II. Put the Psalter bookmark there. Sunday Morning Prayer Week II is the office used for the Second Sunday of Advent.

  3. In the Proper of Seasons, find the Second Sunday of Advent. Mark that with the Proper of Seasons bookmark.

What color ribbon marks the Invitatory Psalm? Where is the Antiphon for the Invitatory Psalm? Look at the reminder on the Proper of Seasons bookmark if unsure. What color ribbon marks the Canticle of Zechariah?

Now pray the office of Morning Prayer for the Second Sunday of Advent. Check Appendix H to see how you did.

EXTRA PRACTICE: Pray the office again, using the breviary and checking yourself against Appendix H.

Lesson 47: Morning and Evening Prayer during the Christmas Octave

Time moves on. Christmas has come and gone. You managed to buy all the gifts you wanted to give and even managed to gift wrap them and add bows! You rejoiced at singing the Christmas hymns at Christmas Mass. Your Christmas dinner was traditional and scrumptious. Ummm. Burp. And now you've moved into the days immediately after Christmas, the Octave.

Christmas is one of the two most solemn and joyous feasts of the Church year, the other being Easter. Therefore its celebration, as well as Easter's, extends through its OCTAVE. **An OCTAVE is the eight days following certain Solemnities. The Christmas Octave lasts from Christmas Day until Evening Prayer II of the Solemnity of Mary, the Mother of God, which is celebrated on January 1.**

During the Octave, the Church rejoices in the birth of Christ. The offices for the Octave of Christmas reflect this eight day celebration.**When praying the Divine Office during the Octave of Christmas, look in the Proper of Seasons and follow whatever instructions are given there.**

DODO
SELF CHECK #47

1. What is an Octave?

2. What is the Church celebrating during the Christmas Octave?

3. How are the Morning and Evening Prayer offices unique during the Christmas Octave?

Turn to the Octave of Christmas in the Proper of Seasons. These will be the days between Christmas, December 25, and New Year's, January 1. Look at the offices on these days. You'll find instructions for certain parts of the offices of those days, referring you to certain parts of the breviary with the pages given.

Don't let this search throw you for a loop. Yes, some of these references refer you to certain saints' feasts and you haven't a clue how to pray them yet. That's just peachy because you'll learn how to pray those feasts in the next part of this book. For now, simply realize that, **for the Octave of Christmas, your breviary's Proper of Seasons tells you exactly where to go to pray the offices correctly.** That's pretty comforting, isn't it?

Lesson 48: Night Prayer during the Christmas Octave

TECHNIQUE

How to pray Night Prayer during the Christmas Octave:

   1. On Christmas Eve, use Sunday Night Prayer I unless you attend Midnight Mass in which case you are exempt from praying Night Prayer.

   2. From Christmas night (December 25) through December 30, you may use either Sunday Night Prayer I or II (the choice is up to you).

   3. On the eve of the Solemnity of Mary, the Mother of God (December 31, New Year's Eve), use Sunday Night Prayer I.

   4. On the night of the Solemnity (January 1), use Sunday Night Prayer II.

   5. During the Octave of Christmas, use the Concluding Prayer that begins "Lord, we beg You to visit this house" unless that day of the Octave is actually a Sunday (or eve of a Sunday). In that case, use the other Concluding Prayer which is the one for Sunday's.

   6. On the night of January 2, return to the usual pattern of praying the correct Night Prayer office for the day of the week.

Yawn! Your house or apartment is still. The gifts are opened and some put away. A precious Christmas hush seems to envelop the night. You're tired. But first you wish to spend some time with the Lord. Time to pray Night Prayer. Let's see how to do that.

Because the Octaves are so special, **Night Prayer for each night of the Christmas Octave is taken either from After Evening Prayer I for Sundays and Solemnities or After Evening Prayer II for Sundays and Solemnities.** Use one all the time or bounce between the two. It's up to you.

"In this section, you'll learn about ..."

Morning and Evening Prayer in Lent

Morning Prayer in the Easter Season

Evening Prayer in the Easter Season

Night Prayer for the Easter Triduum

The triple alleluia

Special considerations for Easter Triduum

THE DIVINE OFFICE FOR DODOS

PRAYING MORNING, EVENING, AND NIGHT PRAYER DURING LENT/EASTER

If you have a four volume breviary, you will need the volume for Lent/Easter for the lessons in Section Eight.

Lesson 49: Morning and Evening Prayer during Lent/Easter (Except the Octave)

The year moves on again. It seems as if Christmas were just over and here it is, Ash Wednesday already. No matter when Ash Wednesday comes, it always seems to arrive too early. You must be getting old if the years seem to fly by so.

In the Proper of Seasons, find Ash Wednesday. Page through the Proper of Seasons, looking carefully at all the parts of the Office printed there for use during Lent. Continue to page through the Proper of Seasons until Ordinary Time begins again.

What did you notice about your breviary?

Look at Morning Prayer for the First Sunday of Lent. This will be the first Sunday after Ash Wednesday. Study this carefully. Are there any alternatives for other Sundays of Lent written in your breviary here?

Breviaries are as different as dodos are. Some breviaries have <u>each day's office printed individually</u>. You'll simply advance the Proper of Seasons bookmark through the Proper of Seasons as you pray. You'll know that your breviary is like this if you have only <u>one</u> choice of Antiphon for the Canticle of Zechariah, <u>one</u> set of Intercessions, and <u>one</u> Concluding Prayer (and possibly an alternative prayer) for the First Sunday of Lent.

Other breviaries <u>combine parts of the offices</u>. You'll know that your breviary is like this if you have a heading "Lent—Sunday—Weeks 1 to 4" above this office. In this type of breviary, you'll use this one office for the first four Sundays of Lent. <u>You'll find parts of the office labeled for the proper Sunday.</u> For the First Sunday of Lent in this type of breviary, you'll have <u>four</u> Antiphons

---

DODO SELF CHECK #49

1. Does your breviary combine offices? Or does it have each office printed out separately in the Proper of Seasons?

2. How will you know which selections to use, if your breviary combines offices?

3. Where can you find the Invitatory Antiphon for Lent/Easter? Hint: Refer to the Proper of Seasons bookmark.

---

for the Canticle of Zechariah, but each is marked for the proper Sunday (Sunday 1, 2, 3, or 4). You'll have <u>two</u> groups of Intercessions, but each is marked for the proper Sunday (Sundays 1 and 3 use the same Intercessions; Sundays 2 and 4 use the same Intercessions). You'll find <u>four</u> Concluding Prayers, but each is marked for the proper Sunday (Sunday 1, 2, 3, or 4). In a breviary like this, you'll move the Proper of Seasons bookmark through the week's offices in the Proper of Seasons and then return to Sunday Evening Prayer I for the next week.

In both types of breviaries, the Fifth Week of Lent has its own unique offices as does Holy Week and the Easter Octave.

Page ahead in your breviary's Proper of Seasons to the weeks of Easter following the Easter Octave to Pentecost. Does your breviary combine the offices or have each one separately?

No matter whether your breviary combines offices or has each written separately, the Divine Office is the same in all breviaries. What changes is how you use the breviary to find the correct prayers and readings. I bet you knew that, but isn't it reassuring to see it in print?

Lesson 50: The Easter Triduum

The six weeks of Lent have moved right along. You've managed to find meatless alternatives for Friday's and aren't too tired yet of tuna fish salad sandwiches and macaroni and cheese. Good Friday is tomorrow and you know the fasting might be a little tough. But you'll make it through. You did it on Ash Wednesday and you ate a decent dinner this evening. Better get moving to get to Church for the Mass of the Lord's Last Supper. Yes, it's Holy Thursday evening, the start of the EASTER TRIDUUM.

A TRIDUUM is three days of prayer. The EASTER SEASON opens with the EASTER TRIDUUM which begins with Holy Thursday Evening Prayer and continues through Good Friday, Holy Saturday, and Easter. However, <u>until the SOLEMNITY OF EASTER actually BEGINS, the Church is still in a penitential season. Therefore, until the Solemnity actually BEGINS, the Church CONTINUES TO USE the Hymns, responses, and so on used for Lent.</u> Only with the beginning of the Solemnity of Easter does the Church switch to the Easter Hymns, responses, and other parts

**DODO
SELF CHECK #50**

1. What is a triduum? What is the Easter Triduum?

2. What days make up the Easter Triduum?

3. When does the Easter Season begin?

4. Since the Easter Triduum is part of the Easter Season, why does the Church continue to use, during the Triduum, the parts of the Office for Lent?

of the Office that express the joy of the Resurrection.

Look in your breviary's Table of Contents under the Proper of Seasons. Your breviary may have a special heading for the Easter Triduum or it may include the Easter Triduum under the heading "Holy Week." In either case, if you page through the Holy Week offices, you'll eventually come to a section marked "Easter Triduum."

Lesson 51: Night Prayer during the Easter Triduum

The Mass of the Lord's Last Supper was reverent. You stayed after a bit to venerate the reposed Body of the Lord on its side altar. It's late now, and you want to pray Night Prayer before heading to bed.

Your breviary contains instructions to help you pray Night Prayer during the Easter Triduum.

The Easter Triduum begins with Evening Prayer for Holy Thursday. Let's pre-

---

TECHNIQUE

How the Church prays Night Prayer during the Easter Triduum:

    1. On Holy Thursday, Good Friday, and Holy Saturday, use Night Prayer after Evening Prayer II on Sundays for all three days as instructed in your breviary.

    2. Also as instructed, in place of the usual six line Responsory ("Into your hands, Lord, I commend my spirit" and the five lines that follow) that follows the Night Prayer Reading, the following Responsories are prayed on the nights indicated:

    3. Holy Thursday: For our sake Christ was obedient, accepting even death.

    4. Good Friday: For our sake, Christ was obedient, accepting even death, death on a cross.

    5. Holy Saturday: For our sake, Christ was obedient, accepting even death, death on a cross. Therefore God raised him on high and gave him the name above all other names.

    6. Use the second Concluding Prayer ("Lord, we beg you to visit this house . . . ") for each night of the Easter Triduum.

---

tend that you've already prayed that. Page through until you come to the Concluding Prayer. What instruction follows this in your breviary? What Responsory is given?

Let's skip ahead a bit. Look at the Good Friday and Holy Saturday Evening Prayer offices. Page through each until you come to the Concluding Prayer. What instruction follows in your breviary? What Responsories are given?

Turn back to Holy Thursday. Read the Night Prayer Responsory given. Now read again the Night Prayer Responsory for Good Friday and Holy Saturday. Do you see how each Responsory builds on the previous one like a swelling Hymn?

Now turn to Night Prayer after Evening Prayer II on Sundays. You'll see two Concluding Prayers written there. One begins "Lord, we have celebrated today . . .." This is the one that you've been praying with the Night Prayer offices. The second choice begins "Lord, we beg you to visit this house . . .." Some breviaries tell you to use this second prayer for the Easter Triduum. Others don't. Whether or not your breviary tells you, this second Concluding Prayer is the one that you will use for the Easter Triduum. Now you know!

PRACTICE: Holy Thursday has come and gone. You have managed to fast and abstain without too much difficulty today, Good Friday. It's time for Night Prayer and then bed. Let's practice praying Night Prayer for Good Friday.

Choose an appropriate Hymn in your breviary. Remember, you want a Lenten Hymn. It's not Easter yet. **Move** the bookmark Hymn to the proper spot.

Move the Night Prayer bookmark to Night Prayer after Evening Prayer II on Sundays. **Move** the Proper of Seasons bookmark to the very end of the offices for Good Friday where the Responsory is printed.

Pray Night Prayer for Good Friday. Remember to flip to the Proper of Seasons for the Responsory following the Reading and to pray the second Concluding Prayer.

Lesson 52: Praying Morning and Evening Prayer during the Easter Octave

Easter has come and gone. You'd managed to dye yet another batch of eggs and you sang the Alleluias at Mass as if you've never heard them before. How the joyous ringing of the bells at the Easter Mass still rings in your heart! The Easter baskets are put away for another year, and you hope you've found the last of the jelly beans that rolled under the couch. You're in the days immediately following Easter: the Easter Octave which celebrates for eight days the Resurrection of Our Lord.

The Easter Octave lasts from Easter Day until Evening Prayer II of the Sunday following Easter. The Sunday following Easter is called Mercy Sunday.

DODO
SELF CHECK #52

1. When does the Easter Octave begin? How long does it last? When does it end?

2. How are the Morning and Evening Prayer offices unique during the Easter Octave?

3. What is different about praying the Invitatory on Easter?

4. What dismissal is prayed for Morning and Evening Prayer during every day of the Easter Octave?

Turn to the Octave of Easter in the Proper of Seasons. Page through the offices for the Octave of Easter, looking carefully at the instructions given. Do you see a pattern of joyful celebration here? You'll notice that, **during the Easter Octave, the Hymns, Antiphons, Psalms, and Canticles for Morning and Evening Prayer are the same as those on Easter Sunday.** Yes, the Church prays the Easter Offices day after day for a full week because Easter is the highest feast of the Church year. No other feast is celebrated during the Easter Octave.

Easter Sunday is a unique celebration in that it both opens the Octave and closes the Triduum. There's a special rule for praying the Invitatory on Easter. The regular rule about praying the Invitatory before the first office of the day (whether that is the Office of Readings or Morning Prayer) changes for Easter. **On Easter day only, the Invitatory is <u>always</u> prayed at the beginning of <u>Morning</u> Prayer.** This is the case even if the Office of Readings is prayed before Morning Prayer. Why is it this way? Because the Easter Vigil Mass takes the place of the Office of Readings, if you attend that Mass. And lots of folks do. In medieval times, the Easter Vigil Mass was held very late on Holy Saturday, usually concluding on Easter Sunday Morning. This is how the religious, who prayed the Divine Office, celebrated Easter. So the first office prayed on Easter was Morning Prayer and that would have included the Invitatory.

Here's another difference during the Easter Octave. The Morning and Evening Prayer offices end with a different dismissal. You've been using the following dismissal: "May the Lord bless us, protect us from all evil, and bring us to everlasting life. Amen." This is not the dismissal that's used during the Easter Octave. So where is it?

You may have difficulty locating in your breviary the dismissal that's said. Look at the Easter Octave offices and Hymns and see if you can find the dismissal that's used. **During the <u>entire</u> Easter Octave, the dismissal for both Morning and Evening Prayer is "Go in peace, Alleluia, Alleluia. Thanks be to God,**

Alleluia, Alleluia." If you can't find it in your breviary, you'll just have to remember it or write it in someplace. It's OK to write in your breviary. It belongs to you, doesn't it?

Lesson 53: The Easter Season

Time for a quick lesson on the Easter Season. Won't you feel smart when this lesson's done?

From the SOLEMNITY OF EASTER until the end of the EASTER SEASON is a time of great rejoicing. We pray "Alleluia" many times during this season as a cry of joy.

The SOLEMNITY OF EASTER begins with the Easter Vigil Mass which takes the place of the Office of Readings for Easter. The Office of Readings used to be known as Vigils and used to be the first office of the day. The Solemnity of Easter is the first day on which the Easter parts of the Divine Office are prayed.

The EASTER OCTAVE is part of the Easter Season. The Easter Octave (eight days) lasts from Easter evening until the evening of Mercy Sunday which is the Sunday following Easter.

All during the EASTER SEASON, Easter parts of the Divine Office are prayed. The EASTER SEASON continues for six weeks and ends with Evening Prayer II on the Feast of Pentecost. Nevertheless, Night Prayer for Pentecost is said as it was said all during the Easter Season.

DODO
SELF CHECK #53

1. When does the Solemnity of Easter begin?

2. What office does the Easter Vigil Mass replace?

3. What is the Easter Octave? How long does it last?

4. How long is the Easter Season? When does it end?

5. When does the Church begin to pray Easter parts of the Divine Office? For how many days does the Church pray them? Where do you find these Easter parts of the Office?

6. When is the last time that the Church prays Night Prayer for the Easter Season?

The Easter parts of the Divine Office are in the Proper of Seasons and the Psalter, depending on the day. Use all the parts in the Proper of Seasons first. Use the Psalter for parts not in the Proper of Seasons. Celebrating saints' days adds another dimension to this which we'll get to later. All in good time.

Lesson 54: The Triple Alleluia Antiphon

Easter is such a joyous time. We just can't seem to pray Alleluia enough. Alleluia is a much prettier word than Yippee or Hooray! But it means the same thing. We're so very glad that Jesus died and rose again to save us from sin that we can't contain our joy. Let's look at one time that Alleluia is prayed so wondrously during the Easter Season.

Turn to the Night Prayer offices and page through them (*remember, if you have a four volume breviary, you're using the Lent/Easter volume.*). Look for the Antiphons for the Psalms and Canticles. You'll see the Antiphon that you've been praying for Night Prayer and another Antiphon marked "Easter." The Easter Antiphon is a series of three "Alleluia's." Isn't that beautiful?

Turn to Night Prayer for Wednesday. How many Psalms are prayed in the Psalmody? Two? Correct!

Now look at the Antiphons. Some breviaries have Antiphon 1 and Antiphon 2 written both before and after the Psalms. Others only have the Antiphons written once, before the Psalms. What's your breviary's format?

Now look at the Antiphon marked "Easter." If your breviary writes the Antiphon both before and after the Psalms, do you see the Easter Antiphon written after Psalm 31:1-6 and then again before Psalm 130? Where is the Easter Antiphon written again? You'll notice that the Easter Antiphon is not written again until <u>after the second Psalm</u> which is Psalm 130.

If your breviary only prints the Antiphons before the Psalms but not after, do you see the Easter Antiphon printed before Psalm 130? No? Do you have a misprint in your breviary?

Not at all. You won't see the Easter Antiphon printed between the two Psalms <u>because it's not prayed between the two Psalms</u>. The three Alleluia's are prayed only at the beginning of the Psalmody and again at the end. Here's why: **In the Psalmody, if only one Antiphon is given for a series of two or three Psalms and/or Canticles, then the Antiphon is prayed only <u>at the very beginning of the Psalmody and again at the very end of the Psalmody</u>. The single, unchanging Antiphon is <u>not</u> repeated between the Psalms and Canticles.** That's the rule!

PRACTICE: Pray the Psalmody for Wednesday Night Prayer during the Easter Season. Remember to pray the Triple Alleluia Antiphon only at the very beginning and the very end of the Psalmody. After praying this Psalmody, check how you did against Appendix. I.

Lesson 55: Night Prayer during the Easter Octave

Ah, in our little game of pretend, we're still in the Easter Octave. The days move along, each Morning and Evening Office being the one for Easter Sunday. You're feeling the incredible joy of this season that clings to the offices like a cloud of Triple Alleluias. You want to pray Night Prayer, too, at this happy time. How do you do it?

Praying Night Prayer during the Easter Octave can be a bit tricky, but you've proven that you're a pretty smart dodo. It won't take you long to learn this technique.

Turn to Night Prayer in your breviary (*remember, you are using the Lent/Easter volume if you have a four volume breviary*). Look at the Antiphons for the Psalmody. Do you see the Antiphons marked "Easter?" Yep, they're the Triple Alleluia Antiphons!

Just as the Antiphons are different for the Easter Octave, so is the Responsory. Instead of "Into your hands, Lord, I commend my spirit" and the five following lines, you'll be using another Responsory. Where is it?

Throughout the <u>entire</u> Easter Octave, the Responsory that follows the Reading for <u>all</u> the Morning, Evening, and Night Prayer Offices is <u>exactly the same</u>. Let's find it.

TECHNIQUE

How the Church prays Night Prayer during the Easter Octave:

    1. On Easter evening, use Sunday Night Prayer II. Use either Sunday Night Prayer I or Sunday Night Prayer II for the days within the Octave of Easter (the choice is yours).

    2. For the eve of Mercy Sunday (the Sunday after Easter), use Sunday Night Prayer I. For the night of Mercy Sunday, use Sunday Night Prayer II which concludes the Octave.

    3. In the Psalmody, use the string of three "Alleluia's" as the Psalmody Antiphon.

    4. For the Responsory after the Reading, use the words, "This is the day the Lord has made, Alleluia. Let us rejoice and be glad, Alleluia."

    5. When praying the Antiphon for the Gospel Canticle ("Protect us, Lord, as we stay awake . . . "), pray after it the "Alleluia" that is in parentheses.

    6. No matter whether you are using Sunday Night Prayer I or II, always conclude with the Concluding Prayer for Sunday which begins "Lord, be with us throughout this night . . . " or "Lord, we have celebrated today . . .".

**DODO
SELF CHECK #55**

1. During the Easter Octave, what Night Prayer offices are used? Which are used on which days?

2. What is the joyful Antiphon for the Psalmody?

3. How does the Responsory after the Reading read?

4. What joyous word do you pray after the Antiphon for the Gospel Canticle?

5. What Concluding Prayer do you always use?

In your breviary, find Easter Morning Prayer. Find the Reading. What is the Responsory following it?

Page ahead and look at Evening Prayer for Easter. What is the Responsory following the Reading?

Keep paging through all the offices of the Easter Octave. In every single Morning and Evening Prayer office during the Easter Octave , the Responsory reads, "This is the day the Lord has made, Alleluia. Let us rejoice and be glad, Alleluia." **During the Easter Octave, this same Responsory is used during every Night Prayer <u>even though the Responsory may not be written out in your breviary's Night Prayer offices.</u>** If you don't have it in your breviary, write it in. Or write it on a card and put it into your breviary. It's OK to do whatever you need to do to help you pray better.

Here's another change, although an easier one. In the Night Prayer offices, look at the Antiphon for the Gospel Canticle. It reads, "Protect us, Lord, as we stay awake; watch over us as we sleep, that awake, we may keep watch with Christ, and, asleep, rest in his peace." In one volume breviaries, an Alleluia in parentheses follows this Antiphon. In four volume breviaries, the Alleluia in parentheses is found only in the volume for Lent/Easter. **During the Easter Octave, pray this Alleluia as part of the Antiphon**. That was fairly easy, right?

Now for a review. Do you remember what was unique about Night Prayer during the Christmas Octave? That's right. All the Night Prayer Offices during the Octave were from either After Evening Prayer I on Sundays and Solemnities or After Evening Prayer II on Sundays and

---

TECHNIQUE

How to pray Night Prayer during the Easter Season after the Easter Octave:

1. Use the Night Prayer section of the breviary that corresponds to the day of the week.

2. Choose an appropriate Hymn.

3. Use the parts of the offices marked "Easter."

4. Pray all the Alleluia's that are in parentheses.

5. Pentecost is the last day that Morning, Evening, and Night Prayer are prayed in the special Easter Season manner. On Monday following Pentecost, return to praying the offices as you do during Ordinary Time.

Solemnities. I bet you deduced that it's the same for the Easter Octave. Every day of the Easter Octave, just like every day of the Christmas Octave, is a SOLEMNITY, the highest celebration of the Church. On Solemnities, only Night Prayer that follows either Sunday Evening Prayer I or Sunday Evening Prayer II is used. Since the Octave is part of the Solemnity of Easter, the first Concluding Prayer is used every night during the Octave.

PRACTICE: Pretend that it's the Eve of Mercy Sunday and you're ready to pray Night Prayer. How will you do that?

      1. **Move** your Hymn bookmark to an appropriate Easter Hymn.

      2. Are you going to **move** your Night Prayer bookmark to Sunday Night Prayer I or II? Check the above technique if you're not sure.

TECHNIQUE

How to pray Morning and Evening Prayer during the Easter Season following the Octave:

1. **Choose one of the Easter Hymns.**

2. **Begin with the Psalter. Pray the Psalmody, using the Psalms and Canticles with the Antiphons marked "Easter."**

3. **Turn to the Proper of Seasons for the remainder of the Office.**

4. **Say all the "Alleluia's" in parentheses during the entire Easter Season.**

---

3. Following the technique, **pray** Night Prayer for the Eve of Mercy Sunday. Check how you did by comparing your prayer with the office as written out in Appendix J.

DODO SELF CHECK #56

1. During the Easter Season, where are the Psalms and Canticles that are used for Morning and Evening Prayer? Where are the other parts of the Morning and Evening Prayer offices?

2. During the Easter Season, how do you treat the Alleluias in parentheses?

3. When do you return to praying Morning, Evening, and Night Prayer as you do during Ordinary Time?

4. What Concluding Prayer do you always use?

Lesson 56: Praying the Offices during the Easter Season after the Easter Octave

Time is moving right along. Mercy Sunday, the first Sunday after Easter, is over. You've come this far and you want to keep praying Morning, Evening, and Night Prayer offices. It's easy to do so.

Remember that we're still in the Easter Season, all the way up to Pentecost. So you've got to look in the Proper of Seasons first when setting up the offices to pray. Remember?

Page through the Proper of Seasons following Mercy Sunday. What do you notice about every single Morning and Evening Office?

Now page through the Psalter, looking at the Antiphons for the Psalmody and remembering that, during the Easter season, you're so happy that Jesus died and rose to save us that you're going to pray every one of those Alleluias in parentheses.

PRACTICE: Pray Morning and Evening Prayer for Wednesday during the Second Week of Easter. Use Week II of the Psalter. Set up your breviary according to the above instructions.

EXTRA PRACTICE: Pray Wednesday Night Prayer for the Second Week of Easter. Follow the instructions above.

SECTION NINE
Propers and Commons

"In this section, you'll learn about ..."

The Proper of Saints

Various commons

Ferial days

Solemnities and feasts

Memorials and commemorations

THE DIVINE OFFICE FOR DODOS

PROPERS AND COMMONS

Those with four volume breviaries will need all four volumes for these instructions and for the remainder of this book.

Lesson 57: The Proper of Saints I

OK. You're doing great. Really great! You're learning to pray the Divine Office. There are only a few more major parts of the Office about which you feel really dodo-y at this point. And they really are major parts of the Office. The Proper. The Commons. How do you use these confusing sections of the breviary? Maybe you could just skip them?

No, you don't want to skip them. In these sections you're going to make some wonderful friends in the Church. The saints! Let's get started in making our acquaintance with them.

Actually anyone in heaven is a SAINT. However, the Church canonizes certain people who have lived lives of exceptional holiness. This means that experts have studied the lives of these people and deemed their sanctity heroic, exceptional. Those for whom the canonization process is complete are called "saints." Those who are deemed extraordinarily holy but for whom some procedures are not yet complete are called "blessed." Some of these saints have special feast days. These are celebrated in the Divine Office.

One of those initially confusing parts of the breviary has special parts of the Office for each particular saint that the Office celebrates. Let's find that part and soon it won't seem confusing at all.

Look in the Table of Contents. Read the various headings. I bet you can easily find the part that has the offices for the saints. The PROPER OF SAINTS, right?

Let your webbed dodo feet skip through the Proper of Saints as you savor all the saints named there. Did you find some old familiar saintly friends? And what of all the unfamiliar saints? Look how many holy guides you can ask to pray for you when you use this section of the breviary. Isn't it great!

Time for some detective work. Does every saint have the same parts of the Office written under his or her heading? Check and see. What are some parts of the Office written in the Proper of Saints? What parts do you see most frequently? Less frequently? Feeling a bit confused? That's a normal reaction. Keep keeping on. The saints will help you understand their section of the breviary if you ask them to.

The PROPER OF SAINTS contains the entire Office or portions of the Office

for all the saints celebrated during the Church year. Each saint has his or her own office for one day of the year.

Keep paging through the Proper of Saints. Do you see how nearly every saint has a brief biography printed at the beginning of the day? **When praying the Office for the saint, read the biography of the saint <u>silently</u> before beginning the office.**

Those with four volume breviaries will notice that many saints' celebrations in the Proper of Saints have Readings and Responsories for the Office of Readings. Since we haven't yet learned to pray this office, we'll ignore these for now. The Concluding Prayer is used for Morning and Evening Prayer as well as for the Office of Readings.

We haven't put any bookmarks into the breviary for a while. But now we get to use one. Guess which? You got it! **Place the Proper of Saints bookmark anywhere in the Proper of Saints section of your breviary.**

Here's the rule for using the Proper of Saints. It's similar to the rule for using the Proper of Seasons. **When celebrating a saint's day, use all the parts of the saint's office that are printed in the Proper of Saints. When the Proper of Saints is missing some parts of the office, use those parts from other sections of the breviary.** Later lessons will discuss what other parts of the breviary to use. That wasn't so hard, was it?

DODO
SELF CHECK #57

1. Who is a saint? Who is a canonized saint? What is the difference between a saint and a blessed?

2. Do all saints have an office in the breviary?

3. What is the name of the section of the breviary that has offices of the saints?

4. When praying the office of a saint, do you read aloud the biography of the saint that is printed in the breviary?

5. What bookmark marks the Proper of Saints?

6. *In four volume breviaries, where in the Proper of Saints is the Concluding Prayer for Morning and Evening Prayer?*

Lesson 58: The Proper of Saints II

Let's examine some of the celebrations in the Proper of Saints. Don't let the terms throw you. We're not going to try to understand all the terms just yet. We simply want to get familiar with this part of the breviary.

Begin at the beginning of the Proper of Saints. Do you see that **the Proper of Saints is arranged chronologically by date from January 1 to December 31. Not every day has a saint's celebration.**

Look at the celebration for February 10. It's for Saint Scholastica, a lovely saint who wanted to spend more time speaking of the Lord with her brother St.

Benedict who kept saying that he had to get back to the monastery. Scholastica prayed and God sent a violent rainstorm so Benedict couldn't leave. Four days later, Scholastica died. Now that you know a bit about Saint Scholastica, let's look at her celebration. Do you see, at the beginning of this celebration, the words "Memorial" and "Lent: Commemoration?" Again, don't worry about the words yet. Just recognize that they're there.

Now look at February 11, the celebration of Our Lady of Lourdes, the apparition of the Blessed Mother to St. Bernadette at Lourdes, France.. You won't see the word "Memorial" but only "Lent: Commemoration." Page through the Office and find some other celebrations that are marked both "Memorial" and "Lent: Commemoration" and some that are marked only "Lent: Commemoration."

Now flip ahead in the Proper of Seasons to May. Look at May 26 for Philip Neri. Philip was a great saint who had a problem with patience. One day he prayed for patience before the tabernacle and felt that the Lord told him that God would grant his request. Pleased with God's answer, Philip went about his daily work only to lose his violent temper twice in the same morning. Upset that God hadn't kept His promise, Philip returned to the tabernacle and complained, "Lord, I prayed for patience and You said You'd give it to me. Yet I've blown up twice just this morning." You know what God said to Philip? "Philip, you asked for the virtue of patience. Now I am multiplying your opportunities to practice it." May God grant us dodos patience as we work through this manual!

Does the celebration of St. Philip Neri say "Memorial" and/or "Lent: Commemoration?" You know why it doesn't say "Lent: Commemoration." We can't possibly be celebrating Lent in May.

Now look at May 27 for Saint Augustine of Canterbury, the first bishop of Canterbury, England. When many of his forty companions wanted to head back to Rome where they'd come from, Augustine made them hold their ground. Because of them, Christianity blossomed in the British Isles.

Does the celebration for Saint Augustine of Canterbury say "Memorial?" No. It doesn't say anything.

Are you puzzled? That's normal. Let's look a bit more and raise even more questions.

Now look at May 25. Can you see an office for Venerable Bede, an English doctor of the Church and talented author, and another for St. Gregory VII, medieval Pope and reformer of the Church, and another for Saint Mary Magdalene de Pazzi, a Carmelite nun who was a mystic and who had the gift of healing. All three of these saints have an office on May 25 and none of them say "Memorial."

Now look at May 31. This is not a saint's celebration. It is titled "Visitation" and celebrates Mary's visitation to Elizabeth when Mary was pregnant with Jesus and Elizabeth with John. What word is at the beginning of this celebration? Yep. "Feast."

Compare the office for the Visitation with that of Saint Augustine of Canterbury on May 27. Which office is longer? What parts are written under the office for the Visitation that are omitted under the office for Saint Augustine of Canterbury?

Now page ahead to June 24. This office if for the "Birth of John the Baptist." What's the designation at the head of this office? Yes. "Solemnity."

Compare the office for the Birth of John the Baptist (June 24) with that of the Visitation (May 31). What parts are in both offices? What parts are in the office for the Birth of John the Baptist that are not in the office for the Visitation?

Are you really confused now? Not to worry. We're just exploring. The confusion will clear up in good time. God is giving you an opportunity to practice patience.

Let's compare the offices for Memorials, Feasts, and Solemnities. Which offices have more parts to them? What are some of those parts?

Another thing to look for in the Proper of Saints. Turn to September 9, the office for Saint Peter Claver, the apostle to the slaves brought to the New World. A Jesuit priest cut to the quick by the horrors of seventeenth century slavery, St. Peter Claver vowed to be "the slave of the Negroes forever," bringing them food, medicine, solace, and prayer. St. Peter Claver's celebration reads "Memorial." After the biography of Saint Peter Claver is a small instruction that reads "From the common of pastors, p. ___, or of holy men: those who worked for the underprivileged, p. ___." Oh, no! Is the office telling you that you are going to have to some more flipping around to pray? Yes, but don't fret. You'll learn how to do this shortly.

DODO
SELF CHECK #58

1. How does your first experience with the Proper of Saints make you feel? Confused? Frustrated? Not to worry. These are very common reactions.

2. What are some of new terms that you discovered in the Proper of Saints?

Now look at September 14, the Triumph of the Cross. Does this give any sort of beginning instruction?Page ahead to September 15, Our Lady of Sorrows, a celebration of the Blessed Virgin Mary which commemorates the sad events in her life. What instruction does this give? It should say, "From the common of the Blessed Virgin Mary, p. ___, except the following."

Look ahead for the instructions for each office in September. What do you notice about them?

Whew! That was some lesson and you might feel as if it put you through the food grinder, so to speak. You might be ready to take the Proper of Saints and rip it out of your breviary, at this point! But don't do that because you really are going to learn how to use this section. Instead, go make yourself a nice cup of coffee, tea, hot chocolate, lemonade, or cod liver oil, whatever you like best, and relax. You deserve a break.

Lesson 59: The Commons

All rested up? Great! Let's proceed, then, in our common fashion and explore the Commons. If you're good at history, you might remember that, in medieval and colonial times, the Common was a large field where townsfolk used to gather to chat and to graze their livestock. Many towns still have a Common. The Common belongs to the town, not to any one individual. In the breviary, **a COMMON is an office that can be used for a number of celebrations.** It's a section used "in common."

The Proper of Saints often instructs you to go the "common" of someone (pastors, virgins, the Blessed Virgin, martyrs, and so on). Let's find this section of the breviary.

**DODO
SELF CHECK #59**

1. What is a Common?

2. How do you feel about your first experience with the Commons? Frustrated? Confused? You're a normal dodo! Soon you'll learn how to use the Commons.

3. Which two bookmarks mark the Commons? How are they distinguished from each other?

4. If you have a choice between certain options within a Common, how do you know which option to select?

Look in your breviary's Table of Contents. Find the section marked COMMONS. What are the commons listed under this general heading? You'll find over a dozen there.

Let's page through some of the commons, getting familiar with them. Start with the first common, the Common of the Dedication of a Church. Page through this and on into the Common of the Blessed Virgin Mary. Keep paging through a few more commons. Do you notice any similar sections in them?

Two bookmarks mark the Commons. One says "Common: Primary Office" and the other "Common: Secondary Office." Place these in any two different sections of the breviary marked Commons.

Let's talk about these two bookmarks for just a second. One says "Primary Office" and the other "Secondary Office." Think about that a minute. Does this mean that you will primarily use one office for some celebrations but may also use the secondary office at the same time, for the same celebration? Oh, tell me it isn't true! But it is true. Can you really learn how to pray the Commons? Maybe using two commons for one celebration? Really and truly learn to use this part of the breviary? Yes, you'll learn. All in good time, all in God's time.

Need to catch your breath about now? Don't be surprised if you do. Many folks find the Commons to be the most confusing parts of the Divine Office. Soon you'll understand them. So take a deep breath and, when you're ready, let's move along.

Look again at the Common of the Blessed Virgin Mary. Look at the Intercessions for Evening Prayer I, Morning Prayer, and Evening Prayer II. How many sets of Intercessions are listed for each of those offices?

Now look at the Concluding Prayer. How many do you see listed? Notice that your breviary uses the word "Or" as a heading when it lists more than one option for each section of the Office. Page through some of the other Commons. Do you see options for certain parts of those offices? What parts of the offices have these options? Are you getting the sense that there is a smorgasbord of information and options in the Commons? There sure is! So what do you select?

If you have a choice of options for certain parts of the Divine Office, as indicated by the word "Or," you may choose whichever option you wish, provided that it corresponds with the current season of the Church year.

Lesson 60: Ferial Days

Ferial Days have nothing to do with those beady eyed popular pets called ferrets nor with amusement park rides that take you skyward and back down again in a dizzying circle. **The weekdays of the year on which no saint is celebrated are called FERIAL DAYS (pronounced fair-ee-al).** Sundays are <u>not</u> Ferial Days. Sundays are SOLEMNITIES.

Ferial Days are "hidden" days in the breviary, so, in this regard, they are like ferrets, who, in the wild, are seldom seen. In the Proper of Saints, turn to July. Do you see any saint's office for July 1? July 2? No? That's because there are no saints celebrated those days. Those are Ferial Days. Page through the July

**DODO
SELF CHECK #60**

1. What is a Ferial Day? Do you use the Proper of Saints or the Commons on Ferial Days?

2. What is today's date? Find it in the Proper of Saints. Is a saint assigned to today? If not, today would be a Ferial Day. If today has a saint's celebration, page through the Proper of Saints and look for the next Ferial Day. On the Ferial Day, where do you find the parts of the Office to pray? Hint: Check back in this lesson for the answer.

offices. What other days in July are Ferial Days? All the days you don't see listed, that's what.

So far, except for certain Feasts and Solemnities during Lent/Easter and
Advent/Christmas, you've been praying each office as if it fell on a Ferial Day.
You know how to do that. **To pray the Divine Office on Ferial Days, use only
the Psalter and, in Lent/Easter and Advent/Christmas, the Proper of Seasons
as well.**

Lesson 61: Solemnities, Feasts, Memorials, Commemorations

I hope you like vocabulary because this lesson deals with some new vocabulary
words you need to understand to pray the Divine Office. We'll learn these
words in order of importance regarding their celebration, the most important
celebration first and the least important last. If you're an organized dodo, mak
ing a chart of these just might intrigue you. Go ahead and put flowers and
curlicues on it if you like!

Do you remember the four headings you saw when you paged through the
Proper of Saints? Yes? Great! "Solemnity," "Feast," "Memorial,"
"Commemoration." Some celebrations had no headings. Does that seem weird
or what?

**SOLEMNITIES, FEASTS, MEMORIALS, and COMMEMORATIONS are spe-
cial celebrations in the Church. Both the Proper of Saints and the Commons
are used in praying the offices for these days.**

To understand these celebrations, let's begin at the beginning, always the best
place to start anything. You've already learned to pray the Sunday offices for
Ordinary Time and during the Seasons of the year. **Every Sunday is a SOLEM-
NITY. A SOLEMNITY is a solemn celebration in the Church, the highest
Church holiday. It is celebrated by the whole Church.** SOLEMNITY is your firs
vocabulary word. And it's not new as you had it earlier.

What are some of the Solemnities of the Church? Besides every Sunday, you
already know some other Solemnities. Easter, Christmas, and their Octaves are
celebrated as Solemnities.

Some celebrations in the Proper of Saints are also Solemnities. For example,
look at June 24, the Birth of John the Baptist and August 15, the Assumption o
Mary. These are two Solemnities celebrated in the Proper of Saints. There are
other Solemnities in the Church year. How about going on a Solemnity treasure hunt and seeing how many you can find? Where will you find these gems?
Yes! In the Proper of Seasons and Proper of Saints. If you can find a dozen
Solemnities, go reward yourself with a candy bar or a veggie burger, whatever

you prefer!

Remember, Solemnities are the highest celebrations of the Church year.

Let's look at the second highest celebration. Check out September 14, the Triumph of the Cross, and September 29, the office for the Archangels Saints Michael, Gabriel, and Raphael. These are marked "Feasts." **A FEAST is a high celebration of the Church but not quite as important as a Solemnity. However, it is still celebrated by the whole Church.** FEAST is your second vocabulary word.

That wasn't too difficult, was it? So what's the next lowest celebration? Did you guess Memorial? Right on! Many celebrations in the Proper of Saints are labeled "Memorial" and many other offices aren't labeled at all. Here's where the terms get a little tricky, but hang on, you'll soon understand. **The offices labeled "Memorial" as well as those with no labels are MEMORIALS. A MEMORIAL is a lesser celebration of the Church.** MEMORIAL is your third vocabulary word for today.

Of course, if you are at all awake, you have a question. Why are some Memorials labeled "Memorial" and others aren't? Unlike some questions, this one does have an answer.

Some Memorials ARE celebrated by the Church, but others MAY be celebrated (a parish, religious order, or an individual may choose to celebrate them if desired). Which do you think ARE celebrated, the ones labeled "Memorial" or the ones not labeled?

If you answered "the ones labeled Memorial," you're pretty sharp! **The offices labeled "Memorial" are called OBLIGATORY MEMORIALS. Obligatory means that these Memorials are to be celebrated by the whole Church.** OBLIGATORY is your fourth vocabulary word. Hold on because here comes vocabulary word number five. **The underlined offices are OPTIONAL MEMORIALS. Optional means that any individual or parish MAY celebrate the Memorial if desired.** OPTIONAL is the fifth vocabulary word. We're not done yet!

Look at the office for February 14 for Saints Cyril, Monk, and Methodius. These are two saints, not three. Saint Cyril was a monk. His brother was Saint Methodius. Together, in the 800's, they evangelized the Slavic nations. The celebration for Saints Cyril, Monk, and Methodius is marked "Memorial" and "Lent: Commemoration." Turn to the offices for December 21 and December 23. Do you see that these, too, are marked "Commemoration?" Page ahead to December 29, the office for Saint Thomas Becket, the famous English archbishop and chancellor who was martyred at the command of King Henry II. What's the designation for this office?

A COMMEMORATION is similar to an Optional Memorial. This means that a parish or individual may choose to celebrate a Commemoration if desired.

Commemoration is the sixth vocabulary word.

Here's another tidbit of information. Commemorations are celebrated a bit differently than Optional Memorials, and they occur only during Lent/Easter and Advent/Christmas.

Let's discuss Lent first. Lent is a very special time during the Church year. **During Lent until Palm (Passion Sunday), all Memorials, whether Obligatory or Optional, become Commemorations. During Holy Week and the Easter Octave, no Commemorations are celebrated because, as you learned earlier, every day during Holy Week has its own special office.**

Now let's see what happens during Advent/Christmas. **During the last week of Advent and the Christmas Octave (December 17 to January 1), all Memorials become Commemorations.**

Were you good with math? Here are some crazy looking equations to summarize these rules:

Lent/Easter Memorials=Commemorations
Palm Sunday to Divine Mercy Sunday=No Memorials or Commemorations
Last Week of Advent to January 1 Memorials=Commemorations

So now you know. Every single day of the Church year is either a Solemnity, Feast, Obligatory Memorial, Optional Memorial, Commemoration, or Ferial Day. How about them vocabulary words!

Now for some Divine Office Trivia. What if a Solemnity, Feast, Obligatory Memorial, Optional Memorial, or Commemoration fall on a Sunday?

All Sundays are Solemnities. They are celebrated as such. Therefore, no Feast, Memorial (Obligatory or Optional), or Commemoration takes the place of the Sunday celebration. However, if another Solemnity falls on a Sunday during Ordinary Time, the other Solemnity is celebrated instead of the Sunday for Ordinary Time. This is why, if the Solemnity of the Assumption of Mary (August 15) or the Solemnity of All Saints (November 1) falls on a Sunday, the Solemnities of the Assumption and All

1. What is a Solemnity? How do you know when a day is a Solemnity? What day of the week is always a Solemnity?

2. What is a Feast? How do you know when a day is a Feast? Does the whole Church celebrate every Feast?

3. What is an Obligatory Memorial? How do you know when a day is an Obligatory Memorial? Does the whole Church celebrate every Obligatory Memorial?

4. What is an Optional Memorial? How do you know when a day is an Optional Memorial?

5. What is a Commemoration? How do you know when a day is a Commemoration? Does the whole Church celebrate every Commemoration?

6. What is a Ferial Day? On a Ferial Day, where do you find the prayers for the Office?

7. Are Feasts, Memorials, or Commemorations celebrated on Sundays?

Saints are celebrated in place of the Sunday celebrations. We've all been familiar with this happening during Sunday Masses.

**The Sundays during Lent/Easter and Advent/Christmas have special celebra-
tions for the seasons. If a Solemnity coincides with a Sunday during the
Lent/Easter and Advent/Christmas Seasons, the Solemnity may be celebrated
on Sunday, on another day (Saturday or Monday), or may be skipped. What
happens depends on the Solemnity.** You will learn more about which
Solemnities are skipped and which celebrated later.

Do you still have your wits about you? Give yourself a pat on the back, if you
can reach that far around yourself. You've learned a lot in this chapter.
Congratulations!

And slide your vocabulary list inside your breviary's front or back cover. You're
gonna refer to it often from here on out.

SECTION TEN
Praying Morning, Evening and Night Prayer on Solemnities and Feasts

"In this section, you'll learn about ..."

Sunday Morning Prayer: Week I

Using the Propers of Saints and Commons

Morning and Evening Prayer on solemnities

Night Prayer on solemnities

Morning, Evening and Night Prayer on feasts

PRAYING MORNING, EVENING, AND NIGHT PRAYER ON SOLEMNITIES AND FEASTS

Lesson 62: Sunday Morning Prayer, Week I

You've had some pretty grueling lessons lately. So you deserve a break. Let's start this chapter with something a bit easier. We're going to do some prowling around in the breviary, looking for something pretty specific. Curious? Tear off several strips of scrap paper, not from this manual but maybe from some old junk mail, and let's get started.

We're going to look in the Proper of Saints. Take a strip of paper and mark each of these offices as you find them so you'll be able to locate them easily for this lesson.

Find the offices for each of these days: February 22, April 25, July 3, August 6, September 14, November 30. Now look at each day and answer these questions:

What saint is being celebrated on each day?

What is the designation of each day (Solemnity, Feast, Memorial, Commemoration)?

Look at Morning Prayer for each of these Feasts. Do you see a designation under Antiphon 1 that reads, "Psalms and Canticle from Sunday, Week I, p. ___"? Hmm. Interesting.

The Psalms and Canticle from Sunday, Week I, are often used in praying the Divine Office on Feasts and sometimes on Solemnities and Memorials as well. Why? Because these Psalms and Canticle are especially joyful and praiseworthy of God. They express the emotions we ought to have on special Church celebrations.

In the Psalter of your breviary, find Sunday Morning Prayer, Week I. *If you have a four volume breviary, find Sunday Morning Prayer, Week I, in each volume.* Find the first Psalm of Sunday Morning Prayer, Week I. What Psalm is it? What is the Canticle? The last Psalm?

The Psalms and Canticle of Sunday Morning Prayer, Week I, are special. They are Psalm 63:2-6, the Canticle of Daniel 3:57-88, 56, and Psalm 149. They are special because they are prayed in the Morning Office on particular celebrations that do not fall on Sunday.

Do you remember how we mark certain stationary places in the breviary that we'll be referring to often? Yep! With the restful ribbons. We have a ribbon we've not used yet. **Draw the green ribbon (green for the spiritually life giving Psalms and Canticle of Sunday Week I) down through your breviary to mark the first Psalm of Sunday, Week One, Psalm 63:2-9 in your Psalter.** *If you have a four volume breviary, do this in every volume.*

Was I right in telling you that this lesson would be a snap?

Lesson 63: General Instructions on Using the Proper of Saints and the Commons

We'll get to a little more nitty gritty in this chapter. When you paged through the Proper of Saints, you noticed that some saints had a great deal written in their offices and others had very little. Compare the offices for December 7, St. Ambrose, the great bishop of Milan who converted St. Augustine, with those of December 8, the Immaculate Conception of Mary, who was conceived without original sin. In one volume breviaries, you'll see only a prayer listed for St. Ambrose *(four volume breviaries will also have a Second Reading for the Office of Readings and its Responsory)* while the Immaculate Conception is pages long. Does this mean that, on December 7, your entire Office consists of one little prayer? You should have it so easy!

Under Saint Ambrose you will see an instruction that reads, "From the Common of Doctors, page ___." This means that the <u>parts of the Office not in the Proper of Saints</u> are going to be found in the Common of Doctors and in the Psalter (you will learn which parts later).

What are the parts of the Office for Morning Prayer (if it's the first prayer of the day) and Evening Prayer? Let's list them in order:

> Introduction
> Invitatory Antiphon (Morning Prayer only)
> Invitatory (Morning Prayer only)
> Hymn
> Psalmody, Psalm Prayers, and Antiphons
> Reading
> Responsory
> Canticle of Zechariah (Morning) or Canticle of Mary (Evening) and
Antiphon

Intercessions
Our Father
Concluding Prayer, and Conclusion.

All these parts of the Office are prayed during every Morning and every Evening Prayer time no matter how little is written in the Proper of Saints. But then, you already knew that, didn't you? You'll soon learn where to look for those parts of the Office that are missing from the Proper of Saints.

Now look back at that lonely prayer under Saint Ambrose's celebration. You'll pray that lonely little prayer as the Concluding Prayer to the Morning Prayer office. If Saint Ambrose's celebration occurred on most any other day of the year, you'd also pray that prayer as the Concluding Prayer for Evening Prayer. But you won't pray it on this night. Can you figure out why?

What celebration comes the day after St. Ambrose's Memorial? Go ahead and peek. Yes, the Immaculate Conception. The Immaculate Conception is a Solemnity which is a higher Church celebration than Ambrose's Memorial. So Ambrose gets bumped, if you will. You won't be praying Evening Prayer for Saint Ambrose on December 7 because, that night, the Church will be praying Evening Prayer I for the next day, the Immaculate Conception. Check out your breviary and see what I mean. Don't worry about St. Ambrose. I don't think he minds a bit that Our Lady bumped him out of Evening Prayer. He always had a great devotion to her and yielded to her will in his earthly life.

Page ahead in the Proper of Saints to December 11, a celebration in honor of Saint Damascus I, Pope, the patron of Saint Jerome and the pope who published what we now accept as the Canon of Sacred Scripture, the books of the Bible. In one volume breviaries, the celebration for Saint Damascus, like Saint Ambrose's celebration, has only one Concluding Prayer *(four volume breviaries will give a Second Reading for the Office of Readings and its Responsory as well)*.

Under the celebration for Saint Damascus is an instruction which refers you to the Common of Pastors for the parts of the Office not here in the Proper of Saints. However, Saint Damascus has his own Concluding Prayer. His own prayer will conclude both the Morning and Evening Prayer Offices. The Concluding Prayer for Saint Damascus takes the place of the Concluding Prayer in the Common of Pastors.

Here's why: **If the Proper of Saints lists a Concluding Prayer, it's prayed in place of any other Concluding Prayer. Even though the Concluding Prayer is written only once, it concludes both Morning and Evening Prayer.**

Now turn to the celebration for Saint Lucy on December 13. St. Lucy is the patron of those suffering eye problems because her eyes were put out during her martyrdom in 304. What parts of St. Lucy's office are printed under this celebration? Under Morning Prayer, the listing says "Canticle of Zechariah" and has an Antiphon. Does this mean that the Church prays only the Antiphon on this day? You know that's not true! The Church uses the Antiphon under St. Lucy's celebration with the Canticle of Zechariah that you have already marked with a silver ribbon. For Evening Prayer, the "Canticle of Mary" has an Antiphon. It's prayed with the Canticle of Mary that you've marked with the blue ribbon.

Do you think that the Church prays the Antiphon written under the celebration for Saint Lucy as well as another Antiphon elsewhere in the breviary? No. **The Church uses only one Antiphon at a time.** In this case, the Antiphon is written under the celebration of the saint.

Look in your breviary for the celebration for St. Martin of Tours, November 11. St. Martin of Tours was a bishop who, while still a soldier in the world, cut his cloak in two and gave half to a freezing beggar. That evening he had a vision of Christ wearing the half-cloak. Wasn't that neat? What instruction is given for the celebration of St. Martin of Tours? You are referred to the Common of Pastors. Does this mean that the Church prays all the parts listed under Saint Martin and the same parts from the Common of Pastors? No. The Church prays all the parts under Saint Martin but does <u>not</u> pray those <u>same</u> parts in the Common of Pastors. The Church uses the Common of Pastors only for any <u>missing</u> parts.

The Office for Saint Martin of Tours appears to be very complete. However, one part is missing. Can you find which? Yes! The Intercessions. Does this mean that the Church skips praying them? Nope. Where will you find the Intercessions? In the Common of Pastors.

> ## DODO
> ## SELF CHECK #63
>
> 1. If a celebration in the Proper of Saints lists only a Concluding Prayer, where are the other parts of the Office printed?
>
> 2. If one part of the Office is listed in the Proper of Saints and the same part in the Common, which is prayed?
>
> 3. If you have a choice of Commons, how do you know which to choose?
>
> 4. How will you mark the Common that you are using?

Now look at the celebration for June 27. This is for St. Cyril of Alexandria, bishop and Doctor of the Church who is known for his writings on the Incarnation and the Trinity. What instruction regarding the Common is given in St. Cyril's Memorial? It reads, "From the common of pastors, p. ____, or of doctors of the Church, p. ____." Which common is used? **When a celebration lists a choice of Commons, you really do have a choice. Select one Common or the other.** How do you decide? That's up to you. You could do it by deciding if you like your pastor or your doctor better. Or maybe you could flip a coin or ask your dog for an opinion. Any way you make a choice, it's up to you. Once you choose, mark the Common you are using with the "Common: Primary Office" bookmark.

Lesson 64: Evening Prayer I, Morning Prayer, and Evening Prayer II on Solemnities

Following our pattern of going from the most important celebrations to those of lesser importance, we'll start with Solemnities. **Solemnities are the highest celebrations in the Church.** You'll recall that Sunday has Evening Prayer I and Evening Prayer II because **Sunday is a Solemnity.**

All Solemnities begin with Evening Prayer I. Evening Prayer I is always prayed as the Vigil (that is, the night before) office of a Solemnity.

Look in the Proper of Seasons for August 15, the Solemnity of the Assumption. This celebration begins with Evening Prayer One. **Evening Prayer One for these special high celebrations <u>takes the place of</u> the regular Evening Prayer that you might be saying that day whether that Evening Prayer would be in the Psalter or in the Proper of Saints.**

For example, August 14 is a new Memorial in honor of Saint Maximilian Kolbe. Maximilian Kolbe was a holy priest who began the Knights of the Immaculata and who gave up his life for another in the German concentration camp of Auschwitz. The Memorial of Saint Maximilian Kolbe will be in newer breviaries but not in older ones (older ones may have a supplement of new celebrations which would contain the office for the Memorial of Saint Maximilian Kolbe). On August 14, the Memorial for Saint Maximilian Kolbe is said for Morning Prayer, but Evening Prayer for August 14 is Evening Prayer I for the Solemnity of the Assumption which is August 15. Why? Because a Solemnity is a higher celebration than a Memorial.

Let's check out Evening Prayer I for the Solemnity of the Assumption. You'll see that the entire office is printed in the breviary. Now check out Morning Prayer and Evening Prayer II for the Assumption. You'll see that both entire offices are printed in the Proper of Saints.

It's a snap to pray Morning and Evening Prayer on the Solemnity of the Assumption. Simply follow what's written in the Proper of Saints.

Is it this easy with all Solemnities? Ah, you wish!

First, let's look in the Proper of Saints to see if there is any celebration on March 18. Yep, there is. March 18 is a Commemoration in honor of Saint Cyril of Jerusalem, bishop, catechist, and Doctor of the Church. If you chose to observe this Commemoration (and you do have a choice during Lent), then you'd pray Morning Prayer from the Memorial of Saint Cyril, but you wouldn't pray Evening Prayer for him. Why not? Because March 19 is a Solemnity with its own Evening Prayer I.

What Solemnity falls on March 19? No one expects you to remember it. Go ahead and look. Did you know that it was the Solemnity of Saint Joseph, Husband of Our Lady and Foster Father of Our Lord? For this Solemnity, you'll see complete offices for Evening Prayer I, Morning Prayer, and Evening Prayer II. But are they really complete? Let's look more closely.

Look at Evening Prayer I for the Solemnity of Saint Joseph. Under Antiphon 1, you'll find an instruction that tells you that the "Psalms and canticle (are) from the common of holy men, p. _____." It doesn't take a rocket scientist to figure out that you have to go to the Common of Holy Men to pray this office.

In order to pray Evening Prayer I for the Solemnity of Saint Joseph, you would have your Proper of Saints bouncing bookmark at March 19. You would have your "Common: Primary Office" bouncing bookmark at the Psalms for Evening Prayer I for the Common of Holy Men.

Let's bounce over to the Common of Holy Men. Does your breviary have the Psalms written out for Evening Prayer I or does it refer you to the Common of Pastors for the Psalms? Here's where you get to use the "Common—Secondary Office" bookmark.

Oh, no, the two Commons bookmarks! They're easier to use than you think.

<u>Always</u> use the Common—Primary Office bookmark to mark the <u>first</u> common referred to in your breviary. For most celebrations, the Common-Primary Office bookmark will be the only one you'll use. However, if the "Primary" Common (the first common you went to) refers you to a <u>second</u> common, use the Common-Secondary Office bookmark to mark the appropriate places in that "Secondary" Common. Remember. Primary Common first (like primary school) and Secondary Common second (like secondary school). Got it? Good for you!

Now let's apply this information to the Solemnity of St. Joseph. **If the Common of Holy Men, in your breviary, refers you to the Common of Pastors for the Psalms for Evening Prayer I, then move the "Common: Secondary Office" bouncing bookmark to that spot.**

What are the Psalms and Canticle for Evening Prayer I for the Solemnity of Saint Joseph? The Psalms are 113 and 146 and the Canticle is Ephesians 1:3-10. These Psalms and Canticle are the same for both the Common of Holy Men and the Common of Pastors.

OK. This has been a painstaking lesson. If you need a break, go get a coffee, soft drink or glass of lemonade and come back when you feel refreshed. How about getting me a milkshake? Vanilla, please.

DODO
SELF CHECK #64

1. Which day of the week is always a Solemnity?

2. What office begins a Solemnity? On what night does this office fall?

3. Does Evening Prayer I for a Solemnity take the place of whatever other Evening Prayer would be said that night?

4. Where do you find the office Prayers and Readings for Solemnities?

Ready to roll again? OK! Let's look farther into the office for the Solemnity of Saint Joseph. Do you notice that two different Responsories are given for each office? One Responsory is marked "Lent" and the other "Easter." If you take a deep breath, you can figure this out. It's quite simple. Should the Solemnity fall during Lent, the Lenten Responsory is used. Should it fall during the Easter celebration (which rarely happens), the Easter Responsory is used.

Now look at Morning Prayer. The ground is a little more familiar here. You're referred to Sunday, Week I, for the Psalms and Canticle. You've already got those marked with the green ribbon. Look at Evening Prayer II. More familiar territory. You are again referred to the Common of Holy Men for the Psalms and Canticle and you've got those marked with the Primary Commons bookmark.

Is it really so very difficult to pray Evening Prayer I, Morning Prayer, and Evening Prayer II for the Solemnity of Saint Joseph? Not really. All parts of the office are in the Proper of Saints. You are referred to the proper pages for those parts of the office that are written in the Commons. You mark these pages in advance with the bookmarks.

A Solemnity is clearly marked in the breviary. Its Office will be in either the Proper of Saints or the Proper of Seasons, and you will know which because you will be moving your bookmarks along as you pray the Divine Office. The breviary will tell you where to find any parts of the Office that are not printed in the Proper.

PRACTICE: **Pray** Evening Prayer I for the Solemnity of Saint Joseph.

EXTRA PRACTICE: **Pray** Evening Prayer II for the Solemnity of the Assumption.

Lesson 65: Night Prayer on Solemnities

Have you been discovering that you're a smarter dodo than you thought you were? I hope so! This lesson might be pretty easy for you. You may already suspect what it teaches. Let's see.

Solemnities, you know, are the highest celebrations in the Church. You already have an inkling of how to treat Night Prayer for Solemnities. You learned about that when we talked about the Easter and Christmas Octaves. Let's take what we learned there and apply it to all Solemnities.

Find Night Prayer after Evening Prayer I on Sundays and Solemnities (marked "Saturday" in some breviaries) and Night Prayer after Evening Prayer II on Sundays and Solemnities (marked "Sunday" in some breviaries). Did you catch that designation "and Solemnities?" That's a clue that, **on Solemnities, Night Prayer after Evening Prayer I (Saturday) and Night Prayer after Evening Prayer II (Sunday) are prayed instead of whatever the Night Prayer would be for the weekday.**

Look for the Concluding Prayer. You'll notice two of them. Up until now, you've been praying only the first Concluding Prayer. Let's say a Solemnity falls on a Sunday. If it does, pray what you've been praying all along. The first Concluding Prayer. Now let's say a Solemnity falls on a day other than Sunday. In that case, **on Solemnities that don't fall on a Sunday,** pray the second Concluding Prayer to the Night Prayer offices.

Now, some review. On Easter, which Concluding Prayer will you pray? The first one because Easter always falls on a Sunday.

If the Solemnity of Christmas falls on a Sunday, which Concluding Prayer will you say? The first.

If Christmas falls on a weekday, what Concluding Prayer will you say? The second.

PRACTICE: Pray Night Prayer I (Saturday) as you would for Christmas Eve if Christmas came on a Tuesday.

EXTRA PRACTICE: Pray Night Prayer I (Saturday) for Christmas Eve as you would if Christmas fell on a Sunday.

**DODO
SELF CHECK #65**

1. On a Solemnity, which Night Prayer offices are the only ones used?

2. When is the second Concluding Prayer to the Night Prayer offices used?

3. If a Solemnity falls on a Sunday, what Night Prayer offices are used? What Concluding Prayer?

4. If a Solemnity falls on any day other than a Sunday, what Night Prayer offices are used? What Concluding Prayer?

5. If Christmas fell on a Monday, what Night Prayer office would be prayed on Christmas Eve (Sunday Night)? What Concluding Prayer? What Night Prayer office would be prayed on Christmas Day (Monday Night)? What Concluding Prayer? (Hint: If you're not sure about the answers to these questions, reread the last paragraph about the 1998 Monday Solemnity of Saints Peter and Paul.)

Here is another "supposes." Suppose a Solemnity falls on a Monday as the Solemnity of Saints Peter and Paul (June 29) did in 1998?

What Night Prayer was said on Sunday night which was the Eve of the Solemnity? Night Prayer after Evening Prayer I (marked "Saturday" in some breviaries) with the second Concluding Prayer.

What Night Prayer was said for Monday night, June 29, the day of the Solemnity? Night Prayer after Evening Prayer II (marked "Sunday" in some breviaries) with the second Concluding Prayer.

What Night Prayer was prayed on the night after the Solemnity, that is, Tuesday, June 30? The correct Night Prayer for the corresponding day of the week, in this case Night Prayer for Tuesday Night.

Lesson 66: Morning, Evening, and Night Prayer on Feasts

We've concluded discussing Solemnities, at least for now. What's the second highest celebration of the Church? Did you remember Feasts? Good for you!

A FEAST is a high celebration of the Church. It has its own offices. Because a Feast is not as high a celebration as a Solemnity, **a Feast does not usually have an Evening Prayer I. The Divine Office for the Feast usually begins on the day of the Feast itself. This is true even though the Common may have an Evening Prayer I.**

When praying the Divine Office on a Feast, follow what is in the Proper of Saints first. If the Proper of Saints tells you to use Evening Prayer I from the Common or elsewhere (as, for example, it does if the Triumph of the Cross, September 14, occurs on a Sunday), then use Evening Prayer I.

If the Proper of Saints does not mention any special Evening Prayer I, then use whatever Evening Prayer would be appropriate for that evening, just as though the next day were not a Feast.

Feasts are clearly marked in the breviary. They are found in either the Proper of Saints or the Proper of Seasons. You'll know a Feast because you'll be moving your bookmarks along as you pray. The breviary will refer you to any parts of the Divine Office that are not found in the Feast itself.

It's easy to pray Morning and Evening Prayer on a Feast. **To pray Morning and Evening Prayer on a Feast, use the Proper of Saints first. Follow any instructions given there about where to find parts of the Office. Take everything else from the Common to which the Feast refers.**

A mathematical like equation for this would be:

FEASTS=Proper of Saints First + Common Second

It's easy to pray Night Prayer on a Feast. A Feast is not as high as celebration as a Solemnity. Therefore, it has no effect on Night Prayer. **On a Feast, pray the same Night Prayer that you would pray were it simply a regular weekday.** That really was easy, wasn't it?

Let's see how this works. Turn to July 3, the Feast of St. Thomas the Apostle, you know, the doubter. In 1998, July 3 fell on a Friday.

Will there be an Evening Prayer I for the Feast of St. Thomas the Apostle? No, because you use the Proper of Saints first, and it lists no Evening Prayer I under St. Thomas's Feast. Since July 2 is a Ferial Day (no saint is celebrated), Evening Prayer on July 2 will be from the Psalter just as if the next day were no big celebration at all.

Look at the instruction for the Feast of St. Thomas. What two parts of the breviary are used to pray Morning and Evening Prayer? Right! Proper of Saints first. Then, if a part of the Office isn't in the Proper, use the Common of Apostles. The Common of Apostles is the Primary Common and the <u>only </u>common used for this feast.

Where are the Psalms and Canticles for the Morning Prayer Psalmody? The breviary tells you to go to Sunday, Week I. You've already got those marked with your green ribbon.

DODO
SELF CHECK #66

1. What is a Feast? How does it differ from a Solemnity?

2. Does a Feast usually have Evening Prayer I? Why or why not? How will you know if it does have Evening Prayer I?

3. What two parts of the breviary are used for praying Morning and Evening Prayer on Feasts? How does one use them?

4. What Night Prayer office is used on a Feast?

Where are the Psalms and Canticles for Evening Prayer? The breviary tells you to go to the Common of Apostles. Where are the Antiphons for them? The instructions tell you to use the ones from Morning Prayer of the Feast. All the instructions are in the breviary.

Where is the Invitatory Psalm? The Canticle of Zechariah? The Canticle of Mary? You've already ribbon marked them!

What Night Prayer Office is used? Remember the rule for Feasts? The one for the day of the week on which the Feast falls (in 1998, Friday Night Prayer).

PRACTICE: No matter what day it is, let's pretend that today is July 3. If you are in the USA, you might be going to a fireworks display tonight. And maybe to the beach or the pool before that. But before everything else, you want to pray Morning Prayer for the Feast of St. Thomas the Apostle.

First, move the bookmarks to the correct locations. **The Proper of Saints bookmark will be at the Feast of Saint Thomas the Apostle (July 3). The "Common: Primary Office" bookmark will be at the Common of the Apostles** (be sure to put it at the Morning Prayer location and not at Evening Prayer I since Evening Prayer I is not prayed on a Feast unless you are specifically told to pray it. You aren't told to pray it for the Feast of St. Thomas.).

The ribbons should already be in place since they don't move. **The white ribbon should be marking the Invitatory Psalm. The green ribbon should be marking the Psalmody for Sunday Morning Prayer, Week I. The silver ribbon should be marking the Canticle of Zechariah.**

When you have the parts of the Morning Prayer office correctly marked, you are ready to pray. Pray Morning Prayer for the Feast of St. Thomas all the way through using your breviary. When you finish, check how you did by referring to Appendix K.

"In this section, you'll learn about ..."

Night Prayer on memorials

Prayer on obligatory memorials

Prayer on optional memorials

Praying the Office on commemorations

Getting to know the Ordo

Special cases and seasons

THE DIVINE OFFICE FOR DODOS

PRAYING MORNING, EVENING, AND NIGHT PRAYER ON MEMORIALS AND COMMEMORATIONS

Lesson 67: Memorials and Night Prayer on Memorials

Praying the Office on Feasts is a piece of cake, don't you think? Well, some Memorials are a little trickier. More like eating taffy with false teeth. Ready to tackle Memorials? Not sure? Oh, let's give it a go!

Some saints' celebrations have a heading that says either "Memorial," "Commemoration," "Feast," or "Solemnity." And some have no headings at all. We've tackled Feasts and Solemnities. Let's approach the others.

First, some review. **A MEMORIAL is a lesser celebration of the Church. All offices labeled "Memorial" and all offices with no labels are Memorials.** However, wouldn't you know that labeled and unlabeled offices are celebrated a bit differently. Well, you've come this far. Might was well go all the way and learn these distinctions.

In the Proper of Saints, compare the celebrations for St. Lawrence of Brindisi on July 21 with that of St. Mary Magdalene on July 22. St. Lawrence of Brindisi was a Capuchin Franciscan, a terrific preacher, and a Doctor of the church. You know St. Mary Magdalene, the first follower of Jesus to see Him after the Resurrection.

Now for a little review. You'll note that St. Lawrence's celebration has no label while St. Mary Magdalene's is labeled "Memorial." St. Lawrence's celebration is a Memorial, too, but it is an OPTIONAL MEMORIAL. **An OPTIONAL MEMORIAL is not labeled in the breviary. An individual or parish may <u>choose</u> to celebrate it if desired.** St. Mary Magdalene's celebration is an OBLIGATORY MEMORIAL. **An OBLIGATORY MEMORIAL is labeled "Memorial" in the breviary. The whole Church celebrates Obligatory Memorials.**

Look at St. Bridget's celebration on July 23. St. Bridget was a wife, mother, and mystic known for her prophecies, revelations, and holiness. Is St. Bridget's celebration an Optional or Obligatory Memorial? Apply the above definitions and figure it out! How about Saints Joachim and Ann, the parents of Our Lady, on July 26? St. Martha, who waited on Jesus while Mary sat at His feet and prayed, on July 29? Saint Peter Chrysologus, the golden tongued preacher, bishop, and Doctor of the Church, on July 30?

Now check these four celebrations again, comparing the Concluding Prayers.

How many Concluding Prayers are listed for each celebration? Right. Only one. So which office do you use it with? Or do you use it with all the offices?

Time for a memory jog. Do you recall that, in the Proper of Seasons, a single Concluding Prayer was used to conclude both the Morning and Evening Prayer offices? The same applies here. **The Concluding Prayer listed in the Proper of Saints is used to conclude** <u>both</u> **the Morning and Evening Prayer offices.**

All Memorials, whether Optional or Obligatory, are minor celebrations of the Church. They do not have Evening Prayer I. The Night Prayer office used is the one for the day of the week on which the Memorial falls. Shortly you will learn how to pray Morning and Evening Prayer on a Memorial.

Lesson 68: Praying Morning and Evening Prayer on Obligatory Memorials

Go get yourself a cup of coffee and a sandwich. This is a long lesson. Might as well be comfortable going over it.

When praying the Divine Office on Feasts and Solemnities, you learned to use first all the parts of the Office that are in the Feast or Solemnity as listed in either the Proper of Saints or the Proper of Seasons. Any parts not in the Proper of Saints or the Proper of Seasons are taken from the Common.

Here's a mathematical-like formula for that:

SOLEMNITIES AND FEASTS=Proper of Saints/Proper of Seasons First + Commons Second

Memorials aren't found in the Proper of Seasons. They're all in the Proper of Saints. Memorials use the Proper of Saints. They use the Commons. They use the Psalter. Now hang in there with me, will you? In order to pray the Divine Office on a Memorial, you need to know which parts of the breviary to use and

11-3

when to use them. First you'll learn to pray Morning and Evening Prayer on Obligatory Memorials. Later on Optional Memorials.

Now take a sip of that coffee before moving on. Feel better now?

Praying Morning and Evening Prayer on OBLIGATORY MEMORIALS		
Part of Office	**Use 1st**	**Use 2nd**
Invitatory Antiphon	Memorial	Common or Psalter
Hymn	Memorial	Common
Psalmody	Memorial	Psalter
Reading/Responsory	Memorial	Common or Psalter
Antiphon for Canticle of Zechariah	Memorial	Common or Psalter
Antiphon for Canticle of Mary	Memorial	Common or Psalter
Intercessions	Memorial	Common or Psalter
Concluding Prayer	Memorial	Common

On OBLIGATORY MEMORIALS, the Office is taken first from the Memorial in the Proper of Saints. Those portions of the Office not in the Proper of Saints are taken from the Common or the Psalter. <u>For certain parts of the Office, the Church allows a choice between the Common or Psalter.</u>

This is too much information for a simple math-like equation. We need a chart here. So here it is:

Let's review the chart. And do feel free to look back at it at any time. That's why it's here.

Where do you first look for all parts of the Office? In the Memorial.

If the Memorial has no Invitatory Antiphon, where do you find it? In the Common or the Psalter (your choice).

Which Hymn will you use to celebrate an Obligatory Memorial if the Memorial has no Hymn? The one in the Common only.

Which Psalmody will you use if the Memorial has no Psalmody? The one from the Psalter only.

Other than the Invitatory Antiphon, what four parts of the Office can be taken either from the Common or the Psalter (your choice) if those parts are not in the Memorial? The Reading and Responsory, the Antiphon for the Canticle of Zechariah, the Antiphon for the Canticle of Mary, and the Intercessions.

If the Memorial has no Concluding Prayer, which prayer will you use? Only the one from the Common.

OK. You are doing great. Another sip of coffee and a bite of that sandwich before moving on.

How about a summary? **On OBLIGATORY MEMORIALS, use first all the parts of the Office in the Memorial. If the Memorial does <u>not</u> have a Hymn, use the Hymn from the Common. If the Memorial does <u>not</u> have a Psalmody, use the Psalmody in the Psalter. If the Memorial does <u>not</u> have a Concluding Prayer, use the Concluding Prayer from the Common. For any other parts of the Office not in the Memorial, use the corresponding parts from <u>either</u> the Psalter <u>or</u> the Common. The choice is up to you.**

How in the world will you remember all this? Well, take a peek at that sandwich you're munching on. Think of the Morning and Evening Prayer offices on an Obligatory Memorial as a sandwich. How about a meat and cheese one?

The Hymn, which begins the offices and is like the top slice of bread, and the Concluding Prayer, which concludes the offices and is like the bottom slice of bread, are both taken from the **M**emorial (think of **M**olasses Bread), if they are in the Memorial. But, if they aren't, take them from the **C**ommon (think of **C**rusty Wheat Bread).

The Psalmody, which is like the sandwich filling, is taken from **M**emorial (think of **M**eat), if it's in the Memorial. But, if it's not, it's taken from the **P**salter (think of **P**rovolone Cheese).

All the other parts of the offices, which are like the condiments in a sandwich, are taken either from the **C**ommon (think of **C**risp Lettuce) or the **P**salter (think of **P**ickles). It's your choice.

What does this tell you about sandwiches? They're basically the same but there are variations in their makeup. Same thing with praying Memorials. Basically the same but with variations in their makeup. Just as you don't think twice about making a sandwich, except to decide what to put in it, so you'll soon not be thinking twice about Memorials.

Let's see how this works. **Move your Proper of Saints bookmark to the Memorial for Saint Justin Martyr which is June 1.** Saint Justin Martyr was, to state the obvious, a martyr. He was the first layman to serve as an apologist and met his death by beheading in 165. Not a nice way to go, but then, he flew right into the Lord's Presence where his head was, in his spiritual body, promptly restored. The celebration for this great Christian debater is marked "Memorial." So you know it's Obligatory which means that the whole Church celebrates it.

The instruction given says, "From the common of one martyr, page ___." The only parts of the Office under the Memorial for Saint Justin Martyr are the Antiphons for Canticles of Zechariah and Mary and the Concluding Prayer *(those with four volume breviaries will have the Second Reading for the Office of Readings and its Responsory as well)*. This means that all the other parts of the Office for Saint Justin Martyr will be taken either from the Common or from the Psalter.

First mark the Common. The Common of One Martyr is the Primary Common and the only Common used for this Memorial. **Move your "Common: Primary Office" bookmark to the Common of One Martyr.** What do you do with the Common—Secondary Office bookmark? Just leave it someplace in the Commons but pay no attention to it. In 1998, June 1 fell on Monday, Week I. Let's pretend it's that day. **Move your Psalter bookmark to Monday Morning Prayer, Week I.**

We can use either the Common or the Psalter for certain parts of this Office. Let's decide to do things alphabetically. Why not? That means we'll the Common. Now, referring to the above chart and using your breviary, answer the following questions:

> Where will you find the Hymn?
> The Invitatory Antiphon?
> Psalmody?
> Reading and Responsory?
> Antiphon for Canticle of Zechariah?
> Intercessions?
> Concluding Prayer?

All right! You are about ready to pray. But first, another sip of coffee and you might want to finish that sandwich. I hope it was a tasty one.

PRACTICE: Pray Morning Prayer for the Memorial of Saint Justin Martyr <u>using the Common wherever you have a choice</u>. See how you did by checking yourself against Appendix L.

EXTRA PRACTICE: Pray Morning Prayer for the Memorial for Saint Justin Martyr but <u>use the Psalter wherever you have a choice</u>. Check how you did by referring to Appendix M.

Now compare the parts of the two offices. What parts are alike? What are different?

If you're a thinking dodo, you may have a few questions.

Does the Church permit use of the Reading from one part of the breviary and the Responsory from another part? No, that's not an acceptable practice. **The Responsory used is always the one that follows the Reading in the breviary.** If the Reading from the Psalter is chosen, then the Responsory that follows it is also chosen. If the Reading from the Common is chosen, the Responsory that follows it is also chosen. The Reading and Responsory always go together—sort of like putting black olives or green ones in your sandwich. You'd not think of pulling the red pimento out of the green olives and putting it with the black olive in your sandwich, would you? Green olive and pimento go together, just like Reading and Responsory.

Does the Church allow use of one part of the Office from the Psalter and another from the Common, or ought the Psalter or Common be used consistently when there is a choice? **With the exception of not mixing the Reading and Responsory, those praying may choose, when choice is allowed, to pray one part of the Office from the Psalter and the other part from the Common.** This means that, for the Memorial of Saint Justin Martyr, one could use the Invitatory Antiphon from the Common of One Martyr, the Reading and Responsory from the Psalter, and the Intercessions from the Common. Or one could mix and match these parts in other ways. However, since the Antiphon for the Canticle of Zechariah, the Antiphon for the Canticle of Mary, and the Concluding Prayer are written under the Memorial of Saint Justin, these are the ones the whole Church uses. You can see what variety the Memorial "sandwich" can take.

Suppose a Memorial falls on a Sunday? Or during Holy Week or during the Octave of Easter? Does the Church celebrate the Memorial? No. **Memorials are <u>never</u> celebrated on Sundays or during Holy Week and the Easter Octave. These days have special offices**. The Sunday, Holy Week, and Easter Octave celebrations are used at these times.

Are there any exceptions to the above guidelines? Very few. To take one example, the Memorial for St. Agnes, child martyr of the early Church, on January 21 tells the reader to use Sunday Week I Psalms for Morning Prayer Psalms and the Psalms and Canticle from the Common of One Martyr for Evening Prayer II. We wouldn't expect this

**DODO
SELF CHECK #68**

Use the chart in this chapter to answer these questions, now or later!

1. On an Obligatory Memorial, what parts of the Divine Office are used from the Memorial?

2. What parts of the Office may be taken from either the Common or the Psalter if they are not in the Memorial?

3. What parts of the Office are to be taken from the Common if they are not in the Memorial?

4. What parts of the Office are to be taken from the Psalter if they are not in the Memorial?

5. What is the "sandwich hint?"

6. Does the Church ever mix a Reading from the Psalter and a Responsory from the Common? Why not?

7. If you have a choice of whether to use the Common or Psalter, is it acceptable to use one part from each?

because Memorials use the Psalmody from the Psalter unless the Memorial has its own Psalmody. So what makes St. Agnes so special? Because her day used to be celebrated as a Feast so it has offices written for a Feast. Now we celebrate her day as a Memorial. Anybody but a saint would see this as a demotion, but St. Agnes doesn't care because she knows that it's Christ Who receives the glory, not her.

So what to do? You'll be all right if you remember this simple guideline. The breviary has all "special" instructions written in it. **Always follow first whatever instructions are given in the Proper of Saints. If no instructions are given, follow the rules summarized in the chart shown earlier.**

**DODO
SELF CHECK #69**

1. What is an Optional Memorial? How is it marked in the Proper of Saints?

2. Does the Church celebrate every Optional Memorial? If you choose not to celebrate it, how do you pray the Office of the day?

3. If two or more Optional Memorials fall on the same day, is it proper Church usage to celebrate both? Do you have to celebrate either?

4. On what days of the year does the Church never celebrate Memorials?

Lesson 69: Optional Memorials

Believe it or not, this is going to be an easier lesson. But, despite the title of this lesson, it's not an optional lesson. It's one any wanting-to-be-wise dodo will gladly do.

You've bumped into Optional Memorials before. Remember? **An OPTIONAL MEMORIAL is a Memorial that may be celebrated.** That means you don't have to celebrate it. So one real way to deal with an Optional Memorial is to skip it. Do you really want to do that and miss out on some pretty fantastic saints? I don't think so.

In the Proper of Saints, turn to December 11. What saint is celebrated that day? Saint Damascus I. Remember him? He's the patron of Saint Jerome; St. Damascus I published the Canon of Sacred Scripture, the Bible. Now you remember, don't you? Saint Damascus I doesn't have a heading to his celebration. This means that the celebration for Saint Damascus I is an OPTIONAL MEMORIAL.

Now for some review. Optional means something that may or may not be chosen. **OPTIONAL MEMORIALS are saints' celebrations that have no heading in the breviary. These unlabeled offices may be celebrated if desired. If they are not celebrated, the day is treated as a Ferial Day (a day on which no celebration is held).** On Ferial Days, use only the Psalter and, during Lent/Easter and Advent/Christmas, the Proper of Seasons as well.

More review. **The Church doesn't celebrate any Memorial, whether Optional or Obligatory, on Sundays, during Holy Week, or during the Easter Octave.** These days have their own special offices.

Sometimes two or more Optional Memorials are celebrated on the same day (this does not happen with Obligatory Memorials). Look at November 16. Whose offices are celebrated that day? Are either one marked "Memorial?" No, neither is. This means that the offices for both Saint Margaret of Scotland and Saint Gertrude are OPTIONAL MEMORIALS.

When two or more Optional Memorials fall on the same day, you may choose to celebrate neither saint. Or you may choose to celebrate one saint or the other. Generally only one saint, if any, is celebrated, even if two or three are listed.

Lesson 70: The Easiest Way to Pray Morning and Evening Prayer on Optional Memorials during Ordinary Time

You mean there's an easiest way to do something in the Divine Office? Oh, tell me! Puullleees!

There is one very, very easy way to pray Optional Memorials. So simple you might fall out of your chair when you learn it, so hold on! As you know, Optional Memorials fall during Ordinary Time and also during the Seasons of the Church year. Here's the easy prayer method for praying Morning and Evening Prayer on Optional Memorials during Ordinary Time. **In Ordinary Time, when praying Morning and Evening Prayer on Optional Memorials, use every part of the Office in the Proper of Saints. Use the Psalter for those parts _not_ in the Proper of Saints.** In this easy method, the Common is not used, even through the breviary will have a Common as a reference.

Here's a simple mathematical-like equation for this:

MP and EP Optional Memorials Ordinary Time=Saints first + Psalter second.

Let's see how this works. Suppose today is October 16. The Proper of Saints bookmark would already be at October 16 as you will be moving it through the Proper of Saints as you pray.

Find October 16 in the Proper of Saints. Are any saints celebrated on this day? Two great ones—Saint Hedwig, duchess and mother of seven children who, upon being widowed, became a Cistercian nun who had to leave her convent to make peace among her battling kids. Sound like someone you can identify with? The other saint is gentle Margaret Mary Alacoque, to whom were given

DODO
SELF CHECK #70

1. If you choose to observe an Optional Memorial during Ordinary Time, what is the easiest method to use?

2. What parts of the office from the Proper of Saints do you use? What parts do you use from the Psalter?

the revelations regarding the Sacred Heart of Jesus, a devotion many practice in the Church today. Are the celebrations of these two saints Optional Memorials? How do you know? Does the Church permit a choice on whether or not to celebrate these?

Suppose you decide to celebrate an Optional Memorial on October 16. Let us say that the year is 1998. In 1998, October 16 fell on Friday of Week IV. This was Friday during the 28th week of Ordinary Time. Since you would be praying the Office daily, your Psalter bookmark would already be at Friday, Week IV, in the Psalter.

On October 16, ought you celebrate both Saint Hedwig and Saint Margaret Mary Alacoque? Gosh, do you have to choose? I'm afraid so. You could celebrate one saint this year and the other next year, if you like. Let's say your kids can't agree on who gets the remote for the tv so you choose Saint Hedwig. Under her office there is only one Concluding Prayer. So that's all you'd use from her celebration. The rest of the office will be in the Psalter.

PRACTICE: Pray the entire Morning Prayer office using the Psalter. When you get to the Concluding Prayer, use the one from the Optional Memorial for Saint Hedwig instead of the Concluding Prayer in the Psalter. This is the simplest way to observe this Optional Memorial.

If you don't want to leave out St. Margaret Mary Alacoque, go back and pray an office for her, too, using everything from the Psalter except the Concluding Prayer which is the only part of this office that's in the Proper of Saints.

Did you find this to be an easy method?

Lesson 71: Two Other Ways to Celebrate Morning and Evening Prayer on Optional Memorials

Look, I don't even have to observe Optional Memorials. Just to be nice, I just learned a super simple way to pray them. Now you want to give me two options for the options? No way, Jose. OK, if you want to skip this chapter, go right ahead. But if you like choice or are a curious dodo about what's coming up, read on. What have you got to lose? You don't have to use these options even if you know about them.

There are four ways to pray Morning and Evening Prayer on Optional Memorials.

One you just learned. It applies only to Optional Memorials during Ordinary Time. What's that method?

A second method you also know. That is to **pray the Morning and Evening Prayer offices as you would pray them on Obligatory Memorials.**

A third way is to:

> **1. Use all the parts of the office found in the Proper of Saints.**
>
> **2. Use the Psalter <u>only</u> for the Psalmody and its Antiphons and Psalm-Prayers.**
>
> **3. Use <u>everything else</u> from the Common.**

At first glance, this seems similar to how the Office is prayed on Obligatory Memorials, but it's a bit different. It's simpler. Compare the three directives above with those in Lesson 68 and you'll see what I mean. Look at the celebration for Saint John Damascene on December 4 in the Proper of Saints. St. John Damascene is a Doctor of the Church who authored 150 religious works and who defended the veneration of icons. Next time you dust off your statue of St. Anthony or St. Joseph or Our Lady, you can thank St. John Damascene for the Church allowing it in your house. Do you see a small instruction under St. John's biography? The instruction reads, "From the common of doctors of the Church" and a page number in your breviary is given.

This means that, if you so choose, you can use the common of doctors of the Church to pray the office on this Optional Memorial. Let's see how using the Common works for a celebration of Saint John Damascene on December 4, 1998.

Place your Proper of Saints bookmark at Saint John's Optional Memorial on December 4. What part of the Office is printed there?

In 1998, the Optional Memorial of St. John Damascene fell on Friday, Week I of the Psalter. **Mark this with the Psalter bookmark.** Remember, in this option, you'll be using only the Psalms, Antiphons, and Psalm-Prayers from the Psalter. The rest will come from, first, the Proper of Saints, and, second, from the Common of Doctors.

On December 4, 1998, the Proper of Seasons bookmark would have been at Friday of the First Week of Advent in the Proper of Seasons. Will you use the Proper of Seasons if you follow this option for praying the Divine Office on Optional Memorials? No, in this option you will not use the Proper of

DODO
SELF CHECK #71

1. What are three ways to pray Morning and Evening Prayer on Optional Memorials? Describe each way in detail.

2. Do you use the Psalmody in the Commons for Morning and Evening Prayer on Optional Memorials? Where do you find the Psalms for the Psalmody?

Seasons. You will learn how to use it later. **Move the "Common: Primary Office" bookmark to the Common of Doctors of the Church (the page number will be under Saint John Damasene's day).** Will you use the Common in this option? Yes, you will use it for everything but the Psalmody (from the Psalter) and the Concluding Prayer (which is under St. John Damascene's celebration).

Now page through the Common of Doctors, just to be sure that all the parts of the office are there. Remember the parts? Hymn—Psalms and Antipohns—Reading/Responsory—Canticle of Mary—Intercessions—Our Father—Concluding Prayer. Yikes! Something's missing! The Common of Doctors has no Intercessions? Do you skip them? You already know the answer to that question. So what do you do?

First thing to do is to think ahead. **When using any Common, always look back at its very first page to see if there are any special instructions.** Different breviaries give different instructions. You probably won't find the words "Primary Common" and "Secondary Common" used, but you don't need them, do you? You remember that the first Common you use is the Primary Common and any Common that one refers you to is the Secondary Common. Some breviaries tell you that you are to take everything from the another common except the parts written in this common. Other breviaries get more specific and refer you to another common for certain well marked parts of the Divine Office.

Whatever instruction your breviary gives, the parts of the Office will be the same. You need only know how to find the parts that you need. Put the bookmarks in the locations given and you're ready to pray!

So how do you pray the Optional Memorial of St. John Damascene? The Primary Common bookmark is at the Common of Doctors. The Common of Doctors refers you to the Common of Pastors for parts not in the Common of Doctors. Does this mean that you have to use that Commons—Secondary Office bookmark? You betcha. The parts of the office not in the Common of Doctors, in this case the Intercessions, will be in the Common of Pastors. **Go to that spot and put the Commons-Secondary Office right there, at the Intercessions.**

PRACTICE: Pray Morning Prayer for an Optional Memorial for Saint John Damascene using only the Proper of Saints, the Psalmody from the Psalter, and the Common.

After praying Morning Prayer for the Optional Memorial of Saint John Damascene, using this option, check how you did by looking at Appendix N.

Lesson 72: Praying Morning and Evening Prayer on Optional Memorials during Seasons of the Church Year

Wait a minute. Didn't we say that there are four ways to pray the Divine Office on Optional Memorials? We've already discussed three. What's number four? The fourth way deals with praying the Divine Office during Lent/Easter and Advent/Christmas.

Praying the Divine Office on Optional Memorials during Lent/Easter and Advent/Christmas is a bit more complicated than praying the Office during Ordinary Time. Oh, great! Wait a moment. Hang in there. If you don't want to pray an office for an Optional Memorial, you don't have to. It's optional. If you read this instruction over, you can decide what you'd like to do. Agreed?

OK, what's the first thing you have to do? Well, first you note whether the Optional Memorial becomes a COMMEMORATION. A Commemoration has its own procedures. More about that later.

First let's see how to celebrate an Optional Memorial during a Church Season when that Memorial does <u>not</u> become a Commemoration. This would be during the first three weeks of Advent and after the Easter and Christmas Octaves (the eight days following the Solemnities). During these times, as you already know, the Church is using the Proper of Seasons. The guidelines for using the Proper of Seasons apply, to an extent, here, but with these additional techniques.

**A Fourth Way to Pray Morning and Evening Prayer on Optional Memorials during the First Three Weeks of Advent and during the Easter and Christmas Seasons
after the Octaves**

      1. FIRST—SAINTS: Use all parts of the Office found under the Optional Memorial in the Proper of Saints.

      2. NEXT—SEASONS: Then use all the other parts found in the Proper of Seasons.

      3. LAST—PSALTER: Use the Psalter for parts of the Office in neither the Proper of Saints nor the Proper of Seasons.

Try to memorize these key words. SAINTS. SEASONS. PSALTER. Let's say them again. SAINTS. SEASONS. PSALTER. Got it?

Have you noticed that the Common is not used in this option?

Let's see how this works. Earlier we celebrated the Optional Memorial of Saint John Damascene using the Common. Now let's celebrate it using the Proper of Seasons.

Find the Optional Memorial of Saint John Damascene on December 4 in the Proper of Saints. Is it an Obligatory or Optional Memorial? How do you know? **Move the Proper of Saints bookmark to December 4.**

In 1998, December 4 fell on Friday of the First Week of Advent. **The Proper of Seasons bookmark would be at that spot.**

In the Psalter, the Psalter bookmark would be at Friday, Week I. Put your bookmarks in place.

How do we do this? Remember the order. SAINTS. SEASONS. PSALTER.

To celebrate the Optional Memorial of Saint John Damascene using the Proper of Seasons, look first in the Proper of SAINTS. All that is printed is a Concluding Prayer. Is this used to conclude both the Morning and Evening Prayer offices? You betcha.

Now where do you look? In the Proper of SEASONS. Everything not in the Proper of Saints take from the Proper of Seasons.

What if a part is not in the Proper of Saints or the Proper of Seasons? Where do you find it? Yep. PSALTER.

Go through the Morning Prayer office section by section. Follow the above rules. Remember the key words: SAINTS. SEASONS. PSALTER.

First look in the Proper of Saints. Use all the parts of the office there.

Next look in the Proper of Seasons. Use all the parts of the office there that are not in the Proper of Saints.

Last, look in the Psalter. Use all parts of the office here that are not in either the Proper of Saints or the Proper of Seasons.

What will you use from the Proper of Saints for the Optional Memorial of Saint John Damascene? Only the Concluding Prayer.

What will you use from the Proper of Seasons for this celebration? The Invitatory Antiphon, Reading, Responsory, Antiphon for the Canticle of Zechariah, and Intercessions.

What will you use from the Psalter? The Psalmody and its Antiphons.

What Hymn will you use? One appropriate for Advent (you can find it in a special section of your breviary).

PRACTICE: Pray Morning Prayer for the Optional Memorial of Saint John Damascene for December 4, 1998, using the Proper of Seasons. Check how you did by referring to Appendix O.

EXTRA PRACTICE: Pray Evening Prayer for the Optional Memorial of Saint John Damascene for December 4, 1998. How do you think you did with it?

Lesson 73: Commemorations

Oh, no. Here's that word. Commemorations. Scary. Yes, praying the Divine Office on Commemorations is a bit tricky, but all you need to know are a few simple techniques. And then, presto, it'll seem easy.

A COMMEMORATION is a Memorial, whether Optional or Obligatory, that is celebrated at any time during Lent and also during Advent between December 17 to the 23rd and during the Octave of Christmas (between Christmas and New Year's). All Memorials celebrated at these times become COMMEMORA-TIONS. COMMEMORATIONS are optional **celebrations which means that parishes and individuals may** choose **to celebrate them if desired. Commemorations are not celebrated during Holy Week or the Octave of Easter (eight days after Easter Sunday) even if a saint's celebration coincides with those days. These are special holy days whose individual offices are** never **replaced by a saint's Commemoration.**

Only Memorials, whether Optional or Obligatory, become Commemorations. **Feasts and Solemnities of the Saints** never **become Commemorations. They are always celebrated at the proper time unless they coincide with a Solemnity of the Church year.** No saint's Feast or Solemnity, for example, is ever celebrated during Holy Week, Easter, and the Easter Octave because these are Solemnities of the Church Year that involve our Lord Jesus. A saint's Feast or Solemnity does not replace a Solemnity of Christ. **Feasts that coincide with a Solemnity of the Church simply drop out of the calendar for that year. Solemnities that coincide are transferred to another day so that they will still be celebrated.**

DODO
SELF CHECK #73

1. What is
Commemoration? How
do you know if a
Memorial is a
Commemoration? Does
the Church allow any
choice about whether or
not to celebrate
Commemorations?

2. When do
Commemorations occur?

3. Do Feasts or
Solemnities become
Commemorations?

4. How is Night Prayer
prayed on a
Commemoration?

5. How are the Morning
and Evening Prayer
offices prayed on
Commemorations?

Suppose you bravely choose to observe a Commemoration. You're going to apply a technique called the "Commemoration Combo." Here's how it works:

Night Prayer: On a Commemoration, Night Prayer is the one for the weekday. No changes are made in the Night Prayer office. Oh, that was easy. No Combo here. But read on.

Morning and Evening Prayer: Here's where you do the Commemoration Combo. A Commemoration occurs on special days of the Church year. The Commemoration must take second place to these observances. To do this, **pray the entire office using the Proper of Seasons and the Psalter, just as if the Commemoration did not exist**. Really? Yes, really. **When you get to the Concluding Prayer of the Morning or Evening Office, pray the first part of it but leave off the ending ("through Our Lord Jesus Christ" and so on). Now, if praying Morning Prayer, add the Morning Prayer Antiphon for the Canticle of Zechariah from the Proper of Saints (if there is one) and for Evening Prayer, add the Evening Prayer Antiphon from the Canticle of Mary (if there is one)**. Oh, oh. This is the Combo, isn't it? Sure is. You mean I combine the Antiphon right here, in the middle of the Concluding Prayer? Yes, that's exactly what I mean. Weird, isn't it? **Pray the Antiphon right here even though it seems odd. Then pray the Concluding Prayer for the saint.** Did you say the saint's Concluding Prayer? You mean I combine that prayer with the Proper of Seasons Concluding Prayer? Yep. More weird. **End the offices with the usual "May the Lord bless us, protect us from all evil, and bring us to everlasting life. Amen." Then make the Sign of the Cross as usual**.

There you have it. The Commemoration Combo!

Do you want to see how this works? If you're any kind of incredulous dodo, you sure do! Turn in the Proper of Saints to March 23. March 23 is a Commemoration in honor of St. Turibius de Mongrovejo, St. Turibius is a marvelous bishop who defended the rights of the native Indians of Peru who were suffering terribly under the Spaniards. In 1998, March 23 fell on Monday of the Fourth Week of Lent. It was also Monday of Week IV in the Psalter. To pray Morning Prayer on the Commemoration of St. Turibius, you would pray the entire office using the Psalter for the Psalmody and the Proper of Seasons for the rest of the Office as you've already learned. The Commemoration would only be noted at the end of the offices as part of the Concluding Prayer.

How would you compose this prayer? First find the Concluding Prayer for the Proper of Seasons. Next find the Antiphons for the Canticles of Zechariah and Mary in the Proper of Saints. Finally find the Concluding Prayer for the Commemoration of St. Turibius.

PRACTICE: Follow the above instructions and **pray** the Concluding Prayer for Morning Prayer as it should be prayed for the Commemoration of St. Turibius.

EXTRA PRACTICE: Pray the Concluding Prayer for Evening Prayer as it should be prayed for the Commemoration of St. Turibius. **Check** how you did on both prayers by referring to Appendix P.

Now go to December 29, the Commemoration of St. Thomas Becket, the well known English Archbishop of Canterbury and martyr under King Henry II of England. You'll note that December 29 has an office both in the Proper of Saints for St. Thomas Becket and in the Proper of Seasons for December 29. That's OK. Follow the Commemoration Combo Procedure listed above.

PRACTICE: Pray the Concluding Prayer for the Morning Prayer office for a Commemoration of St. Thomas Becket.

EXTRA PRACTICE: Pray the Concluding Prayer for the Evening Prayer office for St. Thomas Becket. **Check** how you did on both prayers by referring to Appendix P.

**DODO
SELF CHECK #74**

1. How will you know if a certain Memorial is Obligatory to your country and not to other places?

2. How do you pray the Divine Office if the Primary Common that you are using refers you to another Common? How do you use the bookmarks in these cases?

Lesson 74: Special Cases

You didn't think you were going to get by without some exceptions, did you? Life if full of exceptions and the Divine Office is no exception to the norm. The good thing about the exceptions is that they present no problem because the breviary tells you how to deal with them. So let's dig in and see what they are.

Look, for example, at October 19. Two offices fall on the same day. Are either of these marked "Memorial?" One, the one for Sts. Isaac Jogues and John de Brebeuf, who were two of the North American Martyrs who died at the hands of the Native Americans whom they were trying to convert, says, "In the dioceses of the United States: Memorial." What do you suppose that means? If you guessed that this office is an <u>Obligatory Memorial</u> only in the United States, you guessed correctly. So if you live in Alaska, Hawaii, Maine, or any other state in the USA, you'd celebrate this memorial. But if you live in Timbuktu, Antarctica, or any other place other than in the USA, you've got a choice regarding which Memorial to celebrate—either that of Saints Isaac Jogues and companions or that of Saint Paul of the Cross, the founder of the Passionists, because both of these would be Optional Memorials for you. For the Passionists, however, the office of their founder St. Paul of the Cross is not a Memorial but a Solemnity which is so marked for them in a special breviary supplement for their Order. Passionists worldwide will celebrate the office of St. Paul of the Cross as a Solemnity.

For certain celebrations, two Commons may be used. Look, for example, at the Memorial for November 10, that of St. Leo the Great, Pope and Doctor of the Church who stabilized the Church during a time of invasion and heresy. What two Commons does this celebration use? Your breviary will say, "From the common of pastors, p. ___, or of doctors of the Church, p. ____."

Suppose that you decide to use the Common for Doctors of the Church. Oh, you might remember that Common. We used it for the Optional Memorial of St. John Damascene. Do you recall that the Common for Doctors of the Church refers you to the Common of Pastors for any parts not in the Common of Doctors? Use the two Commons bookmarks to mark these offices (Doctors as Primary Common and Pastors as Secondary Common) and you're ready to pray.

PRACTICE: Let's **pretend** it's November 10, 1998, and you wish to pray Morning Prayer for the Memorial of St. Leo the Great, using the Common of Doctors.

> ### DODO
> ### SELF CHECK #75
>
> **1. What is an Ordo?**
>
> **2. Why is an Ordo useful?**
>
> **3. What precautions must be taken in ordering an Ordo?**
>
> **4. How long can you use an Ordo?**

    1. First, **move the Proper of Saints bookmark to November 10, the Memorial of St. Leo the Great.**

    2. Next, **place the "Common: Primary Office" bookmark at the Common of Doctors.** Everything in that Common you will use first.

    3. Now **place the "Common: Secondary Office" bookmark at the Common of Pastors**. If parts of the Office are not in the Common of Doctors, you will take them from the Common of Pastors.

    4. November 10, 1998 (the Memorial of St. Leo) fell on Tuesday of Week IV. **Move the Psalter bookmark to that spot.**

5. **Pray** Morning Prayer for the Memorial of St. Leo, using the Common of Doctors as the Primary Office. **Follow** Lesson 68's guidelines for praying the Office on Obligatory Memorials. For this practice, whenever you have a choice between using the Psalter and the Common, use the Common. After you pray the Office through, check how you did by referring to Appendix Q.

Lesson 75: The Ordo

The what? Is an ORDO the cousin of a dodo? Far from it. An ORDO is a smart and handy way to know just what to pray each day in the Divine Office. You might want to get one.

An ORDO, also called a "Guide for Christian Prayer," is a daily guide to praying the Divine Office for a specific year. Maybe you received one with your breviary. An Ordo costs a few bucks, and **you have to buy a new one each year**, but it's worth its weight in gold, because it tells <u>exactly</u> where to find the offices for each day.

You know that the Divine Office is the same all over the world, no matter who published your breviary. However, different publishers arrange the breviary a bit differently. **In order for the page numbers in the Ordo to correspond to the page numbers in <u>your</u> breviary, the Ordo that <u>you</u> get must be the one written for the breviary that <u>you</u> are using.** Makes perfect sense, doesn't it?

Where do you get an Ordo? From a Catholic bookstore. When you request one, tell the clerk the name of your breviary and the publisher so that you receive the Ordo that corresponds to your breviary. If a bookstore seems unable to help, contact the publisher of your breviary by mail, email, or phone.

Ordos are filled with abbreviations. They look pretty confusing, but you'll be able to figure them out. The abbreviations are for the different parts of the Divine Office. Your Ordo may abbreviate Morning Prayer as MP, for example. If all the parts of the Office are taken from one part of the breviary, the Ordo may write ALL. Commons may be abbreviated as Com. and so on. Others will list only the Proper or the Week of the Psalter and you will have to find the correct section and day of the week. With a little study, you'll soon understand your Ordo's system. If you have difficulty, ask your parish priest or a member of a religious order to show you what the abbreviations mean. Or contact the publisher of your Ordo with your questions.

An Ordo is especially helpful when certain Solemnities and Feasts replace Sunday celebrations or, because they coincide with a Sunday celebration, are transferred to Monday. Without an Ordo, you won't know if this is the case. However, if you don't have an Ordo, you can always call your parish priest and ask if such a transferal will occur.

DODO
SELF CHECK #76

1. If you don't have an Ordo, what two ways will tell you what week of the Psalter to use during Ordinary Time?

2. What week of the Psalter does Ash Wednesday always fall in? Why?

3. On Monday of the Second Week of Easter, what office will you use?

4. How will you know what week of Ordinary Time to resume after Pentecost? How will you know what week of the Psalter to use?

Lesson 76: Finding Your Place without an Ordo

If you have an Ordo or intend to purchase one, you can skip this lesson. No one's going to make you read it.

If you don't have an Ordo, don't wish to buy one, or have poor access to Catholic bookstores, on line or in your local area, you'll be glad for this lesson. Don't feel you have to memorize all that's in here. Keep the manual someplace safe, like under your bed, and look back here whenever you've got a question about where you are in the Divine Office. You can even write the page of this lesson inside the front cover of the manual if you want. It's your book. Do what you want with it!

Right off the bat, you'll want to find out where the Church is in the Divine Office for today. You'll need to find your spot in the Proper of Seasons as well as in the Psalter. To do this, phone a priest or a religious community or look in your church's weekly missalette to see what Sunday of the year you are currently celebrating. Find that Sunday's offices in the Proper of Seasons. All the Sunday offices for Ordinary Time should tell you what week of the Psalter to use.

Ordinary Time begins on the Monday following the Baptism of Our Lord (Monday, Week I), is interrupted by Lent, and continues after Pentecost until Advent. If your breviary's Proper of Seasons doesn't tell you what week of the Psalter you're using for Ordinary Time, you can figure out the week by this trick: Keep it in mind and maybe it will come in handy on a quiz show some day. Here's the trick: Divide the number of the Week of Ordinary Time by 4 and look at the remainder. Remainder 1 means use Week I of the Psalter; Remainder 2 means use Week II; Remainder 3 means use Week III; Remainder 0 means use week IV. For example, for the 22nd Week of Ordinary Time, you would divide 22 by 4 (22/4 = 5, remainder 2). The remainder is 2. Thus, for the 22nd week of Ordinary Time, use Week II of the Psalter. Turn in your breviary's Proper of Seasons to the 22nd Sunday of Ordinary Time. It may already say "Psalter Week II." Is that clever or what?

But you may not be in Ordinary Time. You may be in one of the Church seasons, either Lent/Easter or Advent/Christmas. What are the guidelines for those seasons?

The First Sunday of Advent is <u>always</u> Sunday, Week I. Follow the weeks in order (Week I, Week II Week III Week IV, and then repeat the cycle) until the Sunday of the Baptism of Our Lord. After the Baptism of the Lord, Ordinary Time begins with Monday, Week I and continues until Ash Wednesday. Pretty straight forward, right?

No matter what week you're in when praying the Tuesday before Ash Wednesday (Shrove Tuesday), Ash Wednesday is <u>always</u> Wednesday of Week IV. This means that no matter if Shrove Tuesday was Tuesday of Week I, Week II, Week III, or Week IV, you go to <u>Week IV</u> for Ash Wednesday. Why? Because this makes the Easter cycle work out correctly. Nifty, eh?

After Ash Wednesday, proceed with Thursday, Friday, and Saturday of Week IV so that the first Sunday of Lent is Sunday, Week 1. Continue to use the Psalter in order. Recall that the Triduum and Easter Octave have their own offices in the Proper of Seasons.

On Monday of the second week of Easter, use Monday, Week II of the Psalter. Follow the Psalter in order until Pentecost.

To resume Ordinary Time after Pentecost, ask a priest or a religious community two questions: What week of Ordinary Time are we now in? And what week of the Current Daily Psalter are we now in? Mark your breviary accordingly and proceed with the weeks in order until Advent.

Or you may consult a Mass missalette and then follow the division and remainder guidelines given earlier. Now you know! Don't you feel smart?

Lesson 77: Praying the Office Daily

Congratulations! You did it! You can pray Morning, Evening, and Night Prayer daily. Honest! See how smart you are! All you need do is set your breviary up for today and get praying. You know how to find your place. So why not begin? Get those bouncing bookmarks and restful ribbons in place and you're ready to roll.

Here's a guarantee. If you faithfully pray the Office every day, moving your bookmarks ahead to the next office as you finish one office, you're going to soon discover that all the difficulty and confusion you felt when you first turned to this manual has miraculously cleared up.

Now I know there are several bookmarks you've not used, printed with terms we've not really talked much about. If you want to find out about them, you'll have to read the next section. But this section completes what you need to know to pray the three main offices of the day, Morning, Evening, and Night Prayer.

Good luck, and God bless you!

SECTION TWELVE

The Minor Offices

"In this section, you'll learn about ..."

The gradual psalms

Daytime prayer

Praying the "little offices"

Daytime prayer on feasts and memorials

The Office of Readings

THE MINOR OFFICES

Lesson 78: The Gradual Psalms (Complementary Psalmody)

Ever hear of the Gradual Psalms? The Complementary Psalmody? No? These aren't psalms you pray gradually and they don't pay you any compliments. But they're very important if you want to pray an office we've not discussed much, the Office of Daytime Prayer.

DODO
SELF CHECK #78

1. What are the Gradual Psalms? Where are they found?

2. What bookmark indicates the Complementary Psalmody?

3. How are the Psalms divided up? At what time of the day are the Midmorning Psalms prayed? Midday Psalms? Midafternoon Psalms?

Daytime Prayer sometimes uses the GRADUAL PSALMS. You've got 'em in your breviary. **The GRADUAL PSALMS are Psalms 120 through 128. They're found in the breviary in the section entitled COMPLEMENTARY PSALMODY.**

Look in your breviary's Table of Contents for the Complementary Psalmody. Turn to that section and place the Complementary Psalmody (gradual psalms) bookmark at the beginning of this Psalmody.

Page through the Complementary Psalmody. Do you see that the Psalms are divided into groups of three and are labeled Midmorning, Midday, and Midafternoon? You know what this means, I bet. Of course. It means that certain Psalms are prayed at certain times of the day. Would the Church pray the Midmorning Psalms at 3 p.m.? Not in your life! Midmorning Psalms are prayed about 9 a.m. Way back in Lesson 4, we discussed the times for Midmorning, Midday, and Midafternoon Prayer Want to check back there? Go right ahead!

Lesson 79: Daytime Prayer

If you don't intend to pray Daytime Prayer, you could skip this lesson and the following ones and proceed to Lesson 84 on praying the Office of Readings. If you do want to pray Daytime Prayer, read on.

You've already learned that the complete Divine Office contains how many individual offices of prayer? Did you remember seven? Good for you. **Three of these offices are called MIDMORNING, MIDDAY, and MIDAFTERNOON PRAYER, sometimes called the "LITTLE HOURS." The Little Hours are prayed between Morning and Evening Prayer.** Why do you suppose they're called "Little" Hours? Might they be short offices? If you figured that out, you figured correctly.

Many religious communities and lay people pray only one of the Little Hours. **When only <u>one</u> Little Hour is prayed, that office is called DAYTIME PRAYER.**

Different breviaries print Daytime Prayer in different sections. *The four volume breviary prints Daytime Prayer in the Psalter between the Morning and Evening Prayer offices.* **Some one volume breviaries do the same. Other one volume breviaries have a section called "Daytime Prayer" which has the Daytime Prayer offices.**

Breviaries also differ in how much of the Daytime Prayer offices they print. That's probably because publishers realize that not too many people today pray this office and so they may try to get away with minimizing their attention to it. You can be an aware dodo about Daytime Prayer if you keep the following notions in your little bird brain:

All four volume breviaries and some one volume breviaries print all the Daytime Prayer offices. The offices are different for every day of the four week cycle. There are special parts of the Daytime Prayer Offices during Lent/Easter and Advent/Christmas Seasons and in some celebrations of the Saints and some Commons.

However, some one volume breviaries have only one week's worth of Daytime Prayer—prayer for Sunday, Monday, Tuesday, Wednesday, Thursday, Friday, and Saturday. Then the prayers repeat. These breviaries don't have special Daytime Prayer Offices for the Proper of Seasons or the celebrations of the Saints. You may pray Daytime Prayer using these offices, even though they're incomplete.

<u>Shorter Christian Prayer</u>, the "traveler's breviary," doesn't print Daytime Prayer at all.

That said, suppose you want to pray Daytime Prayer. First thing you've got to do is decide at what time of the day you'll pray it. You've got three approximate times to choose from. **If you pray Daytime Prayer about 9 a.m., you will use the MIDMORNING parts of the Office. If you pray Daytime Prayer about noon, you will use the MIDDAY parts of the Office. If your Daytime Prayer will be about 3 p.m., then you will use the MIDAFTERNOON parts of the Divine Office.** Makes sense, doesn't it?

Once you decide on the time to pray Daytime Prayer, you'll use the Hymn, Reading, Responsory, and Prayer that correspond to the time that you choose. Where in the breviary are these?

Begin by finding Daytime Prayer in your breviary. Look first in the Psalter to see if Daytime Prayer is printed there. If not, look in the Table of Contents for a Daytime Prayer Section.

Next, a Hymn for Daytime Prayer. The Daytime Prayer Hymns will probably be in one of three places:

1. In some breviaries, a Hymn precedes Daytime Prayer.
2. In others, there's a Daytime Prayer Hymn section. You can find that section by looking in the Hymn index or guide for Daytime Prayer Hymns.

DODO
SELF CHECK #79

1. What are the Little Hours? Why are they called "Little?"

2. What is Daytime Prayer? At approximately what three times of day is Daytime Prayer prayed? How many times a day do you wish to pray Daytime Prayer?

3. How does your breviary deal with Daytime Prayer? With Daytime Prayer Hymns?

4. How will you know whether to pray the Midmorning, Midday, or Midafternoon sections of the Office?

5. In breviaries that contain the complete Daytime Prayer offices, where is Daytime Prayer during Ordinary Time found? Where is Daytime Prayer during the Lent/Easter and Advent/Christmas Seasons? On Memorials? Feasts? Solemnities?

3. Still other breviaries, *including four volume breviaries*, list the Daytime Prayer Hymns as part of the Ordinary. Find the Ordinary in the Table of Contents and page through it until you come to a section entitled "Daytime Prayer." This section should begin with Daytime Prayer Hymns.

If your breviary prints Daytime Prayer hymns in a special section, mark that section now with the Daytime Prayer Hymns bookmark. If the Daytime Prayer Hymns are part of a general section of Hymns, the Hymn bookmark will suffice because you can use it to mark the Daytime Prayer Hymn once you finish praying Morning Prayer.

To pray Daytime Prayer, first choose a Hymn. The Hymn should correspond to the time of day that you will be praying Daytime Prayer. If a Hymn is not printed at the beginning of the Daytime Prayer Office, select a Hymn and mark it with the "Daytime Prayer Hymns" bookmark.

How you will now proceed depends on your breviary.

If your breviary only has one week's worth of Daytime Prayer offices, in a separate section, you need only pray the correct office for today's day of the week. You've got three bookmarks for Daytime Prayer, with the time of day (Midmorning, Midday, and Midafternoon) printed on them Mark, with the appropriate bookmark, that section that corresponds to the time of day that you'll be praying Daytime Prayer.

If your breviary has all the Daytime Prayer offices for the year and its various seasons and celebrations, you won't need a bookmark to mark this office. The following techniques will help you find your place:

Find today in the Psalter. If you don't know what week of the Psalter you're in, follow the guidelines in Lesson 76 to find out. **For Ordinary Time, all of the Daytime Prayer will be printed in the Psalter (already marked with the Psalter bookmark).**

In the Lent/Easter and Advent/Christmas seasons, the Daytime Prayer Psalms will be in the Psalter but the Antiphons, Readings, Responsories, and Concluding Prayers will be in the Proper of Seasons (already marked with the Proper of Seasons bookmark).

If today you are celebrating a Memorial, Feast, or Solemnity, follow the instructions in the breviary regarding Daytime Prayer. If no part of the Daytime Prayer Office is written in the Proper of Saints (already marked with the Proper of Saints bookmark), you will use Daytime Prayer from the Psalter for Memorials and Feasts, and Daytime Prayer from the Common for Solemnities.

Lesson 80: General Instructions for Praying Daytime Prayer

TECHNIQUE

Praying Daytime Prayer using a one-volume breviary with a daytime prayer sections:

1. Make the Sign of the Cross silently while saying "God, come to my assistance." Respond, "Lord, make haste to help me."

2. Pray the Glory Be. Say, "Alleluia." (Omit Alleluia during Lent.)

3. Sing, chant, or recite the Hymn you have chosen.

4. Go to Daytime Prayer and pray the Psalmody (Psalms, Canticles, Antiphons, Psalm-Prayers) as you do for any other office. Pray the "Glory Be" as prayed in the Divine Office, after each Psalm and Canticle.

5. Read the Reading and Responsory for the appropriate time of day. Pause briefly for reflection.

6. Say, "Let us pray." Pray the Concluding Prayer. Add the ending printed on the Psalter bookmark.

7. End the office by saying, "Let us praise the Lord." Respond with, "And give him thanks" while making the Sign of the Cross.

**DODO
SELF CHECK #80**

1. How do you begin Daytime Prayer?

2. How do you pray the Psalmody?

3. Where is the Concluding Prayer?

4. How do you conclude the Daytime Prayer Office?

I bet you already suspected this. But in case you didn't, here goes. Just as with the other offices, not all parts of Daytime Prayer may be written out in full in the breviary. Whether or not they're written out, this is the format that is followed:

PRACTICE: This practice is <u>only for those who have a one volume breviary that has a Daytime Prayer Section. If you do not have a one volume breviary with a Daytime Prayer Section, do not do this practice as your Psalmody and Readings will be different.</u> You will practice in the next lesson.

Turn to the Daytime Prayer section. Look at the Sunday Daytime Prayer office. Page through this office, looking for the Concluding Prayer. Where is it?

Let's pretend that this is the Fifth Sunday of Lent. You're getting close to Easter and making plans on where you're going to go for Easter Dinner. Maybe folks will be coming to your place. Right now, you want to stop thinking about whether Easter dinner will be turkey, ham, or both. You want to spend some time with the Lord, praying Daytime Prayer.

Move the Proper of Seasons bookmark to the Fifth Sunday of Lent. Select the Alternative Prayer for Morning Prayer as the Concluding Prayer for your Daytime office.

Now, with your one volume breviary, pray Daytime Prayer at Midday for the Fifth Sunday of Lent. Follow the above format. Check how you did by consulting Appendix R.

Lesson 81: Praying Daytime Prayer

<u>This lesson is for those who have Daytime Prayer written in each office of the four week Psalter.</u> If this doesn't match your breviary, skip this lesson. If it does match your breviary, your breviary should have the complete Daytime Prayer offices in it for the year.

Look at the Psalter. You will find the Daytime Prayer office written out there. *If you have a four volume breviary, first look at the Psalter in the volumes for Ordinary Time.* You'll see that it is easy to pray Daytime Prayer. First decide what time of day you'll be praying. Then choose an appropriate Hymn. Then pray the office straight through, following the format in Lesson 80.   During the seasons of Lent/Easter and Advent/Christmas, however, and on Feasts and Solemnities, the Proper of Seasons or Proper of Saints are used to pray parts or all of the Daytime Prayer office. Yes, I'm sorry, but you'll have to be flipping around between offices again. Think of it as the Divine Office cha cha.

Before you start the fancy footwork, you need to learn a new step. It's called the Single Antiphon Sashay. Let's check this out in your breviary.

You'll find an example of the Single Antiphon Sashay in the Common of Virgins. Find the Midmorning, Midday, and Midafternoon Prayer parts of the Common. How many Antiphons are under each heading? You bet. Only one. Does this mean you pray only one Psalm for these offices, one Psalm for one Antiphon. Nope. You're going to pray the usual number of psalms which is as many as are in the Trinity—three. So where are the other two antiphons? There ain't two other antiphons. How about them apples?

Hey, wait a minute. Just a second. Go jump into the Proper of Seasons. Check out the Lent and Advent offices. How many Antiphons are usually written under the Daytime Prayer heading? Yep. Only one again.

What's going on here?

The Single Antiphon Sashay, that's what. Here's what it's all about:

When only one Antiphon is written under the Daytime Prayer heading, that Antiphon replaces all the other Antiphons used in praying Daytime Prayer. The single Antiphon is prayed once before the first of the three Daytime Prayer Psalms/Canticles and then repeated after the third Psalm's (or Canticle's) final Glory Be and Psalm prayer. The single Antiphon is <u>not</u> prayed <u>between</u> the Psalms/Canticles, but only before you pray them all and after you have prayed them all.

Would you like to see the Single Antiphon Sashay in action? Okey dokey. Find Daytime Prayer for the Solemnity of the Assumption, August 15 and mark it with the Proper of Seasons bookmark. You'll notice that the Office for the Assumption refers you to the Gradual Psalms, and you've already got them marked with a bookmark.

Pretend that you're going to pray Daytime Prayer on your lunch hour. It's a good time. You can eat your sardine and pickle sandwich quickly, scarf down that cup of lukewarm lemonade, and still have time to pray. Since you're going to be praying in the middle of the day, you'll be using the Midday Psalms. Locate the Gradual Psalms for Midday and mark them with the Complementary Psalmody bookmark.

Cha cha back to the Daytime Prayer office for the Solemnity of the Assumption. You'll notice only one Antiphon under the Midday section. Time for the Single Antiphon Sashay. How do you sashay here? You'll pray this Antiphon before Psalm 123 (the first Psalm under the Midday section in

1. If only one Antiphon is given for Daytime Prayer, how is it used?

2. Where are the Antiphons, Readings, Responsories, and Prayers for Solemnities and Feasts? During the Lent/Easter and Advent/Christmas Seasons? During Ordinary Time?

the Complementary Psalmody) and again after the Glory Be following Psalm 125 (the last Psalm in the Midday Complementary Psalmody). Then read the Reading and Responsory as listed under the Solemnity of the Assumption for Midday and end with the Concluding Prayer used for the Morning Prayer office.

PRACTICE: Pray Midday Prayer for the Solemnity of the Assumption. **Check** how you did by comparing your prayer with that written in Appendix S.

Now look at any one of the days in Lent or Advent in the Proper of Seasons. You'll see only one Daytime Prayer Antiphon listed. But no Psalms. Now what in the world?

The Psalms are in the Psalter. But so are Antiphons! What to do?

In Lent/Easter and Advent/Christmas Seasons, the order changes in how you substitute Antiphons. Because the seasons are so special, the order becomes

---

TECHNIQUE

If you wish to daily pray Midmorning, Midday, **and** Midafternoon Prayer, use the Readings, Responsories, and Prayers for the current day for **all three of the "Little Offices."** Use the Daytime Prayer Psalms for the current day for one of the three "Little Offices." For the **other two** offices, you have a choice of Psalms to use.

1. You may use the Gradual Psalms. The Church always uses the Gradual Psalms on any non-Sunday Solemnity of the Church including during the Octaves of Easter and Christmas, Holy Week, and the Easter Triduum. However, for Sundays (which are always Solemnities) and other days, the Church allows the choice of the Gradual Psalms or one of the following options:

2. You may use the Daytime Prayer Psalms for the current weekday in the following two weeks of the Psalter.

3. You may use the Daytime Prayer Psalms for the current weekday in the preceding two weeks of the Psalter.

4. You may use the Daytime Prayer Psalms for the current weekday in the one week prior to this current week and the one week following this current week.

SEASONS—PSALTER.
Use the Psalms from the Psalter to pray Daytime Prayer during Lent and Advent, but don't use the Antiphons from the Psalter. Following the rule—SEASONS—PSALTER—you'll remember that everything in the Proper of Seasons replaces the same parts in the Psalter. So you'd use the single Antiphon in the Proper of Seasons to replace all three Antiphons in the Psalter. You'd only pray that single Antiphon once, before the first Daytime Prayer Psalm and after the final Psalm's (or Canticle's) Glory Be and Psalm Prayer.

SEASONS—PSALTER. The Reading, Responsory, and Prayer follow from the Proper of Seasons. They replace the ones in the Psalter.

PRACTICE: Let's pretend it's March 26, 1998, Thursday during the Fourth Week of Lent. You're well into the Lenten routine at this point. It's time to pray Daytime Prayer at the Midafternoon Hour. At that time, the Church was using Week IV of the Psalter. Use your bookmarks to organize your breviary to pray Daytime Prayer at Midafternoon for March 26, 1998. Then pray this office. Compare how you did with Appendix T.

Lesson 82: Praying All "Little Offices": Midmorning, Midday, and Midafternoon Prayer

Option 1:

Use the Complementary Psalmody bookmark to find the Complementary Psalmody. You may decide to use these Gradual Psalms for the other two "Little Offices."

Option 2:

Use the Psalter. You have three choices in how to use it:

    a. Page forward for two weeks, praying Daytime Prayer for Tuesday, Week III, and Tuesday, Week IV, for two of the "Little Offices."

    b. Page backwards for two weeks, praying Daytime Prayer for Tuesday, Week I, and Daytime Prayer for Tuesday, Week IV, for two of the "Little Offices."

    c. Page backward one week to use Daytime Prayer for Tuesday, Week I, for one "Little Office", and then page forward one week to use Daytime Prayer for Tuesday, Week III, for the other "Little Office."

**DODO
SELF CHECK #82**

1. If you want to pray all
three "Little Offices,"
what are your options
regarding the two
Daytime Prayer offices
that are not in the cur-
rent day of the Psalter?

2. If you choose to use
the Psalter for all three
"Little Offices," what
bookmarks will mark the
Daytime Prayer section
in other weeks of the
 Psalter?

Maybe you really like the Divine Office and want
to pray all seven offices. Maybe you're part of a
First, Second, or Third Order or Lay Movements
that prays all the "Little Offices." If so, this lesson's for you. If you're not going to pray any
other "Little Offices," you might as well skip this
lesson and proceed to Lesson 83.

Have you noticed that the breviary has Readings,
Responsories, and Concluding Prayers for
Midmorning, Midday, and Midafternoon Prayer
but only one Daytime Prayer Psalmody? Where
will you find Psalms for the other two offices?
Would you believe that you have four choices
here? Sort of like choosing between chocolate,
vanilla, strawberry, or cookies 'n cream ice cream.

See the Technique box on the previous page. Are
these techniques clever or what? Let's check out
these options a bit more closely.

**Pretend that this is Tuesday of Week II. Move your Psalter bookmark to that
spot**. Find the Psalms under the Daytime Prayer Office. For one of the "Little
Offices," you will use these Psalms.

Here are the options to use for the other "Little Offices."

**Prayer for all three offices follows the very same for-
mat listed in Lesson 80 under Daytime Prayer.** ➡

**DODO
SELF CHECK #83**

1. When is Daytime
Prayer always taken from
the Proper of Seasons?

2. What are the tech-
niques to follow for
Commemorations?

3. Where do you find
missing parts of the
Daytime Prayer offices
on Optional Memorials?
Obligatory Memorials?
Feasts? Solemnities?

If you intend to pray all three "Little Offices"
using the Psalter, the most common practice is to
use the current day's Daytime Prayer for the
Midday Prayer office. But you don't have to do
that. You can pray the current day's Daytime
Prayer any time you choose. Merely select which
of the above options you'd like, place your bookmarks in the right locations, and you're off and
running.

Here's a wise dodo hint to make your prayer life
smoother. When you complete one of the day's
offices, move the appropriate bookmark to mark
tomorrow's office.

Here's another hint: If you want to pray all three

Guide to Praying Daytime Prayer, Including All Three Little Hours, on Memorials, Feasts, and Solemnities

General Rule—First use <u>everything</u> from the Proper of Seasons.
For parts of Daytime Prayer <u>not</u> in the Proper of Seasons, use the Psalter, Commons, or Proper of Saints, as listed below.

Octave of Easter	Proper of Seasons only
Commemorations	Proper of Seasons only.
All other times	All parts from Proper of Seasons first, Proper of Saints second.

For parts of the Daytime Prayer offices that are <u>missing</u> from either Proper, use the following:

Optional Memorials	
All from Psalter	

Obligatory Memorials	
Hymn	Common
Antiphons	Psalter
Psalms	Psalter
Readings & Responsories	Choose Psalter or Common
Concluding Prayer	Psalter

Feasts	
Hymn:	Common
Antiphons	Psalter
Psalms	Psalter
Readings & Responsories	Common
Concluding Prayer	Common

Solemnities:	
Hymn	Common
Antiphons	Common
Psalms	**Complementary Psalmody** (on Sunday's, Daytime Prayer Psalms for Sunday, Week I, for one of the offices)
Readings & Responsories	Common
Concluding Prayer	Common

offices but, some days, can't pray them at the proper time, it's OK to combine two or three offices once in a while, if you have to. But it's really not kosher proper to do it all the time.

Lesson 83: Daytime Prayer on Memorials, Feasts, and Solemnities

So now you know how to pray one or all of the Little Hours during Ordinary Time. How do you pray it on Memorials, Feasts, and Solemnities? This fine tuning of the Divine Office can get a little tricky. So we've made a chart to help you keep things straight:

PRACTICE: **Use** the chart and find the Daytime Prayer offices for the following celebrations: May 27, the Optional Memorial of St. Augustine of Canterbury; July 22, the Memorial of Saint Mary Magdalene; September 14, the Feast of the Triumph of the Cross; November 1, the Solemnity of All Saints.

Lesson 84: The Office of Readings

In my opinion, the Office of Readings is one of the greatest parts of the Divine Office. But, hey, that's my opinion. If you're not going to pray the Office of Readings, you might as well skip this lesson and the following ones and proceed to Lesson 87.

If you do want to pray this beautiful office, how about checking to see if your breviary has it? Shorter Christian Prayer doesn't and neither do a few one volume breviaries.

How do you suppose this office got its name? From the Readings, you say? Oh, you are so smart. **The OFFICE OF READINGS is so named because two long Readings are part of it. One Reading is from Scripture and the other is from a variety of religious sources.** The parts of the Office of Readings are:
> Hymn
> Three Psalms
> One Biblical Reading followed by Responsory
> One Non-Biblical Reading followed by Responsory
> Te Deum (only on certain days)
> Concluding Prayer

So where are all these in your breviary?

Let's start at the beginning.

Where are the Hymns for the Office of Readings? Are they in the Psalter? They might be. Are they in the Office of Readings Psalter? They might be. If they aren't in either spot, they'll be in the Hymn section which you already have marked with a Hymn bookmark (see Lesson 9).

Next, the Psalms. Always wise to check the Psalter first. Does your breviary have the Psalms for the Office of Readings in the Psalter? If so, the Psalter bookmark will help you find the daily Psalms for the Office of Readings.

If the Psalms for the Office of Readings aren't in the Psalter, they're in a separate section of your breviary. Look in the Table of Contents for the Office of Readings. Turn to that page. You'll find a four week Psalter just for the Office of Readings. **Mark that section with the Office of Readings: Psalter bookmark.**

Now for the Readings. First look in the Proper of Seasons. *In the four volume breviary, you've got the complete set of Readings for this office. Every single day has two Readings, followed by their Responsories—different Readings and Responsories for every day of the year. The Proper of Seasons bookmark marks this section.*

The one volume breviary has only a <u>selection</u> of all the Readings. Each day you'll <u>choose</u> one Biblical and one Non-Biblical Reading, and accompanying Responsories, to pray. Where are the Readings? Page through the Office of Readings Psalter until you come to the Readings. Now page through them. Did you find the Biblical Readings and Non-Biblical Readings sections? Do you suppose we might use two of our bouncing bookmarks to mark these? Right you are.

If you have a one volume breviary, use the "Office of Readings: Biblical" bookmark to mark the "Biblical Readings" section. Use the "Office of Readings: Non-Biblical" bookmark to mark the "Non-Biblical Readings" section which follows. Next is the Te Deum, whatever that is. **The TE DEUM is a Hymn that is prayed in the Office of Readings after the Second Reading and Responsory on Sundays, Feasts, and Solemnities. It is also prayed daily during the Octaves of Christmas and Easter. The Te Deum is prayed at these times whether or not your breviary tells you to do so. The Te Deum <u>is omitted</u> during Lent.**

So where is the Te Deum? Look in your breviary's

**DODO
SELF CHECK #84**

1. What is the Office of Readings? Why is it so named? When is it prayed?

2. How many Readings are read? Describe them. In your breviary, what bookmark(s) mark(s) the Office of Readings?

3. What is the Te Deum? In what part of the Office of Readings is it prayed? Is the Te Deum prayed every day? When is it prayed? When is it omitted? What color ribbon marks the Te Deum?

4. If the Office of Readings is the first office of the day, how does it begin? If it's not the first office of the day, how does it begin?

Table of Contents for the Ordinary of the Divine Office. Turn to the Ordinary and page through the section entitled Office of Readings. You'll come to the Te Deum. Some breviaries also have the Te Deum printed on a special prayer card which you can place in the front or back of your breviary.

Hey, we said this was a Hymn. But it has no musical notes printed with it. Doesn't matter. You can sing or hum your own tune if you wish. If you don't wish, do what most folks do which is reverently pray this glorious song.

Mark the Te Deum with a restful red ribbon (red for the merciful and glorious Blood of Christ, commemorated in the Te Deum).

We conclude with finding the Concluding Prayer. *In the four volume breviary, the Concluding Prayer follows the Readings in the Proper of Seasons.* **In the one volume breviary, use the same Concluding Prayer that you would use for Morning Prayer.** These are, by the way, the same prayer. However, the four volume breviary prints the prayer in more than one spot.

How you begin the Office of Readings depends on whether or not you pray it before Morning Prayer. You've learned to pray Morning Prayer as the first office of the day, and to precede Morning Prayer with the Invitatory. The Office of Readings is the only office that may precede Morning Prayer. It doesn't have to precede it. **You can pray the Office of Readings at any time during the day.**

But, if you do pray the Office of Readings before Morning Prayer, remember that **the Invitatory is be prayed before the __first__ office of the day**. It's prayed only before the first office and not before any other office.

Suppose you decide to pray the Office of Readings before Morning Prayer. Will you begin with the Invitatory? You betcha.

Suppose you pray the Office of Readings any time after Morning Prayer. Will you begin with the Invitatory? Nope, because you'll have prayed the Invitatory before you prayed Morning Prayer.

You already know this, but a little review can be helpful. **The second and all subsequent offices of the day begin, not with the Invitatory, but with the Sign of the Cross, the words, "God, come to my assistance," the response, "Lord, make haste to help me," and the "Glory Be" in its special Divine Office format.**

DODO
SELF CHECK #85

1. Where do you find the Readings on Memorials? Feasts? Solemnities? Commemorations?

2. What Psalmody do you use for Memorials? Feasts? Solemnities? Commemorations?

3. How many Readings are read on a Commemoration? How is it done? What Concluding Prayer is used on Commemorations?

4. When is the Te Deum prayed? When is it omitted?

How to Pray the Office of Readings with Four Volume Breviaries:

FERIAL DAYS

> *Hymn—Psalter or Hymn Index*
> *Three Psalms—Psalter*
> *Readings and Responsories—Proper of Seasons*
> *Concluding Prayer—Proper of Seasons*

COMMEMORATIONS

> *Hymn—Seasonal*
> *Three Psalms—Psalter*
> *Readings and Responsories—Both from Proper of Seasons*
> *Third Reading and Responsory—From Proper of Saints*
> *Concluding Prayer—Proper of Saints*

MEMORIALS

> *Hymn—Proper of Saints; if not there, Proper of Seasons, if not there, Common.*
> *Three Psalms—Memorial first; if no Psalms in Memorial, from Psalter*
> *Readings and Responsories—First Reading: Proper of Saints; if not there, Proper of Seasons. Second Reading: Proper of Saints.*

FEASTS AND SOLEMNITIES

> *Hymn—From Feast or Solemnity; if not there, from Common*
> *Three Psalms—From Feast or Solemnity; if not there, from Common*
> *Readings and Responsories—From Feast or Solemnity; if not there, from Common.*
> *Te Deum (except during Lent)*
> *Concluding Prayer—From Feast or Solemnity*

SUNDAYS

> *Hymn—Proper of Seasons first, if not there, Psalter*
> *Three Psalms—Proper of Seaons first, if not there, Psalter*
> *Readings and Responsories—Proper of Seasons*
> *Te Deum (except during Lent)*
> *Concluding Prayer—Proper of Seasons (your choice of two prayers)*

Lesson 85: The Office of Readings in Four Volume Breviaries

If you have a one volume breviary, the Proper of Saints and the Commons won't have any parts of the Office of Readings. This isn't the case with four volume breviaries. The following instruction is for those with four volume breviaries. If you don't have a four volume breviary, skip this lesson and proceed to Lesson 86.

Quick review. Each Office of Readings (Commemorations excepted) has only <u>two</u> Readings, a Biblical Reading for the First Reading and a Non-Biblical Reading for the Second Reading. Both these Readings are in the Proper of Seasons. Always.

TECHNIQUE

For praying the Office of Readings:

     1. Begin with the Sign of the Cross.

     2. If the Office of Readings is the First Office of the Day: Say, "Lord, open my lips." Respond, "And my mouth will proclaim your praise." Pray the Invitatory with its appropriate Antiphon as taught in Lessons 24, 42, and 57. Follow this with the Glory Be and then the Antiphon repeated.

     3. If the Office of Readings Is NOT the First Office of the Day: Say, "God, come to my assistance." Respond, "Lord, make haste to help me." Pray the Glory Be followed by Alleluia (Omit the Alleluia in Lent and Advent).

     4. To Continue Office of Readings, sing, chant or recite the Hymn.

     5. Pray the Psalms, Canticles, Psalm-Prayers, and Antiphons in the same manner as you have been doing for the other offices.

     6. Pause briefly for reflection. Turn to the Readings. Read the first Reading (from Scripture). Read the Responsory and pause a few moments for silent reflection.

     7. Read the second Reading (non-Biblical) Read the Responsory and pause a few moments for silent reflection.

     8. If this is a Commemoration, read the third Reading (Proper of Saints) and Responsory, then pause a few moments for silent reflection.

     9. On Sundays, Feasts, and Solemnities, and daily during the Christmas and Easter Octaves, pray the Te Deum. Omit it during Lent.

     10. Say, "Let us pray." Read the Concluding Prayer.

     11. Say, "Let us praise the Lord." Respond, "And give him thanks."

     12. Make the Sign of the Cross.

Quick lesson on the Proper of Saints: A few saints have a Hymn, Psalmody and/or First Reading. Every saint has a Second Reading and Concluding Prayer.

Quicker lesson on the Commons: The Commons have a full Office of Readings.

Quickest lesson: On Commemorations, there are three readings—two from the Proper of Seasons and the third from the Proper of Saints. Think of the 3 M's in the word Commemoration to help you remember. So, while this is the quickest lesson, it takes the longest time to pray the Office of Readings on Commemorations. If you decide to commemorate the Commemoration, that is. Remember that observing Commemorations is always optional.

So, how do you pray the Office of Readings?

Remember that this office always has the following and only the following:

> *Hymn*
> *Three Psalms*
> *One Biblical Reading followed by Responsory*
> *One Non-Biblical Reading followed by Responsory*
> *Third Reading followed by Responsory (on C*

Commemorations only)
> *Te Deum (only on certain days)*
> *Concluding Prayer*

Let's see how this works for the various days in the Church year.

Lesson 86: Format for Praying the Office of Readings

Ready to pray the Office of Readings? Find the Office of Readings for today. Let's get praying!

SECTION THIRTEEN

Options

"In this section, you'll learn about ..."

Ordering supplements

Praying in choir

Specific circumstances

OPTIONS

Lesson 87: Order Supplements

Are you a member of a First, Second, or Third Order within the Church? If not, you might want to skip this section.

If you are a member of a First, Second, or Third Order, you might have a Supplement to your breviary. The Supplement contains special offices and parts of offices for saints and celebrations particular to your Order. These won't be in the regular breviary. Some of your Order's saints who are in the breviary may have longer offices in your Order's Supplement. Some celebrations that are Memorials for the whole Church may be Feasts or Solemnities for you. Follow the Supplement's guidelines.

If you purchase an Ordo, be sure to get one that includes the celebrations in your Supplement. Such Ordos are generally available through your religious Order's main office or publisher.

Your Order may also sell nifty plastic breviary covers with a special double cover that will allow you to place the breviary and the Supplement into the same book.

You probably have at least one bookmark that you have not used. If you wish, you can easily adapt that bookmark for use in your Order Supplement. Be creative with your adaptation. Then place that bookmark at today's day of the year, in your Order Supplement.

TECHNIQUE

For using an Order Supplement

If a celebration in the Supplement has no designation, it's an Optional Memorial. If a celebration is marked "Memorial," it's an Obligatory Memorial.

If a celebration is marked "Feast" or "Solemnity," it's a Feast or Solemnity for all members of your Order, no matter how the rest of the Church celebrates it.

If a saint's celebration is marked First, Second, or Third Order <u>without</u> the designation "Memorial," it's an Obligatory Memorial only for the branch of the Order so

Continued on the next page ...

Continued on the next page ...

... continued from previous page

designated. For other branches of the Order, it's an Optional Memorial.

If a celebration is marked, "Feast: First Order," it means that this celebration is a Feast for only First Order members. It's a Memorial for other branches of the Order.

If a Memorial in the Supplement coincides with another Memorial in the breviary, celebrate the Memorial in the Supplement.

If the Supplement has a longer office than in the breviary, use all the parts in the Supplement.

Nightly after Evening Prayer, check the Supplement to see if any saints are to be celebrated the next day. Mark the celebrations with the Supplement bookmark.

You'll discover that there are differences between the Supplement and the breviary. If there are, follow the Supplement. Here are additional tips on how to use a Supplement:

Lesson 88: Praying in Choir

No, you don't have to join your parish choir to pray the Divine Office. You don't have to be able to sing either. So what's this "praying in choir" all about?

Did you know that the Divine Office was written to be prayed OUT LOUD and IN CHOIR? In other words, it was written to be prayed by religious living in communities and by priests praying with others in their churches. You may not be praying the Divine Office in either of these circumstances.

PRAYING IN CHOIR means praying as a group but alternating sides. Obviously, you can't do this if you are praying the Office alone. The Office is

DODO
SELF-CHECK #87

1. How can you get a bookmark to mark the Supplement?

2. If the breviary lists a Memorial on a certain day and the Supplement a different Memorial, whose do you celebrate?

3. If the Supplement has a longer office than the breviary, which office do you use?

4. If a celebration is marked "Second Order," what does that mean?

5. If a Memorial is marked "Memorial," who is to observe it?

6. If a celebration is marked as "Feast: Second Order," what is the celebration for the First and Third Orders?

7. If a celebration in the Supplement has no designation, what sort of celebration is it?

8. If a celebration is marked "Feast" or "Solemnity," do all Order members celebrate it even if it is not so celebrated by the entire Church?

prayed by alternating sides in monasteries and convents and at meetings of laity that pray the Office. Often in choir, the Office is chanted or sung, but it can also be recited.

You can find hints that the Office was intended for praying in choir by looking at your breviary's Responsories and Intercessions. In some breviaries, a V. is before the first line of the Responsories and Intercessions and an R. before the second line. Other breviaries use only the R. or a dash before the second line. The V. stands for "Versicle" and the R., or dash, stands for "Response." When praying in choir, the prayer leader alone says the first part of these prayers (marked with a V. or without the dash) and everyone else answers by praying the second part (marked with an R. or the dash). When praying alone, you obviously pray all parts yourself, as you have been doing. Now remember those terms—Versicle and Response. They might come in handy someday when you're doing a crossword puzzle.

When praying the Office in choir, the Office is prayed straight through without anyone announcing Hymns, pages, or titles for parts of the Office. Any directions or pages are announced <u>before</u> the Office begins. The only exception is that the Reader <u>may</u> announce the Reading with the words, "A Reading from _____," filling in the Scripture book and verses as done at Mass. The Reader <u>may</u> end the Reading by saying "The word of the Lord" to which everyone else would respond, "Thanks be to God."

Now you're going to learn some interesting terms. You've learned so much this far, so why not cap your learning off with some big, important sounding words. Then, if you want to sound impressive at the next dinner party, you can casually make a comment such as "You know, when Bill gets on a roll telling stories, he's a perfect Hebdomedarian." You ought to turn a few heads with that word. Want to know what Bill reminds you of? Read on.

Before we find out about Bill, let's talk about how to pray in choir. To pray in choir, you obviously need two or more people. Divide the group into Side

---

TECHNIQUE

Praying the Divine Office in Choir.

Here is a general summary of how to pray the Office in choir. Once you get the hang of this, you'll be able to adjust the technique for the various offices and various parts of them. The abbreviations are:

| S1—Side One | S2—Side 2 | E—Everyone | C—Cantor |
| R—Reader | P—Prayer Leader | | |

C: In the name of the Father, and of the Son and of the Holy Spirit.
E: Amen

Continued on the next page ...

Continued from the previous page ...

For First Office of the Day
>C: Lord, open my lips
>E: And my mouth will proclaim your praise.
>C: Invitatory Antiphon
>C: 1st line of Invitatory
>S1: First Strophe of Invitatory
>S2: Second Strophe of Invitatory
>S1: Third Strophe of Invitatory
>S2: Fourth Strophe of Invitatory
>S1: Fifth Strophe of Invitatory
>S2: Sixth Strophe of Invitatory
>S1: Glory to the Father and to the Son and to the Holy Spirit
>S2: As it was in the beginning, is now, and will be forever. Amen.
>C: Invitatory Antiphon

All Offices Except First Office of the Day
>C: God, come to my assistance.
>E: Lord, make haste to help me.
>C: Glory to the Father and to the Son and to the Holy Spirit
>E: As it was in the beginning, is now, and will be forever. Amen.

Morning and Evening Prayer
>E: Hymn
>C: Antiphon 1
>C: First Line of First Psalm or Canticle
>S1: First Strophe (verse)
>S2: Second Strophe (verse)
>S1: Third Strophe (verse)
>S2: Fourth Strophe (verse)

Continue alternating sides until Psalm or Canticle is done. When it comes time to say the Glory Be, the Side whose turn it would be begins with "Glory to the Father, and to the Son, and to the Holy Spirit." The other side concludes, "As it was in the beginning, is now, and will be forever. Amen."
>C: Psalm-Prayer
>C: Antiphon 1

Pause briefly
>C: Antiphon 2
>C: First Line of 2nd Psalm or Canticle
>S1: First Strophe
>S2: Second Strophe

(continue as for First Psalm, ending with Glory Be as explained earlier)
>C: Psalm-Prayer
>C: Antiphon 2

Continued on the next page ...

Continued from the previous page ...

Pause briefly
    C: Antiphon 3
    C: First Line of Third Psalm or Canticle
    S1: First Strophe
    S2: Second Strophe
(continue as for First Psalm, ending with Glory Be as explained earlier)
    C: Psalm-Prayer
    C: Antiphon 3
Pause briefly
    R: Reading
    R: First line of Responsory
    E: Second line of Responsory
    R: Third line of Responsory
    E: Fourth line of Responsory
    R: Fifth line of Responsory
    E: Sixth line of Responsory
Pause briefly
    C: Antiphon for Canticle
    E: Canticle (or alternate sides as done for Psalmody)
    E: Glory Be (or alternate sides as done for Psalmody)
    C: Antiphon for Canticle
Pause briefly
    P: First lines of Intercessions
    E: Second lines of Intercessions
    E: Our Father
    P: Concluding Prayer
    C: May the Lord bless us, protect us from all evil, and bring us to everlasting life.
    E: Amen
    C: In the name of the Father, and of the Son, and of the Holy Spirit.
    E: Amen

One (original name: Chorus Side) and Side Two (original name: Alleluia Side). The Psalms and Canticles are prayed out loud so that each side takes one strophe (verse), alternating sides. Choose individuals to perform the following roles:

Cantor (also called Hebdomedarian or First Cantor): Begins Office. Alone prays the Antiphons, first lines of the Psalms or Canticles, and all Psalm prayers. If two cantors are used, the second cantor is sometimes called the Antiphonarian. Two more good crossword puzzle, or dinner party, words.

Reader: Alone reads the Reading and the odd lines of the Responsory (lines 1, 3, and 5). Everyone else replies on the even lines (lines 2, 4, and 6). Prayer Leader: Alone reads first line of Intercessions and Concluding Prayer.

A few options exist for praying in choir:

The Glory Be may be said by everyone instead of alternating sides.

The Antiphon, when repeated at the end of the Psalm or Canticle, may be prayed in unison by everyone. The Antiphon is never prayed by the cantor and then immediately repeated by everyone else.

You have not been praying the Alleluia when it appears in parentheses when in a Canticle. When praying the Office alone, it is correct to omit this. However, when the Canticle is sung in choir, either the Cantor or the Chorus side sings the part not in parentheses and the others respond with the part in parentheses.

When praying in choir, certain postures are customary:

> Introduction up to end of Hymn: All stand
>
> Psalmody: Sit with exception of Cantor who stands while reading alone, then sits for remainder of Psalmody
>
> Reading, Responsory: Sit except for Reader who stands.
>
> Canticle of Zechariah, Mary until End of Office: All stand or kneel.

If there's any way you can visit a convent or monastery while its members are praying the Office, go for it. You'll learn a lot just by observing.

Lesson 89: Options

Everyone likes choices. You've got some choices (options) in praying the Divine Office.

THE INVITATORY PSALM; You've been using Psalm 95 as the Invitatory Psalm. The Church also allows the use of Psalms 100, 67, or 24.

ANTIPHONS: You've learned to pray the Antiphon before and after the Psalms. The Church allows the option of praying it only before the Psalm and not repeating it after.

PSALM-PRAYERS: You've learned to pray the Psalm-Prayers. The Church allows the option of skipping them.

THE PSALMODY WHEN IT CONTAINS PSALMS BROKEN INTO I, II, AND POSSIBLY III PARTS: When a long Psalm is broken into parts in the Divine Office, the sections are numbered I, II, and III. An Antiphon precedes and ends each section. The Church allows the option of praying all the Antiphons as you have learned with the "Glory Be" between each section of the Psalm. A second option is praying the first Antiphon, then praying the Psalm entirely through to the end without a break, ending with the "Glory Be" and then repeating, if desired, the first Antiphon.

THE OUR FATHER: If you wish, you may introduce the "Our Father" with the spoken words, "Remember us, Lord, when you come into your kingdom and teach us how to pray" or some similar invitation to prayer. Several options are printed in the instruction entitled "Ordinary" in your breviary. Look for this in the Table of Contents.

COMBINING OFFICES: It's best not to combine offices but to pray them at the correctly designated times. However, you may combine some if necessary.
    Morning and Evening Prayer are never combined. Morning Prayer is to be prayed in the morning and Evening Prayer in the evening.
    The Office of Readings may be combined with any other office.

DODO
SELF-CHECK #89

1. What are some options in praying the Office?

2. Can you substitute a Memorial on a Ferial Day?

3. How are offices combined? Which offices may be combined? Which may not be combined?

4. What is unique about the Office of the Dead?

    Evening Prayer may be combined with Night Prayer.
    Two of the Minor Offices (Midmorning, Midday, Midafternoon) may be combined.
    To combine offices, sing only one Hymn at the beginning of the first office. Select a Hymn appropriate for either the first or the second office.
    Pray the first office through but skip the Concluding Prayer and go right into praying the first Psalm's Antiphon for the second office and then the first Psalm. Pray this office through to the end. If you pray Night Prayer right after Evening Prayer, you will include the Examination of Conscience before beginning the Night Prayer Psalmody.

FERIAL DAYS: On a Ferial Day, that is a day on which no official Church celebration is held, you may choose to celebrate a certain office as a Memorial. Follow the guidelines for the office that you choose. You may also choose to pray the Office of the Blessed Virgin or the Office of the Dead on a Ferial Day.

THE OFFICE OF THE DEAD: Whenever the Office of the Dead is prayed, it is always <u>prayed exactly as written in the breviary</u>.

Lesson 90: Specific Circumstances

You've come a mighty long way. You began this manual, thinking you were a real dodo when it came to praying the Divine Office. Now look how much you've learned. This is the very last chapter. Let's make it a good one!

Have you made a promise to yourself, your spiritual director, or your Order or Association to pray the Divine Office? If you're so obligated, you might run into certain specific circumstances. Let's see what some might be.

IF YOU CAN'T PRAY AN OFFICE: Try to raise your mind to God wherever you are and realize that God understands. However, for anyone who has an obligation to pray the Office or who seriously wishes to take on this task, these times should be rare exceptions.

IF CIRCUMSTANCES PREVENT YOU FROM READING THE BREVIARY: You might substitute other prayers. Members of some religious Orders have specific prayers to substitute. For example, members of the Secular Franciscan Order are permitted to say 12 Our Fathers (6 for Morning Prayer and 6 for Evening Prayer) if they cannot pray from the breviary. A priest or spiritual director can guide you on what to do. However, if you've made a commitment to pray the Divine Office, substitution of other prayers for those in the breviary should be a rare exception.

IF YOU FORGET TO SAY AN OFFICE: If you go through the day and then remember that you forgot to say an office, simply raise your mind to God and ask Him to help you remember to pray the office next time. God understands that we are human, for He created us so!

IF YOU HABITUALLY FORGET AN OFFICE: Try to do something to help you remember. Perhaps putting your Office book where you will see it at the time of prayer will help. Try taping a note to something you would be using at the time the office should be prayed. Or give yourself a reward when you remember. Be creative in helping yourself to recall your prayer time. Eventually, you'll form a habit of prayer and won't need reminders.

IF YOU MAKE A MISTAKE: God isn't a legalist. Just pray the office as carefully and prayerfully as you can. Consult a priest or religious if you have a question. If you've been doing something incorrectly, correct it and don't worry about it.

IF YOU CAN'T PRAY THE OFFICE AT THE CORRECT TIMES: Try to pray it as close to the correct times as possible.

IF A MONASTERY OR COMMUNITY PRAYS THE OFFICE DIFFERENTLY THAN IN THIS INSTRUCTION: Follow the community's format. This book has presented some of the more common options. There are others, the discussion of which would make this book too tedious. Some Orders also have different, Church approved offices which they pray daily.

IF YOU WISH TO PRAY THE OFFICE OF READINGS DURING THE NIGHT: Great. You may pray this office at any time.

IF YOU PRAY THE OFFICE OF READINGS AT NIGHT, THEN PRAY MORNING PRAYER WITH SOMEONE ELSE WHO HAS NOT PRAYED THE OFFICE OF READINGS: While the Invitatory is to be prayed before the first office of the day, in this case charity and the law of praying the Office in community prevail. The Invitatory would be said together prior to Morning Prayer.

IF YOU PRAY MORNING PRAYER ALONE BUT EVENING PRAYER WITH SOMEONE ELSE: In this case, pray the Invitatory prior to the first prayer of the day. Your prayer partner will have prayed the Invitatory as part of Morning Prayer also.

IF YOU WISH TO PRAY ONLY MORNING OR EVENING PRAYER: Anyone, unless under obligation to do otherwise, may pray whatever he or she pleases. However, praying only Morning Prayer or only Evening Prayer is not considered as praying the Divine Office. If you are under obligation to pray the Divine Office, praying both of these offices fulfills the obligation.

IF YOU HAVE OTHER QUESTIONS: Consult a priest or religious.

Congratulations on a job well done. And don't forget to remember the author of this manual in prayer now and then. Thanks, from one dodo to another! And may God bless you!

APPENDICES

"In this section, you'll learn about ..."

Actual prayers from the Divine Office

APPENDICES

Appendix A
Praying the Psalmody for Friday Evening Prayer, Week III

Great is the Lord, our God, transcending all other gods.

Praise the name of the Lord,
praise him, servants of the Lord,
who stand in the house of the Lord
in the courts of the house of our God.

Praise the Lord for the Lord is good.
Sing a psalm to his name for he is loving.
For the Lord has chosen Jacob for himself
and Israel for his own possession.

For I know the Lord is great,
that our Lord is high above all gods.
The Lord does whatever he wills,
in heaven, on earth, in the seas.

He summons clouds from the ends of the earth;
makes his lightening produce the rain;
from his treasuries he sends forth the wind.

The first-born of the Egyptians he smote,
of man and beast alike.
Signs and wonders he worked
in the midst of your land, O Egypt,
against Pharaoh and all his servants.

Nations in their greatness he struck
and kings in their splendor he slew.
Sihon, king of the Amorites,
Og, the king of Bashan,
and all the kingdoms of Canaan.
He let Israel inherit the land;
on his people their land he bestowed.

(BOW)
Glory to the Father and the Son and the Holy Spirit

(STRAIGHTEN)
>	as it was in the beginning, is now, and will be forever. Amen.

>	Great is the Lord, our God, transcending all other gods.

(PAUSE BRIEFLY FOR SILENT REFLECTION)
>	House of Israel, bless the Lord! Sing psalms to him, for he is merciful.

>	Lord, your name stands for ever,
>	unforgotten from age to age:
>	for the Lord does justice for his people;
>	the Lord takes pity on his servants.

>	Pagan idols are silver and gold,
>	the work of human hands.
>	They have mouths but they cannot speak;
>	they have eyes but they cannot see.

>	They have ears but they cannot hear;
>	there is not a breath on their lips.
>	Their makers will come to be like them
>	and so will all who trust in them!

>	Sons of Israel, bless the Lord!
>	Sons of Aaron, bless the Lord!
>	Sons of Levi, bless the Lord!
>	You who fear him, bless the Lord!

>	From Zion may the Lord be blessed,
>	he who dwells in Jerusalem!

(BOW)
>	Glory to the Father and to the Son and to the Holy Spirit
(STRAIGHTEN)
>	as it was in the beginning, is now, and will be forever. Amen.

>	Father, your name and your memory last for ever. We stand to pray in
your house and praise you with psalms of joy. We ask you in your kindness to
have mercy on us in our lowliness.

>	House of Israel, bless the Lord! Sing psalms to him, for he is merciful.

(PAUSE BRIEFLY FOR SILENT REFLECTION)
>	All nations will come and worship before you, O Lord.

>	Mighty and wonderful are your works,
>	Lord God Almighty!

A-3

Righteous and true are your ways,
O King of the nations!

Who would dare refuse you honor,
or the glory due your name, O Lord?

Since you alone are holy,
all nations shall come
and worship in your presence.
Your mighty deeds are clearly seen.

(BOW)

Glory to the Father and to the Son and to the Holy Spirit (

STRAIGHTEN)

as it was in the beginning, is now, and will be forever. Amen.

All nations will come and worship before you, O Lord.

(PAUSE BRIEFLY FOR SILENT REFLECTION)

Appendix B
Night Prayer for Friday

(MAKE THE SIGN OF THE CROSS)
God, come to my assistance.
Lord, make haste to help me.

(BOW)
Glory to the Father, and to the Son, and to the Holy Spirit:

(STRAIGHTEN)
as it was in the beginning, is now, and will be for ever. Amen.
Alleluia.

(DURING LENT, OMIT THE ALLELUIA).

(MAKE A SILENT EXAMINATION OF CONSCIENCE)

(PRAY A PRAYER OF FORGIVENESS)

(SING OR CHANT A HYMN OF YOUR CHOICE OR ONE LISTED IN THE
BREVIARY)
Day and night I cry to you, my God.

Lord, my God, I call for help by day;
I cry at night before you.
Let my prayer come into your presence.
O turn your ear to my cry.

For my soul is filled with evils;
my life is on the brink of the grave.
I am reckoned as one in the tomb:
I have reached the end of my strength,

like one alone among the dead;
like the slain lying in their graves;
like those you remember no more,
cut off, as they are, from your hand.

You have laid me in the depths of the tomb,
in places that are dark, in the depths.
Your anger weighs down upon me;
I am drowned beneath your waves.

You have taken away my friends
and made me hateful in their sight.
Imprisoned, I cannot escape;
my eyes are sunken with grief.

I call to you, Lord, all the day long;
to you I stretch out my hands.
Will you work your wonders for the dead?
Will the shades stand and praise you?

Will your love be told in the grave
or your faithfulness among the dead?
Will your wonders be known in the dark
or your justice in the land of oblivion?

As for me, Lord, I call to you for help;
in the morning, my prayer comes before you.
Lord, why do you reject me?
Why do you hide your face!

Wretched, close to death from my youth,
I have borne your trials; I am numb.
Your fury has swept down upon me;
your terrors have utterly destroyed me.

They surround me all the day like a flood,
they assail me all together.

Friend and neighbor you have taken away:
my one companion is darkness.

(BOW)
Glory to the Father and to the Son and to the Holy Spirit

(STRAIGHTEN)
as it was in the beginning, is now, and will be forever. Amen.

ANT. Day and night I cry to you, my God.

(PAUSE)
You are in our midst, O Lord,
your name we bear;
do not forsake us, O Lord, our God!

Into your hands, Lord, I commend my spirit.
Into your hands, Lord, I commend my spirit.

You have redeemed us, Lord God of truth.
I commend my spirit.

Glory be to the Father and to the Son and to the Holy Spirit.
Into your hands, Lord, I commend my spirit.

(PAUSE)
Protect us, Lord, as we stay awake; watch over us as we sleep, that
awake, we may keep watch with Christ, and, asleep, rest in his peace.

(MAKE THE SIGN OF THE CROSS)

Lord, now you let your servant go in peace;
your word has been fulfilled.

my own eyes have seen the salvation
which you have prepared in the sight of every people:

a light to reveal you to the nations
and the glory of your people Israel.

(BOW)
Glory to the Father and to the Son and to the Holy Spirit

(STRAIGHTEN)
as it was in the beginning, is now, and will be forever. Amen.

Protect us, Lord, as we stay awake; watch over us as we sleep, that
awake, we may keep watch with Christ, and asleep, rest in his peace.

A-6

Let us pray:
All powerful God,
keep us united with your Son
in his death and burial
so that we may rise to new life with him,
who lives and reigns for ever and ever.

May the all-powerful Lord grant us a restful night and a peaceful death.
Amen.
(MAKE THE SIGN OF THE CROSS)

(CHOOSE ONE ANTIPHON IN HONOR OF THE BLESSED VIRGIN AND PRAY IT. THE HAIL MARY IS USED HERE AS A SAMPLE.)
Hail Mary, full of grace,
the Lord is with you!
Blessed are you among women,
and blessed is the fruit of your womb, Jesus.
Holy Mary, Mother of God,
pray for us sinners,
now and at the hour of our death.
Amen.

Appendix C, Part One
Canticle of Zechariah for Monday, Week I, Ordinary Time

Blessed be the Lord, our God.

(MAKE THE SIGN OF THE CROSS)

Blessed be the Lord, the God of Israel,
he has come to his people and set them free.

He has raised up for us a mighty savior,
born of the house of his servant David.

Through his holy prophets he promised of old
that he would save us from our enemies,
from the hands of those who hate us.

He promised to show mercy to our fathers
and to remember his holy covenant.

This was the oath he swore to our father Abraham,

A-7

to set us free from the hands of our enemies,
free to worship him without fear,
holy and righteous in his sight
all the days of our life.

You, my child, shall be called the prophet of the Most High,
for you will go before the Lord to prepare his way
to give his people knowledge of salvation
by the forgiveness of their sins.

In the tender compassion of our God
the dawn from on high shall break upon us,
to shine on those who dwell in darkness and the shadow of death, and
to guide our feet into the way of peace.

(BOW)
Glory to the Father and to the Son and to the Holy Spirit

(STRAIGHTEN)
as it was in the beginning, is now, and will be forever. Amen.

Blessed be the Lord our God.

Appendix C, Part Two
Canticle of Mary for Monday, Week I,
Ordinary Time

My soul proclaims the greatness of the Lord, for he has looked with
favor on his lowly servant.

(MAKE THE SIGN OF THE CROSS)
My soul proclaims the greatness of the Lord,
my spirit rejoices in God my Savior
for he has looked with favor on his lowly servant.

From this day, all generations will call me blessed:
the Almighty has done great things for me,
and holy is his Name.

He has mercy on those who fear him
in every generation.

He has shown the strength of his arm,
he has scattered the proud in their conceit.

He has cast down the mighty from their thrones,
and has lifted up the lowly.

He has filled the hungry with good things,
and the rich he has sent away empty.

He has come to the help of his servant Israel
for he has remembered his promise of mercy,
the promise he made to our fathers,
to Abraham and his children for ever.

(BOW)

Glory to the Father and to the Son and to the Holy Spirit

(STRAIGHTEN)

as it was in the beginning, is now, and will be forever. Amen.

My soul proclaims the greatness of the Lord, for he has looked with favor on his lowly servant.

Appendix D
Invitatory for Monday, Week I, Ordinary Time

(MAKE THE SIGN OF THE CROSS)

Lord, open my lips.
And my mouth will proclaim Your praise.

Let us approach the Lord with praise and thanksgiving.

Come, let us sing to the Lord
and shout with joy to the Rock who saves us.
Let us approach him with praise and thanksgiving
and sing joyful songs to the Lord.

Let us approach the Lord with praise and thanksgiving.

The Lord is God, the mighty God,
the great king over all the gods.
He holds in his hands the depths of the earth
and the highest mountains as well.
He made the sea; it belongs to him,

the dry land, too, for it was formed by his hands.

Let us approach the Lord with praise and thanksgiving.

(KNEEL OR BOW)
Come, then, let us bow down and worship,
bending the knee before the Lord, our maker,
For he is our God and we are his people,
the flock he shepherds.
(RISE)
Let us approach the Lord with praise and thanksgiving.

Today, listen to the voice of the Lord.
Do not grow stubborn as your fathers did
in the wilderness when at Meriba and Massah
they challenged me and provoked me
Although they had seen all of my works.

Let us approach the Lord with praise and thanksgiving.

Forty years I endured that generation.
I said, "They are a people whose hearts go astray
and they do not know my ways."
So I swore in my anger,
"They shall not enter into my rest."

Let us approach the Lord with praise and thanksgiving.

(BOW)
Glory to the Father, and to the Son, and to the Holy Spirit:

(STRAIGHTEN)
as it was in the beginning, is now, and will be for ever. Amen.
Let us approach the Lord with praise and thanksgiving.

Appendix E
Intercessions and Conclusion for Morning Prayer, Monday Week I, Ordinary Time

We esteem Christ above all men, for he was filled with grace and the Holy Spirit. In faith let us implore him: *Give us your Spirit, Lord.*

Grant us a peaceful day,
when evening comes we will praise you with joy and

purity of heart.
Let your splendor rest upon us today,
direct the work of our hands.
May your face shine upon us and keep us in peace,
may your strong arm protect us.
Look kindly on all who put their trust in our prayers,
fill them with every bodily and spiritual grace.

(OPTIONAL: YOU MAY ADD HERE INTERCESSIONS OF YOUR OWN,
ADDING THE ITALICIZED REFRAIN, "Give us your Spirit, Lord" AFTER
EACH INTERCESSION.)

Our Father, who art in heaven, hallowed be thy name. Thy kingdom
come, thy will be done, on earth as it is in heaven. Give us this day our daily
bread and forgive us our trespasses, as we forgive those who trespass against us.
And lead us not into temptation but deliver us from evil.

Father, may everything we do begin with your inspiration
and continue with your saving help.
Let our work always find its origin in you
and through you reach completion.
We ask this through our Lord Jesus Christ, your Son,
who lives and reigns with you and the Holy Spirit,
one God, for ever and ever.
May the Lord bless us, protect us, and deliver us from all evil. Amen.

(MAKE THE SIGN OF THE CROSS).

In the name of the Father, and of the Son, and of the Holy Spirit.
Amen.

Appendix F
Intercessions and Conclusion for Evening Prayer, Monday, Week I, Ordinary Time

God has made an everlasting covenant with his people, and he never
ceases to bless them. Grateful for these gifts, we confidently direct our prayer
to him:
Lord, bless your people.

Save your people, Lord
and bless your inheritance.
Gather into one body all who bear the name of Christian,
that the world may believe in Christ whom you have sent.
Give our friends and our loved ones a share in divine life,
let them be symbols of Christ before men.

Show your love to those who are suffering,
open their eyes to the vision of your revelation.
Be compassionate to those who have died,
welcome them into the company of the faithful departed.

(OPTIONAL: YOU MAY ADD HERE INTERCESSIONS OF YOUR OWN, ADDING THE ITALICIZED REFRAIN, "Lord, bless your people" AFTER EACH INTERCESSION.)

Our Father, who art in heaven, hallowed be thy name. Thy kingdom come, thy will be done, on earth as it is in heaven. Give us this day our daily bread and forgive us our trespasses, as we forgive those who trespass against us. And lead us not into temptation but deliver us from evil.

Father, may this evening pledge of our service to you
bring you glory and praise.
For our salvation you looked with favor
on the lowliness of the Virgin Mary;
lead us to the fullness of salvation
you have prepared for us.
We ask this through our Lord Jesus Christ, your Son, who lives and reigns with you and the Holy Spirit, one God, for ever and ever.

May the Lord bless us, protect us, and deliver us from all evil. Amen.

(MAKE THE SIGN OF THE CROSS).

In the name of the Father, and of the Son, and of the Holy Spirit. Amen.

Appendix G
Wednesday Morning Prayer during Holy Week

(MAKE THE SIGN OF THE CROSS).
Lord, open my lips.
And my mouth will proclaim your praise.

(INVITATORY ANTIPHON)
Come, let us worship Christ the Lord, who for our sake endured temptation and suffering.

Come, let us sing to the Lord
and shout with joy to the Rock who saves us.
Let us approach him with praise and thanksgiving
and sing joyful songs to the Lord.

Come, let us worship Christ the Lord, who for our sake endured temptation and suffering.

> The Lord is God, the mighty God,
> the great king over all the gods.
> He holds in his hands the depths of the earth
> and the highest mountains as well.
> He made the sea; it belongs to him,
> the dry land, too, for it was formed by his hands.

Come, let us worship Christ the Lord, who for our sake endured temptation and suffering.

(KNEEL OR BOW)
> Come, then, let us bow down and worship,
> bending the knee before the Lord, our maker,
> For he is our God and we are his people,
> the flock he shepherds.

(RISE)
Come, let us worship Christ the Lord, who for our sake endured temptation and suffering.

> Today, listen to the voice of the Lord.
> Do not grow stubborn as your fathers did
> in the wilderness
> when at Meriba and Massah
> they challenged me and provoked me
> Although they had seen all of my works.

Come, let us worship Christ the Lord, who for our sake endured temptation and suffering.

> Forty years I endured that generation.
> I said, "They are a people whose hearts go astray
> and they do not know my ways."
> So I swore in my anger,
> "They shall not enter into my rest."

Come, let us worship Christ the Lord, who for our sake endured temptation and suffering.

(BOW)
> Glory to the Father, and to the Son, and to the Holy Spirit:

(STRAIGHTEN)
> as it was in the beginning, is now, and will be for ever. Amen.

Come, let us worship Christ the Lord, who for our sake endured temptation and suffering.

(SING, CHANT, OR RECITE THE HYMN YOU HAVE CHOSEN)

(ANTIPHON 1)
      In the day of my distress, I reached out with my hands to seek the Lord's help.

(NOW PRAY PSALM 77 AS WRITTEN IN THE PSALTER FOR WEDNESDAY MORNING PRAYER, WEEK II. END WITH GLORY BE PRAYED IN FULL AS USUAL.)

(PRAY THE PSALM-PRAYER AS WRITTEN IN THE PSALTER.)

(ANTIPHON 1)
      In the day of my distress, I reached out with my hands to seek the Lord's help.

(PAUSE BRIEFLY)

(ANTIPHON 2)
      If we have died with Christ, we believe that we shall also live with Christ.

(NOW PRAY THE CANTICLE FROM SAMUEL 2:1-10 AS WRITTEN IN THE PSALTER FOR WEDNESDAY MORNING PRAYER, WEEK II. END WITH THE GLORY BE PRAYED IN FULL AS USUAL.)

(ANTIPHON 2)
      If we have died with Christ, we believe that we shall also live with Christ.

(PAUSE BRIEFLY)

(ANTIPHON 3)
      God had made Christ Jesus our wisdom and our holiness. By him we have been sanctified and redeemed.

(NOW PRAY PSALM 97 AS WRITTEN IN THE PSALTER FOR WEDNESDAY MORNING PRAYER, WEEK II. END WITH THE GLORY BE PRAYED IN FULL AS USUAL.)

(PRAY THE PSALM-PRAYER AS WRITTEN IN THE PSALTER.)

(ANTIPHON 3)
      God has made Christ Jesus our wisdom and our holiness. By him we

have been sanctified and redeemed.

(PAUSE BRIEFLY)

(READING FROM ISAIAH 50:4B-7)
>The Lord God opens my ear that I may hear;
>And I have not rebelled,
>have not turned back.
>I gave my back to those who beat me,
>my cheeks to those who plucked my beard;
>My face I did not shield
>from buffets and spitting.
>The Lord God is my help,
>therefore I am not disgraced;
>I have set my face like flint,
>knowing that I shall not be put to shame.
>
>By your own blood, Lord, you brought us back to God.
>By your own blood, Lord, you brought us back to God.
>From every tribe, and tongue, and people, and nation,
>you brought us back to God.

(BOW)
>Glory to the Father and to the Son and to the Holy Spirit

(STRAIGHTEN)
>By your own blood, Lord, you brought us back to God.

(PAUSE BRIEFLY FOR SILENT REFLECTION)

(ANTIPHON FOR CANTICLE OF ZECHARIAH)
>Through the eternal Spirit, Christ offered himself to God as the perfect sacrifice. His blood purifies us from sin and makes us fit servants of the living God.

(PRAY THE CANTICLE OF ZECHARIAH ALL THE WAY THROUGH TO THE END AS TAUGHT IN LESSON 23. END WITH GLORY BE PRAYED IN FULL AS USUAL.)

(ANTIPHON FOR CANTICLE OF ZECHARIAH)
>Through the eternal Spirit, Christ offered himself to God as the perfect sacrifice. His blood purifies us from sin and makes us fit servants of the living God.

(PAUSE BRIEFLY)
>Let us pray to Christ our Savior, who redeemed us by his death and resurrection: *Lord, have mercy on us.*

You went up to Jerusalem to suffer and so enter into your glory,
bring your Church to the Passover feast of heaven.
You were lifted high on the cross and pierced by the soldier's lance,
heal our wounds.
You made the cross the tree of life,
give its fruits to those reborn in baptism.
On the cross you forgave the repentant thief,
forgive us our sins.

(OPTIONAL: YOU MAY ADD HERE INTERCESSIONS OF YOUR OWN,
ADDING THE ITALICIZED REFRAIN, "Lord, have mercy on us" AFTER
EACH INTERCESSION.)

(PRAY THE OUR FATHER THROUGH TO THE END)
Father, in your plan of salvation
your Son Jesus Christ accepted the cross
and freed us from the power of the enemy.
May we come to share the glory of his resurrection,
for he lives and reigns with you and the Holy Spirit,
one God, for ever and ever.

May the Lord bless us, protect us from all evil, and bring us to everlasting life. Amen.

(MAKE THE SIGN OF THE CROSS).

Appendix H
Morning Prayer for the Second Sunday of Advent

(MAKE THE SIGN OF THE CROSS)
Lord, open my lips.
And my mouth will proclaim your praise.

(INVITATORY ANTIPHON)
Come, let us worship the Lord, the King who is to come.

(PRAY THE INVITATORY PSALM, PSALM 95, REPEATING THE ANTIPHON
BETWEEN THE VERSES AS YOU HAVE BEEN TAUGHT.)

(END WITH THE GLORY BE PRAYED IN FULL.)

(REPEAT INVITATORY ANTIPHON)
Come, let us worship the Lord, the King who is to come.

(NOW SING, CHANT, OR RECITE THE HYMN YOU HAVE CHOSEN)

(ANTIPHON 1)
  Zion is our mighty citadel, our saving Lord its wall and its defense; throw open the gates, for our Lord is here among us, Alleluia.

(YOU SHOULD BE AT SUNDAY MORNING PRAYER, WEEK II, OF THE PSALTER. PRAY PSALM 118 THROUGH TO THE END.)

(PRAY THE GLORY BE)

(PRAY THE PSALM-PRAYER)

(REPEAT ANTIPHON 1)
  Zion is our mighty citadel, our saving Lord its wall and its defense; throw open the gates, for our Lord is here among us, Alleluia.

(PAUSE BRIEFLY)

(ANTIPHON 2)
  Come to the waters, all you who thirst; seek the Lord while he can be found, Alleluia.

(PRAY THE CANTICLE OF DANIEL 3:52-57 ALL THE WAY THROUGH TO THE END)

(PRAY THE GLORY BE)

(REPEAT ANTIPHON 2)
  Come to the waters, all you who thirst; seek the Lord while he can be found, Alleluia.

(PAUSE BRIEFLY)
(ANTIPHON 3)
  Our God will come with great power to enlighten the eyes of his servants, Alleluia.

(PRAY PSALM 150 TO THE END)

(PRAY THE GLORY BE)

(PRAY THE PSALM-PRAYER)

(REPEAT ANTIPHON 3)
  Our God will come with great power to enlighten the eyes of his servants, Alleluia.

(PAUSE BRIEFLY)

(TURN TO THE PROPER OF SEASONS)

(READ THE READING FROM ROMANS 13:11-14)

(READ THE RESPONSORY)

(PAUSE BRIEFLY)

(ANTIPHON FOR CANTICLE OF ZECHARIAH)
   I am sending my angel before me to prepare the way for my coming.

(PRAY CANTICLE OF ZECHARIAH AS TAUGHT IN LESSON 23)

(PRAY GLORY BE)

(REPEAT ANTIPHON FOR CANTICLE OF ZECHARIAH)
   I am sending my angel before me to prepare the way for my coming.

(PRAY INTERCESSIONS BEGINNING)
   "To the Lord Jesus Christ, judge of the living and the dead . . . "

(PRAY OUR FATHER)

(PRAY CONCLUDING PRAYER BEGINNING)
   "God of power and mercy, open our hearts in welcome . . . "

   May the Lord bless us, protect us from all evil, and bring us to everlast
ing life. Amen.

(MAKE THE SIGN OF THE CROSS).

Appendix I
Praying the Psalmody for Wednesday Night Prayer during the Easter Season

Alleluia, Alleluia, Alleluia.

In you, O Lord, I take refuge
Let me never be put to shame.
In your justice, set me free,
hear me and speedily rescue me.

Be a rock of refuge for me,
a mighty stronghold to save me,
for you are my rock, my stronghold.
For your name's sake, lead me and guide me.

Release me from the snares they have hidden
for you are my refuge, Lord.
Into your hands I commend my spirit.
It is you who will redeem me, Lord.

(BOW)

Glory to the Father, and to the Son, and to the Holy Spirit:

(STRAIGHTEN)

as it was in the beginning, is now, and will be forever. Amen.

(PAUSE FOR SILENT REFLECTION)

Out of the depths I cry to you, Lord,
Lord, hear my voice!
O let your ears be attentive
to the voice of my pleading.

If you, O Lord, should mark our guilt,
Lord, who would survive?
But with you is found forgiveness:
for this we revere you.

My soul is waiting for the Lord,
I count on his word.
My soul is longing for the Lord
more than watchman for daybreak.
Let the watchman count on daybreak
and Israel on the Lord.

Because with the Lord there is mercy
and fullness of redemption,
Israel indeed he will redeem
from all its iniquity.

(BOW)

Glory to the Father, and to the Son, and to the Holy Spirit:

(STRAIGHTEN)

as it was in the beginning, is now, and will be forever. Amen.

Alleluia, Alleluia, Alleluia.

Appendix J
Praying Night Prayer on the Eve of Mercy Sunday

(MAKE THE SIGN OF THE CROSS).
>God, come to my assistance.
>Lord, make haste to help me.

(BOW)
>Glory to the Father, and to the Son, and to the Holy Spirit:

(STRAIGHTEN)
>as it was in the beginning, is now, and will be forever. Amen. Alleluia

(MAKE A SILENT EXAMINATION OF CONSCIENCE)

(PRAY A PRAYER OF FORGIVENESS)

(SING OR CHANT A HYMN OF YOUR CHOICE OR ONE LISTED IN THE BREVIARY)
>Alleluia, Alleluia, Alleluia.

>When I call, answer me, O God of justice;
>from anguish you released me; have mercy and hear me.

>O men, how long will your hearts be closed,
>will you love what is futile and seek what is false?

>It is the Lord who grants favors to those whom he loves;
>the Lord hears me whenever I call him.

>Fear him; do not sin: ponder on your bed and be still.
>Make justice your sacrifice and trust in the Lord.

>"What can bring us happiness?" many say.
>Let the light of your face shine on us, O Lord.

>I will lie down in peace and sleep comes at once
>for you alone, Lord, make me dwell in safety.

(BOW)
>Glory to the Father and to the Son and to the Holy Spirit

(STRAIGHTEN)
>as it was in the beginning, is now, and will be forever. Amen.

(PAUSE)

O come, bless the Lord, You are in our midst, O Lord,
your name we bear; do not forsake us, O Lord, our God!

Into your hands, Lord, I commend my spirit.
Into your hands, Lord, I commend my spirit.

You have redeemed us, Lord God of truth.
I commend my spirit.

(BOW)

Glory to the Father, and to the Son, and to the Holy Spirit:

(STRAIGHTEN)

as it was in the beginning, is now, and will be forever. Amen.

Alleluia, Alleluia, Alleluia.

(PAUSE FOR SILENT REFLECTION)

Hear, O Israel! The Lord is our God, the Lord alone! Therefore, you
shall love the Lord your God with all your heart, and with all your soul, and
with all your strength. Take to heart these words which I enjoin on you today.
Drill them into your children. Speak of them at home and abroad, whether
you are busy or at rest.

(PAUSE)

This is the day the Lord has made; let us rejoice and be glad, Alleluia.

(PAUSE)

Protect us, Lord, as we stay awake; watch over us as we sleep, that
awake, we may keep watch with Christ, and, asleep, rest in his peace, Alleluia.

(MAKE THE SIGN OF THE CROSS)

Lord, now you let your servant go in peace;
your word has been fulfilled.

my own eyes have seen the salvation
which you have prepared in the sight of every people:

a light to reveal you to the nations
and the glory of your people Israel.

(BOW)

Glory to the Father and to the Son and to the Holy Spirit

(STRAIGHTEN)

as it was in the beginning, is now, and will be forever. Amen.

Protect us, Lord, as we stay awake; watch over us as we sleep, that awake, we may keep watch with Christ, and asleep, rest in his peace, Alleluia.

Let us pray:

Lord,
be with us throughout this night.
When day comes may we rise from sleep
to rejoice in the resurrection of your Christ,
who lives and reigns for ever and ever.

May the all-powerful Lord grant us a restful night and a peaceful death. Amen.

(MAKE THE SIGN OF THE CROSS)

(CHOOSE ONE ANTIPHON IN HONOR OF THE BLESSED VIRGIN AND PRAY IT. THE HAIL MARY IS USED HERE AS A SAMPLE.)
Hail Mary, full of grace,
the Lord is with you!
Blessed are you among women,
and blessed is the fruit of your womb, Jesus.
Holy Mary, Mother of God,
pray for us sinners,
now and at the hour of our death.
Amen.

Appendix K
Praying Morning Prayer for the Feast of St. Thomas the Apostle

(MAKE THE SIGN OF THE CROSS).
Lord, open my lips.
And my mouth will proclaim your praise.

(INVITATORY ANTIPHON—NOT IN PROPER OF SAINTS/SAINT THOMAS, SO TAKE IT FROM THE COMMON OF THE APOSTLES)
Come, let us worship the Lord, the King of Apostles. Alleluia.

Come, let us sing to the Lord
and shout with joy to the Rock who saves us.
Let us approach him with praise and thanksgiving
and sing joyful songs to the Lord.

Come, let us worship the Lord, the King of Apostles. Alleluia.

The Lord is God, the mighty God,
the great king over all the gods.
He holds in his hands the depths of the earth
and the highest mountains as well.
He made the sea; it belongs to him,
the dry land, too, for it was formed by his hands.

Come, let us worship the Lord, the King of Apostles. Alleluia.

(KNEEL OR BOW)
Come, then, let us bow down and worship,
bending the knee before the Lord, our maker,
For he is our God and we are his people,
the flock he shepherds.

(RISE)
Come, let us worship the Lord, the King of Apostles. Alleluia.

Today, listen to the voice of the Lord.
Do not grow stubborn as your fathers did
in the wilderness
when at Meriba and Massah
they challenged me and provoked me
Although they had seen all of my works.

Come, let us worship the Lord, the King of Apostles. Alleluia.

Forty years I endured that generation.
I said, "They are a people whose hearts go astray
and they do not know my ways."
So I swore in my anger,
"They shall not enter into my rest."

Come, let us worship the Lord, the King of Apostles. Alleluia.

(BOW)
Glory to the Father, and to the Son, and to the Holy Spirit:

(STRAIGHTEN)
as it was in the beginning, is now, and will be for ever. Amen.

Come, let us worship the Lord, the King of Apostles. Alleluia.

(HYMN—NOT IN PROPER OF SAINTS/SAINT THOMAS, SO USE ONE
FROM THE COMMON OF APOSTLES)

(ANTIPHON 1—GIVEN IN PROPER OF SAINTS/SAINT THOMAS)

Lord, we do not know where you are going; how can we know the way?
Jesus replied: I am the way, the truth, and the life.

(NOW PRAY PSALM 63:2-9 FROM SUNDAY, WEEK I, IN PSALTER. END
WITH GLORY BE PRAYED IN FULL AS USUAL.)

(PRAY THE PSALM-PRAYER AS WRITTEN IN THE PSALTER, SUNDAY,
MORNING PRAYER, WEEK I.)

(ANTIPHON 1)
Lord, we do not know where you are going; how can we know the
way? Jesus replied: I am the way, the truth, and the life.

(PAUSE BRIEFLY)

(ANTIPHON 2—GIVEN IN PROPER OF SAINTS/SAINT THOMAS)
Thomas, who was called the Twin, was not present when Jesus
appeared to the apostles; so they told him: We have seen the Lord, Alleluia.

(NOW PRAY THE CANTICLE FROM DANIEL 3:57-88, 56 AS WRITTEN IN
PSALTER, SUNDAY MORNING PRAYER, WEEK I)

(ANTIPHON 2—GIVEN IN PROPER OF SAINTS/SAINT THOMAS)
Thomas, who was called the Twin, was not present when Jesus
appeared to the apostles; so they told him: We have seen the Lord, Alleluia.

(PAUSE BRIEFLY)

(ANTIPHON 3—GIVEN IN PROPER OF SAINTS/SAINT THOMAS)
With your hand, touch the mark of the nails; doubt no longer, but
believe, Alleluia.

(NOW PRAY PSALM 149 AS WRITTEN IN THE PSALTER FOR SUNDAY
MORNING PRAYER, WEEK I. END WITH THE GLORY BE PRAYED IN
FULL AS USUAL.)

(PRAY PSALM-PRAYER FROM SUNDAY MORNING PRAYER, WEEK I)

(ANTIPHON 3—GIVEN IN PROPER OF SAINTS/SAINT THOMAS)
With your hand, touch the mark of the nails; doubt no longer, but
believe, Alleluia.

(PAUSE BRIEFLY)

(READING—GIVEN IN PROPER OF SAINTS/SAINT THOMAS)
You are strangers and aliens no longer. No, you are fellow citizens of
the saints and members of the household of God. You form a building which

rises on the foundation of the apostles and prophets, with Christ Jesus himself as the capstone. Through him the whole structure is fitted together and takes shape as a holy temple in the Lord; in him you are being built into this temple, to become a dwelling place for God in the Spirit.

(PAUSE BRIEFLY FOR SILENT REFLECTION)

(RESPONSORY—GIVEN IN PROPER OF SAINTS/SAINT THOMAS)
   You have made them rulers over all the earth.
   You have made them rulers over all the earth.

   They will always remember your name, O Lord, over all the earth.

   Glory to the Father and to the Son and to the Holy Spirit.
   You have made them rulers over all the earth.

(PAUSE)

(ANTIPHON FOR CANTICLE OF ZECHARIAH—GIVEN IN PROPER OF SAINTS/SAINT THOMAS)
   Because you have seen me, Thomas, you have believed; blessed are they who have not seen me and yet believe.

(PRAY THE CANTICLE OF ZECHARIAH ALL THE WAY THROUGH TO THE ENDS AS TAUGHT IN LESSON 23. END WITH GLORY BE PRAYED IN FULL AS USUAL.)

(ANTIPHON FOR CANTICLE OF ZECHARIAH)
   Because you have seen me, Thomas, you have believed; blessed are they who have not seen me and yet believe.

(PAUSE BRIEFLY)

(INTERCESSIONS—NOT IN PROPER OF SAINTS/SAINT THOMAS, SO USE ONE FROM COMMON OF THE APOSTLES)
   Beloved friends, we have inherited heaven along with the apostles. Let us give thanks to the Father for all his gifts:. *The company of apostles praises you, O Lord.*

(PRAY THE INTERCESSIONS STRAIGHT THROUGH TO THE END AS THEY ARE WRITTEN IN THE BREVIARY. YOU MAY ADD ANY INTERCESSIONS YOU WISH, ENDING THEM WITH THE ITALICIZED REFRAIN, "*The company of apostles praises you, O Lord.*")

(PRAY THE OUR FATHER THROUGH TO THE END)

(PRAYER FOR SAINT THOMAS, FOUND IN THE PROPER OF SAINTS)
   Almighty Father, as we honor Thomas the apostle,

let us always experience the help of his prayers.
May we have eternal life by believing in Jesus,
whom Thomas acknowledged as Lord,
for he lives and reigns with you and the Holy Spirit,
one God, for ever and ever.

May the Lord bless us, protect us from all evil, and bring us to everlasting life. Amen.

(MAKE THE SIGN OF THE CROSS).

Appendix L
Praying Morning Prayer for the Memorial of Saint Justin Martyr Using the Common of One Martyr as Primary Source for the Office for Monday, June 1, 1998 (Week I of Psalter)

(MAKE THE SIGN OF THE CROSS).
Lord, open my lips.
And my mouth will proclaim your praise.

(INVITATORY ANTIPHON—COMMON)
Come, let us worship Christ, the king of martyrs.

Come, let us sing to the Lord
and shout with joy to the Rock who saves us.
Let us approach him with praise and thanksgiving
and sing joyful songs to the Lord.

Come, let us worship Christ, the king of martyrs.

The Lord is God, the mighty God,
the great king over all the gods.
He holds in his hands the depths of the earth
and the highest mountains as well.
He made the sea; it belongs to him,
the dry land, too, for it was formed by his hands.

Come, let us worship Christ, the king of martyrs.

(KNEEL OR BOW)

Come, then, let us bow down and worship,
bending the knee before the Lord, our maker,
For he is our God and we are his people,
the flock he shepherds.

(RISE)

Come, let us worship Christ, the king of martyrs.

Today, listen to the voice of the Lord.
Do not grow stubborn as your fathers did
in the wilderness
when at Meriba and Massah
they challenged me and provoked me
Although they had seen all of my works.

Come, let us worship Christ, the king of martyrs.

Forty years I endured that generation.
I said, "They are a people whose hearts go astray
and they do not know my ways."
So I swore in my anger,
"They shall not enter into my rest."

Come, let us worship Christ, the king of martyrs.

(BOW)

Glory to the Father, and to the Son, and to the Holy Spirit:

(STRAIGHTEN)

as it was in the beginning, is now, and will be for ever. Amen.

Come, let us worship Christ, the king of martyrs.

(HYMN—COMMON)

Christ, in whose passion once was sown . . .

(CONTINUE TO PRAY OR RECITE HYMN UNTIL THE END)

(PSALMODY—PSALTER, MONDAY, WEEK I)
(ANTIPHON 1)

I lift up my heart to you, O Lord, and you will hear my morning
prayer.

(NOW PRAY PSALM 5:2-10, 13-13, THE GLORY BE, AND THE PSALM
PRAYER AS LISTED FOR MONDAY MORNING PRAYER, WEEK I. REPEAT
ANTIPHON 1).

(ANTIPHON 2)
We praise your glorious name, O Lord, our God.

(PRAY THE CANTICLE FROM CHRONICLES 20:10-13 AS LISTED IN THE PSALTER FOR MONDAY MORNING PRAYER, WEEK I, FOLLOWED BY THE GLORY BE. REPEAT ANTIPHON 2).

(ANTIPHON 3)
Adore the Lord in his holy court.

(PRAY PSALM 29 AS WRITTEN IN THE PSALTER FOR MONDAY MORNING PRAYER, WEEK I, FOLLOWED BY THE GLORY BE AND PSALM PRAYER. REPEAT ANTIPHON 3).

(READING FROM THE COMMON OF ONE MARTYR)
Praised be God, the Father of our Lord Jesus Christ, the Father of mercies, and the God of all consolation! He comforts us in all our afflictions and thus enables us to comfort those who are in trouble, with the same consolation we have received from him. As we have shared much in the suffering of Christ, so through Christ do we share abundantly in his consolation.

(PAUSE BRIEFLY)

(RESPONSORY FROM THE COMMON OF ONE MARTYR)
The Lord is my strength, and I shall sing his praise.
The Lord is my strength, and I shall sing his praise.

The Lord is my savior,
and I shall sing his praise.

Glory to the Father and to the Son and to the Holy Spirit
The Lord is my strength, and I shall sing his praise.

(PAUSE BRIEFLY)

(ANTIPHON FOR CANTICLE OF ZECHARIAH FROM MEMORIAL OF SAINT JUSTIN MARTYR)
In every sacrifice let us praise the Creator of all things through his Son Jesus Christ and through the Holy Spirit.

(MAKE THE SIGN OF THE CROSS)
Blessed be the Lord, the God of Israel,
he has come to his people and set them free.

He has raised up for us a mighty savior,
born of the house of his servant David.

Through his holy prophets he promised of old
that he would save us from our enemies,
from the hands of those who hate us.

He promised to show mercy to our fathers
and to remember his holy covenant.

This was the oath he swore to our father Abraham,
to set us free from the hands of our enemies,
free to worship him without fear,
holy and righteous in his sight all the days of our life.
You, my child, shall be called the prophet of the Most High,
for you will go before the Lord to prepare his way
to give his people knowledge of salvation
by the forgiveness of their sins.

In the tender compassion of our God
the dawn from on high shall break upon us,
to shine on those who dwell in darkness and the shadow of death,
and to guide our feet into the way of peace.

(BOW)

Glory to the Father and to the Son and to the Holy Spirit

(STRAIGHTEN)

as it was in the beginning, is now, and will be forever. Amen.

(ANTIPHON FROM MEMORIAL OF JUSTIN MARTYR)

In every sacrifice let us praise the Creator of all things through his Son Jesus Christ and through the Holy Spirit.

(PAUSE BRIEFLY)

(INTERCESSIONS FROM THE COMMON OF ONE MARTYR)

Our Savior's faithfulness is mirrored in the fidelity of his witnesses who shed their blood for the word of God. Let us praise him in remembrance of them:

You redeemed us by your blood.

Your martyrs freely embraced death in bearing witness to the faith,
give us the true freedom of the Spirit, O Lord.
Your martyrs professed their faith by shedding their blood,
give us a faith, O Lord, that is constant and pure.
Your martyrs followed in your footsteps by carrying the cross,
help us to endure courageously the misfortunes of life.
Your martyrs washed their garments in the blood of the Lamb,
help us to avoid the weaknesses of the flesh and worldly allurements.

A-29

(OPTIONAL: ADD ANY INTERCESSIONS YOU WISH. FOLLOW ED BY
THE ITALICIZED REFRAIN, *You redeemed us by your blood.*")

(PRAY THE OUR FATHER)

(CONCLUDING PRAYER FROM THE MEMORIAL OF ST. JUSTIN MARTYR):

> Father,
> through the folly of the cross
> you taught Saint Justin the sublime wisdom of Jesus Christ.
> May we too reject falsehood
> and remain loyal to the faith.
> We ask this through our Lord Jesus Christ, your Son,
> who lives and reigns with you and the Holy Spirit,
> one God, for ever and ever.
>
> May the Lord bless us,
> protect us from all evil
> and bring us to everlasting life.
> Amen.

(CONCLUDE WITH THE SIGN OF THE CROSS).

Appendix M
Praying Morning Prayer for the Memorial of Saint Justin Martyr Using the Psalter as Primary Source for the Office for Monday, June 1, 1998 (Week I of Psalter)

(MAKE THE SIGN OF THE CROSS).
> Lord, open my lips.
> And my mouth will proclaim your praise.

(INVITATORY ANTIPHON—PSALTER)
> Let us approach the Lord with praise and thanksgiving.
>
> Come, let us sing to the Lord
> and shout with joy to the Rock who saves us.
> Let us approach him with praise and thanksgiving
> and sing joyful songs to the Lord.
>
> Let us approach the Lord with praise and thanksgiving.

The Lord is God, the mighty God,
the great king over all the gods.
He holds in his hands the depths of the earth
and the highest mountains as well.
He made the sea; it belongs to him,
the dry land, too, for it was formed by his hands.

Let us approach the Lord with praise and thanksgiving.

(KNEEL OR BOW)
Come, then, let us bow down and worship,
bending the knee before the Lord, our maker,
For he is our God and we are his people,
the flock he shepherds. (RISE)

Let us approach the Lord with praise and thanksgiving.

Today, listen to the voice of the Lord.
Do not grow stubborn as your fathers did
in the wilderness
when at Meriba and Massah
they challenged me and provoked me
Although they had seen all of my works.

Let us approach the Lord with praise and thanksgiving.

Forty years I endured that generation.
I said, "They are a people whose hearts go astray
and they do not know my ways."
So I swore in my anger,
"They shall not enter into my rest."

Let us approach the Lord with praise and thanksgiving.

(BOW)
Glory to the Father, and to the Son, and to the Holy Spirit:

(STRAIGHTEN)
as it was in the beginning, is now, and will be for ever. Amen.

Let us approach the Lord with praise and thanksgiving.

(HYMN—COMMON)
Christ, in whose passion once was sown . . .

CONTINUE TO PRAY OR RECITE HYMN UNTIL THE END)

(PSALMODY—PSALTER, MONDAY, WEEK I)

(ANTIPHON 1)
      I lift up my heart to you, O Lord, and you will hear my morning prayer.

(NOW PRAY PSALM 5:2-10, 13-13, THE GLORY BE, AND THE PSALM PRAYER AS LISTED FOR MONDAY MORNING PRAYER, WEEK I. REPEAT ANTIPHON 1. PAUSE BRIEFLY).

(ANTIPHON 2)
      We praise your glorious name, O Lord, our God.

(PRAY THE CANTICLE FROM CHRONICLES 20:10-13 AS LISTED IN THE PSALTER FOR MONDAY MORNING PRAYER, WEEK I, FOLLOWED BY THE GLORY BE. REPEAT ANTIPHON 2. PAUSE BRIEFLY.).
(ANTIPHON 3)
      Adore the Lord in his holy court.

(PRAY PSALM 29 AS WRITTEN IN THE PSALTER FOR MONDAY MORNING PRAYER, WEEK I, FOLLOWED BY THE GLORY BE AND PSALM PRAYER. REPEAT ANTIPHON 3. PAUSE BRIEFLY.).

(READING FROM THE PSALTER, MONDAY WEEK I)
      Anyone who would not work should not eat. We hear that some of you are unruly, not keeping busy but acting like busy-bodies. We enjoin all such, and we urge them strongly in the Lord Jesus Christ, to earn the food they eat by working quietly. You must never grow weary of doing what is right, brothers.

(PAUSE BRIEFLY)

(RESPONSORY FROM THE PSALTER, MONDAY WEEK I)
      Blessed be the Lord our God, blessed from age to age.
      Blessed be the Lord our God, blessed from age to age.

      His marvelous works are beyond compare,
      blessed from age to age.

      Glory to the Father and to the Son and to the Holy Spirit
      Blessed be the Lord our God, blessed from age to age.

(PAUSE BRIEFLY)

(ANTIPHON FOR CANTICLE OF ZECHARIAH FROM MEMORIAL OF SAINT JUSTIN MARTYR)
      In every sacrifice let us praise the Creator of all things through his Son

Jesus Christ and through the Holy Spirit.

(MAKE THE SIGN OF THE CROSS)

Blessed be the Lord, the God of Israel,
he has come to his people and set them free.

He has raised up for us a mighty savior,
born of the house of his servant David.

Through his holy prophets he promised of old
that he would save us from our enemies,
from the hands of those who hate us.

He promised to show mercy to our fathers
and to remember his holy covenant.

This was the oath he swore to our father Abraham,
to set us free from the hands of our enemies,
free to worship him without fear,
holy and righteous in his sight
all the days of our life.

You, my child, shall be called the prophet of the Most High,
for you will go before the Lord to prepare his way
to give his people knowledge of salvation
by the forgiveness of their sins.

In the tender compassion of our God
the dawn from on high shall break upon us,
to shine on those who dwell in darkness and the shadow of death,
and to guide our feet into the way of peace.

(BOW)

Glory to the Father and to the Son and to the Holy Spirit

(STRAIGHTEN)

as it was in the beginning, is now, and will be forever. Amen.

(ANTIPHON FROM MEMORIAL OF JUSTIN MARTYR)

In every sacrifice let us praise the Creator of all things through his Son
Jesus Christ and through the Holy Spirit.

(INTERCESSIONS FROM THE PSALTER, MONDAY WEEK I)

We esteem Christ above all men, for he was filled with grace and the
Holy Spirit. In faith let us implore him: *Give us your Spirit, Lord.*

Grant us a peaceful day,
when evening comes we will praise you with joy and purity of heart.
Let your splendor rest upon us today,
direct the work of our hands.
May your face shine upon us and keep us in peace,
may your strong arm protect us.
Look kindly on all who put their trust in our prayers,
fill them with every bodily and spiritual grace.

(OPTIONAL: YOU MAY ADD HERE INTERCESSIONS OF YOUR OWN,
ADDING THE ITALICIZED REFRAIN, *"Give us your Spirit, Lord."*)

(PRAY THE OUR FATHER)

(CONCLUDING PRAYER FROM THE MEMORIAL OF ST. JUSTIN MARTYR):

Father, through the folly of the cross
you taught Saint Justin the sublime wisdom of Jesus Christ.
May we too reject falsehood
and remain loyal to the faith.
We ask this through our Lord Jesus Christ, your Son,
who lives and reigns with you and the Holy Spirit,
one God, for ever and ever.

May the Lord bless us,
protect us from all evil
and bring us to everlasting life.
Amen.

(CONCLUDE WITH THE SIGN OF THE CROSS).

Appendix N
Praying Morning Prayer for the Optional Memorial of Saint John Damascene, Friday, December 4, 1998 Using the Common of Doctors of the Church

(MAKE THE SIGN OF THE CROSS).
Lord, open my lips.
And my mouth will proclaim your praise.

(INVITATORY ANTIPHON—COMMON OF DOCTORS)
Come, let us worship the Lord, fount of all wisdom.

Come, let us sing to the Lord
and shout with joy to the Rock who saves us.
Let us approach him with praise and thanksgiving
and sing joyful songs to the Lord.

Come, let us worship the Lord, fount of all wisdom.

The Lord is God, the mighty God,
the great king over all the gods.
He holds in his hands the depths of the earth
and the highest mountains as well.
He made the sea; it belongs to him,
the dry land, too, for it was formed by his hands.

Come, let us worship the Lord, fount of all wisdom.

(KNEEL OR BOW)

Come, then, let us bow down and worship,
bending the knee before the Lord, our maker,
For he is our God and we are his people,
the flock he shepherds.

(RISE)

Come, let us worship the Lord, fount of all wisdom.

Today, listen to the voice of the Lord.
Do not grow stubborn as your fathers did
in the wilderness
when at Meriba and Massah
they challenged me and provoked me
Although they had seen all of my works.
Come, let us worship the Lord, fount of all wisdom.

Forty years I endured that generation.
I said, "They are a people whose hearts go astray
and they do not know my ways."
So I swore in my anger,
"They shall not enter into my rest."

Come, let us worship the Lord, fount of all wisdom.

(BOW)

Glory to the Father, and to the Son, and to the Holy Spirit:

(STRAIGHTEN)

as it was in the beginning, is now, and will be for ever. Amen.

A-35

Come, let us worship the Lord, fount of all wisdom.

(SING, CHANT, OR RECITE A HYMN)

(ANTIPHON 1—PSALTER)
Lord, you will accept the true sacrifice offered on your altar.

(NOW PRAY PSALM 51 AS WRITTEN IN THE PSALTER FOR FRIDAY MORNING PRAYER, WEEK I. END WITH GLORY BE PRAYED IN FULL AS USUAL.)

(PRAY THE PSALM-PRAYER AS WRITTEN IN THE PSALTER.)

(ANTIPHON 1)
Lord, you will accept the true sacrifice offered on your altar.

(PAUSE BRIEFLY)

(ANTIPHON 2)
All the descendants of Israel will glory in the Lord's gift of victory.

(NOW PRAY THE CANTICLE FROM ISAIAH 45-15-25 AS WRITTEN IN THE PSALTER FOR FRIDAY MORNING PRAYER, WEEK I. END WITH THE GLORY BE PRAYED IN FULL AS USUAL.)

(ANTIPHON 2)
All the descendants of Israel will glory in the Lord's gift of victory.

(PAUSE BRIEFLY)

(ANTIPHON 3)
Let us go into God's presence singing for joy.

(NOW PRAY PSALM 100 AS WRITTEN IN THE PSALTER FOR FRIDAY MORNING PRAYER, WEEK I. END WITH THE GLORY BE PRAYED IN FULL AS USUAL.)

(ANTIPHON 3)
Let us go into God's presence singing for joy.

(PAUSE BRIEFLY)

(THE REST OF THE OFFICE IS FOUND IN THE COMMON OF DOCTORS OF THE CHURCH)

(READING)
Simply I learned about Wisdom, and ungrudgingly do I share—

her riches I do not hide away;
For to men she is an unfading treasure:
those who gain this treasure win the friendship of God,
to whom the gifts they have from discipline commend them.

(PAUSE BRIEFLY FOR SILENT REFLECTION)

(RESPONSORY)
Let the peoples proclaim the wisdom of the saints.
Let the peoples proclaim the wisdom of the saints.

With joyful praise let the Church tell forth
the wisdom of the saints.

Glory to the Father and to the Son and to the Holy Spirit.
Let the peoples proclaim the wisdom of the saints.

(PAUSE)

(ANTIPHON FOR CANTICLE OF ZECHARIAH)
Those who are learned will be as radiant as the sky in all its beauty;
those who instruct the people in goodness will shine like the stars for all eternity.

(PRAY THE CANTICLE OF ZECHARIAH ALL THE WAY THROUGH TO
THE ENDS AS TAUGHT IN LESSON 23. END WITH GLORY BE PRAYED IN
FULL AS USUAL.)

(ANTIPHON FOR CANTICLE OF ZECHARIAH)
Those who are learned will be as radiant as the sky in all its beauty;
those who instruct the people in goodness will shine like the stars for all eternity.

(PAUSE BRIEFLY)

(INTERCESSIONS—TAKEN FROM THE COMMON OF PASTORS)
Christ is the Good Shepherd who laid down his life for his sheep. Let
us praise and thank him as we pray: *Nourish your people, Lord.*

Christ, you decided to show your merciful love through your holy
shepherd,
let your mercy always reach us through them.
Through your vicars you continue to perform the ministry of shepherd of souls,
direct us always through our leaders.
Through your holy ones, the leaders of your people, you served as
physician of our bodies and our spirits,

continue to fulfill your ministry of life and holiness through us.
You taught your flock through the prudence and love of your saints,
grant us continual growth in holiness under the direction of our pastors.

(HERE ADD ANY INTERCESSIONS YOU WISH, ENDING THEM WITH
ITALICIZED REFRAIN, *"Nourish your people, Lord"*).

(PRAY THE OUR FATHER THROUGH TO THE END)

(PRAYER FOR SAINT JOHN DAMASCENE)
> Lord,
> may the prayers of Saint John Damascene help us,
> and may the true faith he taught so well
> always be our light and our strength.
> We ask this through our Lord Jesus Christ, your Son,
> who lives and reigns with you and the Holy Spirit,
> one God, for ever and ever.
>
> May the Lord bless us,
> protect us from all evil,
> and bring us to everlasting life. Amen.

(MAKE THE SIGN OF THE CROSS).

Appendix O
Praying Morning Prayer for the Optional Memorial of Saint John Damascene, Friday, December 4, 1998 sing the Proper of Seasons (First Friday of Advent)

(MAKE THE SIGN OF THE CROSS).
> Lord, open my lips.
> And my mouth will proclaim your praise.

(INVITATORY ANTIPHON—PROPER OF SEASONS)
> Come, let us worship the Lord, the King who is to come.
>
> Come, let us sing to the Lord
> and shout with joy to the Rock who saves us.
> Let us approach him with praise and thanksgiving
> and sing joyful songs to the Lord.

Come, let us worship the Lord, the King who is to come.

The Lord is God, the mighty God,
the great king over all the gods.
He holds in his hands the depths of the earth
and the highest mountains as well.
He made the sea; it belongs to him,
the dry land, too, for it was formed by his hands.

Come, let us worship the Lord, the King who is to come.

(KNEEL OR BOW)

Come, then, let us bow down and worship,
bending the knee before the Lord, our maker,
For he is our God and we are his people,
the flock he shepherds.

(RISE)

Come, let us worship the Lord, the King who is to come.

Today, listen to the voice of the Lord.
Do not grow stubborn as your fathers did
in the wilderness
when at Meriba and Massah
they challenged me and provoked me
Although they had seen all of my works.

Come, let us worship the Lord, the King who is to come.

Forty years I endured that generation.
I said, "They are a people whose hearts go astray
and they do not know my ways."
So I swore in my anger,
"They shall not enter into my rest."

Come, let us worship the Lord, the King who is to come.

(BOW)

Glory to the Father, and to the Son, and to the Holy Spirit:

(STRAIGHTEN)

as it was in the beginning, is now, and will be for ever.   Amen.

Come, let us worship the Lord, the King who is to come.

(SING, CHANT, OR RECITE AN ADVENT HYMN)

A-39

(ANTIPHON 1—PSALTER)
Lord, you will accept the true sacrifice offered on your altar.

(NOW PRAY PSALM 51 AS WRITTEN IN THE PSALTER FOR FRIDAY MORNING PRAYER, WEEK I. END WITH GLORY BE PRAYED IN FULL AS USUAL.)

(PRAY THE PSALM-PRAYER AS WRITTEN IN THE PSALTER.)

(ANTIPHON 1)
Lord, you will accept the true sacrifice offered on your altar.

(PAUSE BRIEFLY)

(ANTIPHON 2)
All the descendants of Israel will glory in the Lord's gift of victory.

(NOW PRAY THE CANTICLE FROM ISAIAH 45-15-25 AS WRITTEN IN THE PSALTER FOR FRIDAY MORNING PRAYER, WEEK I. END WITH THE GLORY BE PRAYED IN FULL AS USUAL.)

(ANTIPHON 2)
All the descendants of Israel will glory in the Lord's gift of victory.

(PAUSE BRIEFLY)
(ANTIPHON 3)
Let us go into God's presence singing for joy.

(NOW PRAY PSALM 100 AS WRITTEN IN THE PSALTER FOR FRIDAY MORNING PRAYER, WEEK I. END WITH THE GLORY BE PRAYED IN FULL AS USUAL.)

(ANTIPHON 3)
Let us go into God's presence singing for joy.

(PAUSE BRIEFLY)

(THE REST OF THE OFFICE IS FOUND IN THE PROPER OF SEASONS FOR FRIDAY OF THE FIRST WEEK OF ADVENT)

(READING)
Thus says the Lord:
His leader shall be from Jacob,
and his ruler shall come
from his kin.

When I summon him,

he shall approach me.
You shall be my people,
and I will be your God.

(PAUSE BRIEFLY FOR SILENT REFLECTION)

(RESPONSORY)
Your light will come Jerusalem; the Lord will dawn on you in radiant
beauty.
Your light will come Jerusalem; the Lord will dawn on you in radiant
beauty.

You will see his glory within you.
the Lord will dawn on you in radiant beauty.

Glory to the Father and to the Son and to the Holy Spirit.
Your light will come Jerusalem; the Lord will dawn on you in radiant
beauty.

(PAUSE)

(ANTIPHON FOR CANTICLE OF ZECHARIAH)
Our God comes, born as man of David's line, enthroned as king for
ever, Alleluia.

(PRAY THE CANTICLE OF ZECHARIAH ALL THE WAY THROUGH TO
THE ENDS AS TAUGHT IN LESSON 23. END WITH GLORY BE.)

(ANTIPHON FOR CANTICLE OF ZECHARIAH)
Our God comes, born as man of David's line, enthroned as king for
ever, Alleluia.

(PAUSE BRIEFLY)

(INTERCESSIONS)
Through his Son, God the Father revealed his glory to men and
women. Therefore, let our joyful cry resound: *Lord, may your name be glorified.*

Teach us, Lord, to love each other,
as Christ loved us for God's glory.
Fill us with all joy and peace in faith,
that we may walk in the hope and strength of the Holy Spirit.
Help all mankind, Lord, in your loving mercy,
be near to those who seek you without knowing it.
You call and sanctify the elect,
though we are sinners, crown us with eternal happiness.

(HERE ADD ANY INTERCESSIONS YOU WISH, ENDING THEM WITH
ITALICIZED REFRAIN, *"Lord, may your name be glorified."*)

(PRAY THE OUR FATHER THROUGH TO THE END)

(PRAYER FOR SAINT JOHN DAMASCENE)
> Lord, may the prayers of Saint John Damascene help us,
> and may the true faith he taught so well
> always be our light and our strength.
> We ask this through our Lord Jesus Christ, your Son,
> who lives and reigns with you and the Holy Spirit,
> one God, for ever and ever.

> May the Lord bless us,
> protect us from all evil,
> and bring us to everlasting life. Amen.

Appendix P
Concluding Prayers on Commemorations

(MAKE THE SIGN OF THE CROSS).

**Concluding Prayer to Commemoration of St. Turibius, Morning Prayer, March
23, 1998**

(BEGINNING OF CONCLUDING PRAYER FROM PROPER OF SEASONS)
> Father, creator, you give the world new life by your sacraments.
> May we, your Church, grow in your life
> and continue to receive your help on earth.

(MORNING PRAYER ANTIPHON FROM COMMEMORATION OF SAINT
TURIBIUS)
> It is not you who speak
> but the Spirit of your Father
> who speaks in you.

(CONCLUDING PRAYER FROM COMMEMORATION OF SAINT TURIBIUS)
> Lord, through the apostolic work of Saint Turibius
> and his unwavering love of truth,
> you helped your Church to grow.
> May your chosen people continue to grow
> in faith and holiness.
> Grant this through our Lord Jesus Christ, your Son,
> who lives and reigns with you and the Holy Spirit,
> one God, for ever and ever.

A-42

(USUAL ENDING TO MORNING PRAYER OFFICE)
>May the Lord bless us,
>protect us from all evil,
>and bring us to everlasting life. Amen.

(END WITH THE SIGN OF THE CROSS)

Concluding Prayer to Commemoration of Saint Turibius, Evening Prayer, March 23, 1998

(BEGINNING OF CONCLUDING PRAYER FROM THE PROPER OF SEA-SONS)
>Father, creator, you give the world new life by your sacraments.
>May we, your Church, grow in your life
>and continue to receive your help on earth.

(EVENING PRAYER ANTIPHON FROM COMMEMORATION OF SAINT TURIBIUS)
>This is a faithful and wise steward:
>the Lord entrusted the care of his household to him,
>so that he might give them their portion of food
>at the proper season.

(CONCLUDING PRAYER FOR COMMEMORATION OF SAINT TURIBIUS)
>Lord, through the apostolic work of Saint Turibius
>and his unwavering love of truth,
>you helped your Church to grow.
>May your chosen people continue to grow
>in faith and holiness.
>Grant this through our Lord Jesus Christ, your Son,
>who lives and reigns with you and the Holy Spirit,
>one God, for ever and ever.

(USUAL CONCLUSION FOR EVENING PRAYER OFFICE)
>May the Lord bless us,
>protect us from all evil,
>and bring us to everlasting life. Amen.

(END WITH THE SIGN OF THE CROSS)

Concluding Prayer for Morning Prayer for Commemoration of St. Thomas Becket, December 29 (any year)

(BEGINNING OF CONCLUDING PRAYER FOR DECEMBER 29 FROM PROPER OF SEASONS)
>All-powerful and unseen God,
>the coming of your light into our world

has made the darkness vanish.
Teach us to proclaim the birth of your Son Jesus Christ.

(MORNING PRAYER ANTIPHON FOR CANTICLE OF ZECHARIAH FROM
COMMEMORATION FOR ST. THOMAS BECKET)
Whoever hates his life in this world
keeps it safe for life everlasting.

(CONCLUDING PRAYER FOR COMMEMORATION OF ST. THOMAS BECKET)
Almighty God,
you granted the martyr Thomas
the grace to give his life for the cause of justice.
By his prayers
make us willing to renounce for Christ
our life in this world
so that we may find it in heaven.
We ask this through our Lord Jesus Christ, your Son,
who lives and reigns with you and the Holy Spirit,
one God, for ever and ever.

(USUAL CONCLUSION TO MORNING PRAYER OFFICE)
May the Lord bless us,
protect us from all evil,
and bring us to everlasting life. Amen.

(END OFFICE WITH THE SIGN OF THE CROSS)

**Concluding Prayer to the Evening Prayer Office for the Commemoration of
St. Thomas Becket, December 29 (any year)**

(BEGINNING OF CONCLUDING PRAYER FOR DECEMBER 29 FROM
PROPER OF SEASONS)
All-powerful and unseen God,
the coming of your light into our world
has made the darkness vanish.
Teach us to proclaim the birth of your Son Jesus Christ.

(ANTIPHON FOR CANTICLE OF MARY FROM COMMEMORATION OF ST.
THOMAS BECKET)
The saints find their home
in the kingdom of heaven;
their life is eternal peace.

(CONCLUDING PRAYER FOR COMMEMORATION OF ST. THOMAS BECK-
ET)
Almighty God,
you granted the martyr Thomas

the grace to give his life for the cause of justice.
By his prayers
make us willing to renounce for Christ
our life in this world
so that we may find it in heaven.
We ask this through our Lord Jesus Christ, your Son,
who lives and reigns with you and the Holy Spirit,
one God, for ever and ever.

(USUAL CONCLUSION TO EVENING PRAYER OFFICE)
May the Lord bless us,
protect us from all evil,
and bring us to everlasting life. Amen.

(END OFFICE WITH THE SIGN OF THE CROSS)

Appendix Q
Praying Morning Prayer for the Memorial of St. Leo the Great Using the Common of Doctors for November 10, 1998 (Tuesday, Week IV)

(MAKE THE SIGN OF THE CROSS).
Lord, open my lips.
And my mouth will proclaim your praise.

(INVITATORY ANTIPHON—COMMON OF DOCTORS)
Come, let us worship the Lord, fount of all wisdom.

Come, let us sing to the Lord
and shout with joy to the Rock who saves us.
Let us approach him with praise and thanksgiving
and sing joyful songs to the Lord.
Come, let us worship the Lord, fount of all wisdom.

The Lord is God, the mighty God,
the great king over all the gods.
He holds in his hands the depths of the earth
and the highest mountains as well.
He made the sea; it belongs to him,
the dry land, too, for it was formed by his hands.

Come, let us worship the Lord, fount of all wisdom.

(KNEEL OR BOW)

Come, then, let us bow down and worship,
bending the knee before the Lord, our maker,
For he is our God and we are his people,
the flock he shepherds.

(RISE)

Come, let us worship the Lord, fount of all wisdom.

Today, listen to the voice of the Lord.
Do not grow stubborn as your fathers did
in the wilderness
when at Meriba and Massah
they challenged me and provoked me
Although they had seen all of my works.

Come, let us worship the Lord, fount of all wisdom.
Forty years I endured that generation.
I said, "They are a people whose hearts go astray
and they do not know my ways."
So I swore in my anger,
"They shall not enter into my rest."

Come, let us worship the Lord, fount of all wisdom.

(BOW)

Glory to the Father, and to the Son, and to the Holy Spirit:

(STRAIGHTEN)

as it was in the beginning, is now, and will be for ever.   Amen.
Come, let us worship the Lord, fount of all wisdom.

(HYMN—COMMON OF DOCTORS)

Rise up, O men of God! . . .

(CONTINUE TO PRAY OR RECITE HYMN UNTIL THE END)

(PSALMODY—PSALTER, TUESDAY, WEEK IV)

(ANTIPHON 1)

I will sing to you, O Lord; I will learn from you the way of perfection.

(NOW PRAY PSALM 101, THE GLORY BE, AND THE PSALM PRAYER AS
LISTED FOR TUESDAY MORNING PRAYER, WEEK IV. REPEAT ANTIPHON
1. PAUSE BRIEFLY).

(ANTIPHON 2)

A-46

Lord, do not withhold your compassion from us.

(PRAY THE CANTICLE FROM DANIEL 3:26, 27, 29, 34-41 AS LISTED IN THE PSALTER FOR TUESDAY MORNING PRAYER, WEEK IV, FOLLOWED BY THE GLORY BE. REPEAT ANTIPHON 2. PAUSE BRIEFLY.).

(ANTIPHON 3)
O God, I will sing to you a new song.

(PRAY PSALM 144: 1-10 AS WRITTEN IN THE PSALTER FOR TUESDAY MORNING PRAYER, WEEK IV, FOLLOWED BY THE GLORY BE AND PSALM PRAYER. REPEAT ANTIPHON 3. PAUSE BRIEFLY.).

(READING FROM THE COMMON OF DOCTORS)
Simply I learned about Wisdom, and ungrudgingly do I share—
her riches I do not hid away;
For to men she is an unfailing treasure:
those who gain this treasure win the friendship of God,
to whom the gifts they have from discipline commend them.

(PAUSE BRIEFLY)

(RESPONSORY FROM THE COMMON OF DOCTORS)
Let the peoples proclaim the wisdom of the saints.
Let the peoples proclaim the wisdom of the saints.

With joyful praise let the Church tell forth
the wisdom of the saints.

Glory to the Father and to the Son and to the Holy Spirit.
Let the peoples proclaim the wisdom of the saints.

(PAUSE BRIEFLY)

(ANTIPHON FOR CANTICLE OF ZECHARIAH FROM COMMON OF DOC-
TORS)
Those who are learned will be as radiant as the sky in all its beauty;
those who instruct the people in goodness will shine like the stars for all eternity.

(MAKE THE SIGN OF THE CROSS)

Blessed be the Lord, the God of Israel,
he has come to his people and set them free.

He has raised up for us a mighty savior,
born of the house of his servant David.

Through his holy prophets he promised of old
that he would save us from our enemies,
from the hands of those who hate us.

He promised to show mercy to our fathers
and to remember his holy covenant.

This was the oath he swore to our father Abraham,
to set us free from the hands of our enemies,
free to worship him without fear,
holy and righteous in his sight
all the days of our life.

You, my child, shall be called the prophet of the Most High,
for you will go before the Lord to prepare his way
to give his people knowledge of salvation
by the forgiveness of their sins.

In the tender compassion of our God
the dawn from on high shall break upon us,
to shine on those who dwell in darkness and the shadow of death,
and to guide our feet into the way of peace.

(BOW)

Glory to the Father and to the Son and to the Holy Spirit

(STRAIGHTEN)

as it was in the beginning, is now, and will be forever. Amen.

(ANTIPHON FROM COMMON OF DOCTORS)

Those who are learned will be as radiant as the sky in all its beauty; those who instruct the people in goodness will shine like the stars for all eternity.

(INTERCESSIONS FROM THE COMMON OF PASTORS)

Christ is the Good Shepherd who laid down his life for his sheep. Let us praise and thank him as we pray: *Nourish your people, Lord.*

Christ, you decided to show your merciful love through your holy shepherds,
   let your mercy always reach us through them.
Through your vicars you continue to perform the ministry of shepherd of souls,
   direct us always through our leaders.
Through your holy ones, the leaders of your people, you served as physician of our bodies and our spirits,
   continue to fulfill your ministry of life and holiness through us.

You taught your flock through the prudence and love of your saints,
grant us continual growth in holiness under the direction of our pastors.

(HERE ADD ANY INTERCESSIONS YOU WISH, ENDING THEM WITH THE
ITALICIZED REFRAIN, "*Nourish your people, Lord.*")

(PRAY THE OUR FATHER THROUGH TO THE END)

(CONCLUDING PRAYER FROM THE MEMORIAL OF SAINT LEO):
> God our Father,
> you will never allow the power of hell
> to prevail against your Church,
> founded on the rock of the apostle Peter.
> Let the prayers of Pope Leo the Great
> keep us faithful to your truth
> and secure in your peace.
> We ask this through our Lord Jesus Christ, your Son,
> who lives and reigns with you and the Holy Spirit,
> one God, for ever and ever.
>
> May the Lord bless us,
> protect us from all evil
> and bring us to everlasting life.
> Amen.

(CONCLUDE WITH THE SIGN OF THE CROSS).

Appendix R
Praying Daytime Prayer At Midday for the
Fifth Sunday of Lent Using a One Volume
Breviary That Has a Daytime Prayer Section

(MAKE THE SIGN OF THE CROSS)
> God, come to my assistance.
> Lord, make haste to help me.

(BOW)
> Glory to the Father and to the Son and to the Holy Spirit;

(STRAIGHTEN)
> as it was in the beginning, is now, and will be forever. Amen.

(SING, CHANT, OR RECITE THE HYMN YOU HAVE CHOSEN)

(ANTIPHON 1:)
   What better can we do than take refuge in the Lord! His love will never fail.

(NOW PRAY PART I OF PSALM 118 AS WRITTEN IN YOUR BREVIARY. END WITH THE GLORY BE PRAYED IN FULL. REPEAT ANTIPHON 1)

(ANTIPHON 2:)
   The Lord is my strength, and I shall sing his praise.

(NOW PRAY PART II OF PSALM 118 AS WRITTEN IN YOUR BREVIARY. END WITH THE GLORY BE PRAYED IN FULL. REPEAT ANTIPHON 2)

(ANTIPHON 3:)
   I shall proclaim your goodness, Lord, for you have answered me.

(NOW PRAY PART III OF PSALM 118 AS WRITTEN IN YOUR BREVIARY. END WITH THE GLORY BE PRAYED IN FULL. PRAY THE PSALM-PRAYER AS WRITTEN IN YOUR BREVIARY. REPEAT ANTIPHON 3)

(READING:)
   A man will reap only what he sows. If he sows in the field of the flesh, he will   reap a harvest of corruption; but if his seed-ground is the spirit, he will reap everlasting life.

   Your promise, Lord, will stand for ever.
   In every generation your word is true.

(ALTERNATIVE PRAYER FROM FIFTH SUNDAY OF LENT)
   Father in heaven,
   the love of your Son led him to accept the suffering of the cross
   that his brothers might glory in new life.
   Change our selfishness into self-giving.
   Help us to embrace the world you have given us,
   that we may transform the darkness of its pain
   into the life and joy of Easter.
   Grant this through Christ our Lord
   Who lives and reigns with you for ever and ever. Amen.

   Let us praise the Lord,
   and give him thanks.

(END WITH THE SIGN OF THE CROSS)

Appendix S
Midday Prayer for the Solemnity of the Assumption

(MAKE THE SIGN OF THE CROSS)
>God, come to my assistance.
>Lord, make haste to help me.

(PRAY THE GLORY BE IN FULL)

(SING, RECITE, OR CHANT THE HYMN, ONE APPROPRIATE FOR THE ASSUMPTION)

(ANTIPHON)
>We acclaim you, Mary, as Queen of heaven; the Sun of Justice came forth from your bridal chamber.

(GRADUAL PSALMS AT MIDDAY) (PRAY PSALM 123. END WITH GLORY BE PRAYED IN FULL. PAUSE BRIEFLY FOR REFLECTION)

(PRAY PSALM 124. END WITH GLORY BE PRAYED IN FULL. PAUSE BRIEFLY FOR REFLECTION.)

(PRAY PSALM 125. END WITH GLORY BE PRAYED IN FULL.)

(ANTIPHON)
>We acclaim you, Mary, as Queen of heaven; the Sun of Justice came forth from your bridal chamber.

(PAUSE BRIEFLY FOR REFLECTION)

(READING)
>A great sign appeared in the sky, a woman clothed with the sun, with the moon under her feet, and on her head a crown of twelve stars.

>The holy Mother of God is exalted in glory.
>Above the choirs of angels in the kingdom of heaven.

(PAUSE BRIEFLY)
>Let us pray: All-powerful and ever-living God,
>you raised the sinless Virgin Mary,
>mother of your Son,
>body and soul to the glory of heaven.
>May we see heaven as our final goal
>and come to share her glory.

We ask this through our Lord Jesus Christ, your Son,
who lives and reigns with you and the Holy Spirit,
one God, for ever and ever.

Let us praise the Lord.
And give him thanks.

(END WITH THE SIGN OF THE CROSS).

Appendix T
Daytime Prayer at Midafternoon for
Thursday, March 26, 1998

(MAKE THE SIGN OF THE CROSS)
God, come to my assistance.
Lord, make haste to help me.

(PRAY THE GLORY BE IN FULL)

(SING, RECITE, OR CHANT AN APPROPRIATE LENTEN DAYTIME PRAYER
HYMN)

(ANTIPHON FROM PROPER OF SEASONS)
Armed with God's justice and power, let us prove ourselves through
patient endurance.

(PSALMS FROM DAYTIME PRAYER, WEEK IV OF PSALTER)

(PRAY PSALM 119: 153-160. PRAY GLORY BE IN FULL. PRAY PSALM-
PRAYER. PAUSE BRIEFLY FOR REFLECTION)

(PRAY PSALM 128. PRAY GLORY BE IN FULL. PRAY PSALM-PRAYER.
PAUSE BRIEFLY FOR REFLECTION.)

(PRAY PSALM 129. PRAY GLORY BE IN FULL. PRAY-PSALM PRAYER.)

(ANTIPHON: PROPER OF SEASONS)
Armed with God's justice and power, let us prove ourselves through
patient endurance.

(PAUSE BRIEFLY FOR REFLECTION)

(READING: PROPER OF SEASONS)
Do not surrender your confidence; it will have great reward. You nee
patience to do God's will and receive what he has promised.

My sacrifice to God is a contrite spirit.
A humble, contrite heart, O God, you will not spurn.

(PAUSE BRIEFLY)

Let us pray: Merciful Father,
may the penance of our Lenten observance
make us your obedient people.
May the love within us be seen in what we do
and lead us to the joy of Easter.

Grant this through our Lord Jesus Christ, your Son,
who lives and reigns with you and the Holy Spirit,
one God, for ever and ever.

Let us praise the Lord.
And give him thanks.

(END WITH THE SIGN OF THE CROSS).